AN EXEGETICAL SUMMARY OF
2 TIMOTHY

AN EXEGETICAL SUMMARY OF
2 TIMOTHY

Second Edition

Eugene E. Minor

SIL International

Second Edition
© 1992, 2008 by SIL International

Library of Congress Catalog Card Number: 2008923517
ISBN: 978-155671-191-6

Printed in the United States of America

All Rights Reserved
No part of this publication may be reproduced, stored in a retrieval system, or transmitted in any form or by any means without the express permission of SIL International. However, brief excerpts, generally understood to be within the limits of fair use, may be quoted without written permission.

Copies of this and other publications
of SIL International may be obtained from

International Academic Bookstore
SIL International
7500 West Camp Wisdom Road
Dallas, TX 75236-5699, USA

Voice: 972-708-7404
Fax: 972-708-7363
academic_books@sil.org
www.ethnologue.com

PREFACE

Exegesis is concerned with the interpretation of a text. Exegesis of the New Testament involves determining the meaning of the Greek text. Translators must be especially careful and thorough in their exegesis of the New Testament in order to accurately communicate its message in the vocabulary, grammar, and literary devices of another language. Questions occurring to translators as they study the Greek text are answered by summarizing how scholars have interpreted the text. This is information that should be considered by translators as they make their own exegetical decisions regarding the message they will communicate in their translations.

The Semi-Literal Translation

As a basis for discussion, a semi-literal translation of the Greek text is given so that the reasons for different interpretations can best be seen. When one Greek word is translated into English by several words, these words are joined by hyphens. There are a few times when clarity requires that a string of words joined by hyphens have a separate word, such as "not" (μή), inserted in their midst. In this case, the separate word is surrounded by spaces between the hyphens. When alternate translations of a Greek word are given, these are separated by slashes.

The Text

Variations in the Greek text are noted under the heading TEXT. The base text for the summary is the text of the fourth revised edition of *The Greek New Testament,* published by the United Bible Societies, which has the same text as the twenty-sixth edition of the *Novum Testamentum Graece* (Nestle-Aland). The versions that follow different variations are listed without evaluating their choices.

The Lexicon

The meaning of a key word in context is the first question to be answered. Words marked with a raised letter in the semi-literal translation are treated separately under the heading LEXICON. First, the lexicon form of the Greek word is given. Within the parentheses following the Greek word is the location number where, in the author's judgment, this word is defined in the *Greek-English Lexicon of the New Testament Based on Semantic Domains* (Louw and Nida 1988). When a semantic domain includes a translation of the particular verse being treated, **LN** in bold type indicates that specific translation. If the specific reference for the verse is listed in *A Greek-English Lexicon of the New Testament and Other Early Christian Literature* (Bauer, Arndt, Gingrich, and Danker 1979), the outline location and page number is given. Then English equivalents of the Greek word are given to show how it is translated by commentators who offer their own translations of the whole text and, after a semicolon, all the versions in the list of abbreviations for translations. When reference is made to "all versions," it refers to only the versions in the list of translations. Sometimes further comments are made about the meaning of the word or the significance of a verb's tense, voice, or mood.

The Questions

Under the heading QUESTION, a question is asked that comes from examining the Greek text under consideration. Typical questions concern the identity of an implied actor or object of an event word, the antecedent of a pronominal reference, the connection indicated by a relational word, the meaning of a genitive construction, the meaning of figurative language, the function of a rhetorical question, the identification of an ambiguity, and the presence of implied information that is needed to understand the passage correctly. Background information is also considered for a proper understanding of a passage. Although not all implied information and background information is made explicit in a translation, it is important to consider it so that the translation will not be stated in such a way that prevents a reader from arriving at the proper interpretation. The question is answered with a summary of what commentators have said. If there are contrasting differences of opinion, the different interpretations are numbered and the commentaries that support each are listed. Differences that are not treated by many of the commentaries often are not numbered, but are introduced with a contrastive 'Or' at the beginning of the sentence. No attempt has been made to select which interpretation is best.

In listing support for various statements of interpretation, the author is often faced with the difficult task of matching the different terminologies used in commentaries with the terminology he has adopted. Sometimes he can only infer the position of a commentary from incidental remarks. This book, then, includes the author's interpretation of the views taken in the various commentaries. General statements are followed by specific statements, which indicate the author's understanding of the pertinent relationships, actors, events, and objects implied by that interpretation.

The Use of This Book

This book does not replace the commentaries that it summarizes. Commentaries contain much more information about the meaning of words and passages. They often contain arguments for the interpretations that are taken and they may have important discussions about the discourse features of the text. In addition, they have information about the historical, geographical, and cultural setting. Translators will want to refer to at least four commentaries as they exegete a passage. However, since no one commentary contains all the answers translators need, this book will be a valuable supplement. It makes more sources of exegetical help available than most translators have access to. Even if they had all the books available, few would have the time to search through all of them for the answers.

When many commentaries are studied, it soon becomes apparent that they frequently disagree in their interpretations. That is the reason why so many answers in this book are divided into two or more interpretations. The reader's initial reaction may be that all of these different interpretations complicate exegesis rather than help it. However, before translating a passage, a translator needs to know exactly where there is a problem of interpretation and what the exegetical options are.

Acknowledgments

This volume has been thoroughly reviewed by Richard C. Blight. He has studied the questions and answers and has made a significant contribution in determining their final forms. James E. Mignard and Gerald E. Montgomery have reviewed and commented on the manuscript.

ABBREVIATIONS

COMMENTARIES AND LEXICONS

Alf   Alford, Henry. *Alford's Greek Testament.* Vol. 3. 1871. Reprint. Grand Rapids: Baker, 1980.

BAGD   Bauer, Walter. *A Greek-English Lexicon of the New Testament and Other Early Christian Literature.* Translated and adapted from the 5th ed., 1958 by William F. Arndt and F. Wilbur Gingrich. 2d English ed. revised and augmented by F. Wilbur Gingrich and Frederick W. Danker. Chicago: University of Chicago Press, 1979.

Brd   Bernard, J. H. *The Pastoral Epistles.* 1899. Reprint. Grand Rapids: Baker, 1980.

EBC   Earle, Ralph. *2 Timothy.* In *The Expositor's Bible Commentary,* edited by Frank E. Gaebelein, vol. 11. Grand Rapids: Zondervan, 1978.

EGT   White, Newport J. D. *The First and Second Epistles to Timothy.* In *The Expositor's Greek Testament,* edited by W. Robertson Nicoll, vol. 4. n.d. Reprint. Grand Rapids: Eerdmans, 1980.

El   Ellicott, Charles. *A Critical and Grammatical Commentary on the Pastoral Epistles.* Andover: Warren F. Draper, 1882.

GNC   Fee, Gordon D. *1 and 2 Timothy, Titus.* A Good News Commentary, edited by W. Ward Gasque. San Francisco: Harper and Row, 1984.

Herm   Dibelius, Martin, and Hans Conzelmann. *The Pastoral Epistles.* 2nd ed., 1967. Translated by Philip Buttolph and Adela Yarbro. Hermeneia—A Critical and Historical Commentary on the Bible, edited by Helmut Koester. Philadelphia: Fortress Press, 1972.

HNTC   Kelly, J. N. D. *A Commentary on the Pastoral Epistles.* Harper's New Testament Commentaries, edited by Henry Chadwick. New York: Harper and Row, 1963.

ICC   Lock, Walter. *A Critical and Exegetical Commentary on the Pastoral Epistles.* The International Critical Commentary, edited by S. R. Driver, A. Plummer, and C. A. Briggs. Edinburgh: T. and T. Clark, 1924.

LN   Louw, Johannes P. and Eugene A. Nida. *Greek-English Lexicon of the New Testament Based on Semantic Domains.* New York: United Bible Societies, 1988.

Lns   Lenski, R. C. H. *The Interpretation of St. Paul's Epistles to the Colossians, to the Thessalonians, to Timothy, to Titus and to Philemon.* Minneapolis: Augsburg, 1937.

LSA   Smith, Robert E., and John Beekman. *A Literary–Semantic Analysis of Second Timothy.* Dallas: Summer Institute of Linguistics, 1981.

MNTC   Scott, E. F. *The Pastoral Epistles.* The Moffatt New Testament Commentary, edited by James Moffatt. London: Hodder and Stroughton, 1936.

My   Huther, Joh. Ed. *Critical and Exegetical Handbook to the Epistles to Timothy and Titus.* Translated from the 4th. ed. by David Hunter. Meyer's Commentary on the New Testament. New York: Funk and Wagnalls, 1890.

NCBC   Hanson, A. T. *The Pastoral Epistles.* New Century Bible Commentary, edited by M. Black. Grand Rapids: Eerdmans, 1982.

NTC   Hendriksen, William. *1 & 2 Timothy and Titus.* New Testament Commentary. London: Banner of Truth Trust, 1957.

TG   Bratcher, Robert G. *A Translator's Guide to Paul's Letters to Timothy and to Titus.* London, New York, Stuttgart: United Bible Societies, 1983.

TNTC   Guthrie, Donald. *The Pastoral Epistles.* The Tyndale New Testament Commentaries, edited by R. V. G. Tasker. Grand Rapids: Eerdmans, 1957.

GREEK TEXT AND TRANSLATIONS

GNT   Aland, Kurt, Matthew Black, Carlos Martini, Bruce Metzger, and Allen Wikgren. *The Greek New Testament.* 3d ed. (corrected). London, New York: United Bible Societies, 1983.

KJV   *The Holy Bible.* Authorized (or King James) Version. 1611.

NAB   *The New American Bible.* Camden, New Jersey: Thomas Nelson, 1971.

NASB   *The New American Standard Bible.* Nashville, Tennessee: Holman, 1977.

NIV   *The Holy Bible: New International Version.* Grand Rapids: Zondervan, 1978.

NJB   *The New Jerusalem Bible.* Garden City, New York: Doubleday, 1985.

NRSV   *The Holy Bible: New Revised Standard Version.* New York: Oxford University Press, 1989.

REB   *The Revised English Bible.* Oxford: Oxford University Press and Cambridge University Press, 1989.

TEV   *Holy Bible: Today's English Version.* New York: American Bible Society, 1976.

TNT   *The Translator's New Testament.* London: British and Foreign Bible Society, 1973.

GRAMMATICAL TERMS

act.	active	opt.	optative
fut.	future	pass.	passive
impera.	imperative	perf.	perfect
indic.	indicative	pres.	present
infin.	infinitive	subj.	subjunctive
mid.	middle		

EXEGETICAL SUMMARY OF 2 TIMOTHY

DISCOURSE UNIT: 1:1–2 [EBC, ICC, Lns]. The topic is the address and greeting [ICC, Lns], the salutation [EBC].

1:1 Paul (an) apostle^a of-Christ Jesus
TEXT—Instead of Χριστοῦ ’Ιησοῦ 'Christ Jesus', some manuscripts read ’Ιησοῦ Χριστοῦ 'Jesus Christ'. GNT does not mention this alternative. Only KJV follows the reading 'Jesus Christ'.
LEXICON—a. ἀπόστολος (LN 53.74) (BAGD 3. p. 99): 'apostle' [BAGD, Herm, HNTC, LN, Lns, NTC; all versions], 'special messenger' [LN].
QUESTION—How are the two persons related in the genitive construction ἀπόστολος Χριστοῦ ’Ιησοῦ 'apostle of Christ Jesus'?
  1. He is an apostle who represents Christ Jesus [HNTC, TG]. He is Christ's spokesman [TG]. Christ chose him to be his ambassador [HNTC].
  2. He is an apostle commissioned by Christ Jesus [EBC, ICC, Lns, My, NTC].
  3. He is an apostle sent by Christ Jesus [EGT, LSA, NTC].

through^a (the) will^b of-God
LEXICON—a. διά with genitive object (LN 90.4; 90.44) (BAGD A.III.1.d. p. 180): 'through' [Herm, LN, Lns], 'by' [HNTC, ICC, LN; all versions except TNT], 'because of' [LN]. This prepositional phrase is also translated as a relative clause 'whom God willed to be' [TNT].
  b. θέλημα (LN 25.2; 30.59) (BAGD 2.b. p. 354): 'will' [BAGD, Herm, HNTC, ICC, LN, Lns, NTC; all versions except TNT], 'desire' [LN]. This noun is also translated as a verb: 'to will' [TNT].
QUESTION—What relationship is indicated by διά 'through'?
  It indicates the means by which Paul became an apostle [HNTC, ICC, LSA, My, NCBC; all versions except TNT]: I am an apostle by means of God's will. The direct relationship between 'apostle' and 'will' is result and reason: I am an apostle because God willed that I be one [TG].

according-to^a (the) promise^b of-life^c the (one) in^d Christ Jesus
LEXICON—a. κατά with accusative object (LN 89.8): 'according to' [HNTC; KJV, NASB, NIV], 'in accord with' [Lns], 'in accordance with' [LN; NJB], 'in harmony with' [NTC], 'entrusted with' [Herm], 'for the sake of' [NRSV], 'because' [ICC], not explicit [REB]. This preposition is also translated as a verbal phrase: 'sent to proclaim' [NAB, TEV], '(willed) to proclaim' [TNT].
  b. ἐπαγγελία (LN 33.288) (BAGD 2.b. p. 280): 'promise' [Herm, HNTC, LN, Lns, NTC; KJV, NAB, NASB, NIV, NJB, NRSV, REB], 'what was promised' [BAGD]. This noun is also translated as a verb: 'to promise' [ICC; TEV, TNT].
  c. ζωή (LN 23.88) (BAGD 2.b.α. p. 340): 'life' [BAGD, Herm, HNTC, ICC, LN, Lns, NTC; all versions].

d. ἐν with dative object (LN 89.119): 'in' [Herm, HNTC, NTC; all versions except TEV, TNT], 'in connection with' [Lns], 'in union with' [TEV, TNT], '(which was realized) in' [ICC].

QUESTION—What relationship is indicated by κατά 'according to'?
1. It indicates the purpose for his apostleship [Alf, Brd, EGT, El, Herm, HNTC, My, TG, TNTC; NAB, TEV]: I was appointed to be an apostle in order that God's promise of life might be accomplished, or be made known.
2. It indicates the standard by which God choose him [ICC, NCBC]: I was appointed to be an apostle by God, who did so in accordance with his promise of life. God's appointment was in accord with God's divine plan which involved his promise of life [NCBC].
3. It indicates a result of that promise [NTC]: I was appointed to be an apostle as a result of the promise of life. This does not mean that he was the fulfillment of the promise, but that God appointed him to facilitate its fulfillment [NTC].
4. It indicates an agreement between God's will and God's promise [Lns]: made an apostle by God's will which accords with God's promise of life.
5. It indicates the reason he was appointed [LSA]: appointed to be an apostle because of God's promise.

QUESTION—What relationship is indicated by ἐν 'in'?
It indicates spiritual fellowship with Christ [Brd, EBC, GNC, HNTC, TG, TNTC; TEV, TNT]: the promise concerning life that is in union with Christ Jesus. 'In Christ' means to be in fellowship with Christ and can be considered equivalent to being a Christian [TG]. This life is found only in fellowship with Christ [Brd, EBC, GNC, HNTC, ICC, Lns, LSA, MNTC, My, TG, TNTC]. It is lived in Christ [Brd] and Christ is the center of such a life [NTC, TNTC].

1:2 **to-Timothy (my) beloved**[a] **child:**[b]

LEXICON—a. ἀγαπητός (LN 25.45) (BAGD 2. p. 6): 'beloved' [BAGD, Herm, HNTC, LN, Lns, NTC; KJV, NASB, NRSV], 'dear' [BAGD, LN; NIV, NJB, REB, TEV, TNT], 'well loved' [ICC]. This adjective is also translated as a verbal clause: 'whom I love' [NAB].
b. τέκνον (LN 9.46) (BAGD 2.b. p. 808): 'child' [BAGD, Herm, LN, Lns, NTC; KJV, NAB, NRSV], 'son' [HNTC, ICC; NASB, NIV, NJB, REB, TEV, TNT]. Some translations supply a possessive pronoun with the noun: 'my child/son' [KJV, NAB, NASB, NIV, NRSV, TEV], 'son of mine' [NJB], 'his son' [REB, TNT]

grace,[a] **mercy,**[b] **peace**[c] **from**[d] **God (the) Father and Christ Jesus the Lord of-us.**

LEXICON—a. χάρις (LN 88.66) (BAGD 2.c. p. 877): 'grace' [BAGD, Herm, HNTC, ICC, LN, Lns, NTC; all versions], 'kindness' [LN]. This is a prayer that God will bless him [TG], and be gracious to him [LSA].

b. ἔλεος (LN 88.76) (BAGD 2.a. p. 250): 'mercy' [BAGD, Herm, HNTC, LN, Lns, NTC; all versions], 'help in one's difficulties' [ICC]. This means to be merciful [LSA], and kind [TG].
c. εἰρήνη (LN 22.42) (BAGD 2. p. 227): 'peace' [BAGD, Herm, HNTC, ICC, LN, Lns, NTC; all versions]. This is peace in a person's heart [ICC], 'spiritual strength and well-being' [TG].
d. ἀπό with genitive object (LN 90.15) (BAGD V.4. p. 88): 'from' [BAGD, Herm, HNTC, LN, Lns, NTC; all versions except TEV]. The phrase ἀπὸ θεοῦ 'from God' is also translated as a verb phrase: 'I pray God...to give you grace' [ICC], 'May God...give you grace' [TEV].

DISCOURSE UNIT: 1:3–18 [TEV]. The topic is thanksgiving and encouragement.

DISCOURSE UNIT: 1:3–8 [NCBC]. The topic is personal exhortation to Timothy.

DISCOURSE UNIT: 1:3–5 [Brd, GNC, HNTC, ICC, Lns, LSA, MNTC, TNTC; NAB]. The topic is thanksgiving [Brd, GNC, HNTC, ICC, LSA, MNTC, TNTC], thanksgiving and prayer [NAB], Paul's grateful memories [Lns].

1:3 Thanks[a] I-have to-God,
LEXICON—χάρις (LN 33.350): 'thanks'. The phrase 'to have thanks' is translated: 'to give thanks' [HNTC; REB, TEV], 'to thank' [ICC; KJV, NAB, NASB, NIV, NJB, TNT], 'to acknowledge gratitude to' [NTC], 'to be grateful' [Lns; NRSV].
QUESTION—For what was Paul thankful?
Paul was expressing a general gratitude for God's past and present blessings, including Timothy's faith [EBC, EGT, Lns, NTC]. Most think that this refers specifically to Timothy's past life and the recent reminder of the sincerity of his faith [ICC, LSA, My]. Although the construction is not explicit, the phrase 'taking remembrance' in 1:5 is the implied reason [Brd, EGT, El, GNC]. He was also thankful for God's grace given to Timothy and, in particular, for his godly heritage [EGT, MNTC]. An expression of thankfulness was the customary way to start a letter [EBC, NCBC].

whom I-worship[a] from[b] (my) ancestors[c] with (a) clean[d] conscience,[e]
LEXICON—a. pres. act. indic. of λατρεύω (LN 53.14) (BAGD p. 467): 'to worship' [ICC, LN; NAB, NRSV, REB], 'to serve' [BAGD, Herm, HNTC, Lns, NTC; all versions except NAB, NRSV, REB].
b. ἀπό with genitive object (LN 67.131): 'from' [HNTC, LN, Lns; KJV], 'the way' (LN 10.20) [NASB], 'like' [Lns], 'as' [Herm; NIV, NJB, NRSV, TEV, TNT]. The phrase 'from my ancestors' is translated 'that God whom my forefathers worshipped' [ICC], 'the God of my forefathers' [NAB, REB].

c. πρόγονος (**LN 10.20**) (BAGD p. 704): 'ancestors' [BAGD, Herm, LN; NJB, NRSV, TEV, TNT], 'forefathers' [ICC, NTC; KJV, NAB, NASB, NIV, REB], 'forebears' [HNTC, Lns].

d. καθαρός (LN 53.29) (BAGD 3.b. p. 388): 'clean' [HNTC, LN, Lns], 'clear' [NAB, NASB, NIV, NRSV, REB, TEV], 'pure' [BAGD, Herm, ICC, LN, NTC; KJV, NJB]. The phrase ἐν καθαρᾷ συνειδήσει 'with a clean conscience' is also translated as an adverb: 'honestly' [TNT].

e. συνείδησις (LN 26.13) (BAGD 2. p. 786): 'conscience' [BAGD, Herm, HNTC, ICC, LN, Lns, NTC; all versions except TNT], 'intention' [REB], not explicit [TNT].

QUESTION—What relationship is indicated by ἀπό 'from'?

Most translate it to indicate the manner in which he worships [Herm, ICC, LSA; NASB, NIV, NJB, NRSV, REB, TEV, TNT]: I worship God as my ancestors did. The preposition more strictly indicates the source of the manner in which he worships [Alf, EBC, El, Lns, My]: I worship God in the way I received it from my ancestors. He worshiped in the manner handed down by his ancestors [My]. He worshiped with a faith derived from his ancestors, that is, his faith had its roots in their religion [NTC]. He worshiped with the feelings and principles derived from his ancestors' worship [El]. Such worship was traditional in his family [HNTC].

as/when[a] unceasingly[b] I-have remembrance[c] concerning[d] you in my prayers[e]

LEXICON—a. ὡς (LN 64.12; 67.45): 'as' [LN, Lns; NAB, NASB, NIV, REB, TEV, TNT], 'just as' [NTC], 'when' [Herm, LN; NRSV, REB, TNT], 'whenever' [HNTC, ICC; NAB], 'that' [KJV], not explicit [NJB]

b. ἀδιάλειπτος (LN **68.55**) (BAGD p. 17): 'unceasingly' [BAGD, LN], 'without ceasing' [KJV], 'ceaselessly' [Lns], 'constantly' [Herm; NAB, NASB, NIV, NJB, NRSV, REB], 'constant' [BAGD, NTC], 'always' [TEV, TNT], 'incessantly' [HNTC], 'never fail to do' [ICC].

c. μνεία (LN **29.18**) (BAGD 1. p. 524): 'remembrance' [BAGD, Lns; KJV], 'recollection' [NTC]. The phrase 'to have remembrance' is translated 'to remember' [BAGD, Herm, LN; all versions except KJV, REB], 'to mention' [HNTC; REB], 'to make mention' [ICC]. This phrase has the sense of making mention of them in prayer [TG].

d. περί with genitive object (LN 89.6; 90.24): 'concerning' [LN, Lns], 'of' [ICC, NTC; KJV]. This preposition is omitted when 'you' is translated as the object of a verb: 'to remember/mention you' [Herm, HNTC; NAB, NASB, NIV, NJB, NRSV, REB, TEV, TNT].

e. δέησις (LN 33.171) (BAGD p. 171): 'prayer' [BAGD, Herm, HNTC, ICC, LN; all versions], 'supplication' [NTC], 'petition' [Lns].

QUESTION—What relationship is indicated by ὡς 'as'?

1. It indicates the time when he thanks God [EBC, GNC, ICC, LSA, NCBC, TNTC]: I give thanks to God whenever I remember you, which I do continually.

2. It indicates an accompanying circumstance [EGT, El, Lns, LSA, MNTC, My, NTC]: I give thanks to God while I remember you.
3. It indicates the content of his thanksgiving [KJV]: I give thanks to God that I remember you.

night and day.
QUESTION—What does this phrase modify?
1. It modifies the immediately preceding noun phrase ταῖς δεήσεσίν μου 'my prayers' [EGT, GNC, HNTC, Lns, LSA, NTC]: in my prayers (which I pray) night and day.
2. It modifies the preceding verb phrase ἔχω μνείαν 'I have remembrance' [EBC, El, My, TG; NASB, NIV, TNT]: I constantly remember you night and day.
3. It modifies the following verb ἐπιποθῶν 'longing' [Brd, ICC, MNTC, NCBC, TG]: night and day I long to see you.

1:4 longing[a] to see you,
LEXICON—pres. act. participle of ἐπιποθέω (LN 25.18) (BAGD p. 297): 'to long (for)' [BAGD, Herm, HNTC, LN, Lns, NTC; NASB, NIV, NJB, NRSV, REB, TNT], 'to deeply desire' [LN], 'to greatly desire' [KJV], 'to yearn' [ICC; NAB], 'to want very much' [TEV].
QUESTION—What relationship is indicated by the use of the participial form ἐπιποθῶν 'longing'?
1. It indicates a circumstance accompanying remembering [El, GNC]: I remember you night and day as I long to see you. This deep desire existed before and was contemporaneous with the act of remembering [El]. The mention of remembering Timothy in prayer (1:3) prompted the memory of their last parting and his desire to see him again [GNC].
2. It indicates the reason for remembering him in prayer [My]: I remember you in prayer because I long to see you. The longing for Timothy caused Paul to remember him in prayer continually [My].
3. It indicates a circumstance accompanying giving thanks to God [Lns, LSA]: as I thank God, I long to see you.

remembering[a] your tears,[b]
LEXICON—a. perf. mid. (deponent = act.) participle of μιμνήσκομαι (LN 29.7) (BAGD 1.a.α. p. 522): 'to remember' [BAGD, ICC, LN, Lns; NJB, REB, TEV, TNT], 'to be mindful' [KJV], 'to recall' [Herm, HNTC, LN; NAB, NASB, NIV, NRSV], 'to revive in one's memory' [NTC].
b. δάκρυον (LN 8.73) (BAGD p. 170): 'tear' [BAGD, Herm, HNTC, LN, Lns, NTC; all versions except REB, TNT]. This noun is also translated as a verbal expression: 'to weep' [TNT], 'to shed tears' [REB].
QUESTION—What relationship is indicated by the use of the participial form μεμνημένος 'remembering'?
1. It indicates a reason for the preceding clause [EBC, EGT, El, GNC, HNTC, LSA, My, NTC]: I long to see you because I remember your tears.

2. It indicates a temporal circumstance of the preceding clause [Lns; REB]: I long to see you, when remembering your tears. This implies that it is also the reason for his longing to see Timothy.

QUESTION—Why did Timothy cry?

When Paul and Timothy last parted, Timothy broke down and cried because of being separated from Paul [Alf, Brd, EBC, EGT, El, GNC, HNTC, Lns, MNTC, My, NTC, TG, TNTC].

in-order-that[a] I-may-be-filled[b] with-joy,[c]

LEXICON—a. ἵνα (LN 89.59): 'in order that' [LN], 'that' [KJV], 'so that' [HNTC; NASB, NIV, NRSV, TEV], 'and so' [REB], 'to' [NJB], not explicit [ICC; NAB, TNT].

b. aorist pass. subj. of πληρόω (LN 59.37) (BAGD 1.b. p. 671): 'to be filled' [BAGD, Herm, HNTC, LN, Lns, NTC; KJV, NASB, NIV, NRSV, TEV], 'to make one completely (happy)' [TNT], '(joy) is completed/made complete' [ICC; NAB, NJB, REB].

c. χαρά (LN 25.123) (BAGD 1. p. 875): 'joy' [BAGD, Herm, LN, Lns, NTC; KJV, NASB, NIV, NJB, NRSV, TEV], 'happiness' [HNTC, ICC, LN; NAB, REB]. This noun is also translated as an adjective: 'happy' [TNT].

QUESTION—What relationship is indicated by ἵνα 'in order that'?

This indicates the purpose for seeing him [GNC, Herm, HNTC, Lns, LSA, NTC; NJB] or contemplated result [Brd, ICC; NAB, REB, TNT]: I long to see you in order that I may be filled with joy.

1:5 having-taken remembrance[a] of your sincere[b] faith,[c]

LEXICON—a. ὑπόμνησις (LN **29.10**) (BAGD 2. p. 846): 'remembrance'. The phrase ὑπόμνησιν λαβών 'having taken remembrance' is translated 'I call to remembrance' [KJV], 'I find myself thinking of' [NAB], 'I am mindful of' [NASB], 'I am/have been reminded of' [HNTC, LN; NIV, NRSV, REB], 'I remember' [BAGD, LN; NJB, TEV, TNT], 'in my mind is' [Herm], 'having received a reminder' [Lns, NTC], 'in the recent reminder' [ICC]. Because of the aorist tense of 'having taken', some think that this refers to a specific reminder, such as a letter, a report from someone who knew Timothy, or seeing someone who had a faith like Timothy's [Brd, EBC, EGT, El, HNTC, Lns, TG].

b. ἀνυπόκριτος (LN 73.8) (BAGD p. 76): 'sincere' [BAGD, Herm, HNTC, LN; NAB, NASB, NIV, NJB, NRSV, TEV], 'unhypocritical' [Lns], 'unfeigned' [NTC; KJV], 'genuine' [BAGD, LN]. This adjective is also translated as a noun: 'sincerity' [ICC; REB, TNT].

c. πίστις (LN 31.102; 31.104) (BAGD 2.d.α. p. 663): 'faith' [BAGD, Herm, HNTC, ICC, LN, Lns, NTC; all versions].

QUESTION—What relationship is indicated by the use of the participial form ὑπόμνησιν λαβών 'having taken remembrance'?

1. It indicates the reason for thankfulness (1:3) [Brd, EGT, El, GNC, HNTC, LSA, My]: I thank God because I have been reminded of your sincere

faith. Paul thanked God for God's work in producing such a faith in Timothy [GNC].
2. It is in apposition to 'longing to see you' (1:4) [Alf]: I have been longing to see you and have been remembering your sincere faith.

which dwelt[a] first[b] in your grandmother Lois and in your mother Eunice,
LEXICON—a. aorist act. indic. of ἐνοικέω (LN 85.73) (BAGD p. 267): 'to dwell' [BAGD, HNTC, ICC, Lns, NTC; KJV, NASB, NJB], 'to reside' [LN], 'to be alive in' [REB], 'to live in' [BAGD, Herm; NIV, NRSV], 'to belong to' [NAB]. Faith is also supplied as the object of the verb: 'to have faith' [TEV], 'to possess faith' [TNT].
b. πρῶτον (LN 60.46; 67.18): 'first' [Herm, HNTC, ICC, LN, Lns, NTC; KJV, NAB, NASB, NIV, NJB, NRSV], 'first of all' [TNT], 'before' [LN; REB].
QUESTION—What is implied by the adverb πρῶτον 'first'?
1. The same kind of sincere faith was in Lois (and Eunice) before it was in Timothy [Brd, EGT, LN, MNTC, My]. It does not mean that Lois was the first of her family to have faith [EGT]. Probably it means the faith of a pious Jew [Alf, EGT, Lns, MNTC].
2. Lois was the first of Timothy's family to become a Christian [El, HNTC, LSA, My, NCBC, NTC, TG, TNTC].

and-I-have-been-persuaded[a] that (it dwells) also in you.
LEXICON—a. perf. pass. indic. of πείθω (LN 33.301) (BAGD 4. p. 640): 'to be persuaded' [LN, Lns; KJV, NIV], 'to be confident' [NAB, REB], 'to be sure' [Herm; NASB, NJB, NRSV, TEV, TNT], 'to be convinced' [BAGD, HNTC, LN, NTC], 'to have had proof' [ICC], 'to be certain' [BAGD].

DISCOURSE UNIT: 1:6–18 [NAB, NJB]. The topic is an exhortation to faithfulness [NAB], Timothy's gifts [NJB].

DISCOURSE UNIT: 1:6–14 [Brd, GNC, HNTC, ICC, TNTC]. The topic is an admonition to Timothy [Brd], a challenge to courageous witnessing [HNTC], an appeal for courage and loyalty to the true teaching [ICC], encouragement from experience [TNTC].

DISCOURSE UNIT: 1:6–7 [EBC, Lns, LSA, NTC]. The topic is God's gift to Timothy [EBC], an appeal for loyalty [GNC], an admonition to be unashamed [Lns], a reminder to do what God had equipped him to do [LSA].

1:6 For[a] which reason[b] I remind[c] you
LEXICON—a. διά with accusative object (LN 89.26): 'for' [HNTC, Lns, NTC; NAB, NASB, NIV, NRSV, TEV]. The phrase δι' ἣν αἰτίαν 'for which reason' is translated 'that/this is why' [NJB, REB, TNT], 'feeling this confidence' [ICC], 'wherefore' [KJV], 'therefore' [Herm].
b. αἰτία (LN 89.15) (BAGD 1. p. 26): 'reason' [BAGD, HNTC, LN, NTC; NAB, NASB, NIV, NRSV, TEV], 'cause' [BAGD, LN, Lns].

c. pres. act. indic. of ἀναμιμνῄσκω (LN **29.10**) (BAGD p. 57): 'to remind' [BAGD, Herm, HNTC, ICC, LN, Lns, NTC; all versions except KJV], 'to put one in remembrance' [KJV].

QUESTION—What relationship is indicated by δι' ἣν αἰτίαν 'for which reason'?

1. It indicates an exhortation grounded on the fact of Timothy's sincere faith [Alf, Brd, EBC, EGT, El, GNC, HNTC, ICC, NTC]: since you have a sincere faith, I remind you to fan the flame of God's gift. The verb 'to remind' contains the idea of exhortation [My].
2. It indicates an exhortation grounded on Paul's assurance of Timothy's faith [EGT, El, GNC, HNTC, LSA, MNTC, My, TNTC]: since I have been persuaded that this faith really dwells in you, I remind you to fan the flame of God's gift.

fan-into-flame[a] God's gift[b]

LEXICON—a. pres. act. infin. of ἀναζωπυρέω (LN **68.8**) (BAGD 1. p. 54): 'to fan into flame' [NIV, NJB], 'to fan into live flame' [Lns], 'to stir up' [KJV], 'to stir/stir up into flame' [NAB, REB, TNT], 'to stir into a living flame' [NTC], 'to stir into full life' [ICC], 'to kindle afresh' [NASB], 'to rekindle' [BAGD, Herm, HNTC, **LN**; NRSV], 'to keep alive' [TEV], 'to reactivate' [LN].

b. χάρισμα (LN 57.103) (BAGD 2. p. 879): 'gift' [BAGD, Herm, HNTC, ICC, LN, NTC; all versions], 'charisma' [Lns].

QUESTION—What is meant by fanning the gift into flame?

Two commentators consider this to be a dead metaphor in which the comparison with fire was not intended [ICC, LSA], and the meaning is simply 'to do fervently' [LSA]. Most treat this as a live metaphor comparing the fanning of a fire into a flame with intensifying the use of the gift given by God. 'Gift' is the work and manifestation of the Holy Spirit which often in Scripture is symbolized or manifested by fire [Brd, ICC, MNTC, NTC, TG]. The gift is like a fire which can and should be stirred up or fanned into a flame [EBC, HNTC, Lns, LSA].

1. It is implied that the gift had been neglected [Brd, Herm, HNTC, ICC, LN, My, NTC; NASB]: fan the embers to make them flame up again. The fire was burning low [NTC]; there were only embers [ICC]. His former zeal has weakened because of the suffering Paul had gone through [My].
2. There is no implication that the gift had been neglected [Lns, MNTC, TNTC; TEV]: fan the fire to keep it burning brightly. He has not weakened in zeal [MNTC], and Paul tells him to continue with the same ardor he has shown [Lns].

QUESTION—What is meant by χάρισμα 'gift'?

It is a special grace God gave Timothy to fit him for his ministry [Alf, Brd, EBC, EGT, El, GNC, HNTC, My, NCBC, TNTC]. It was the ability for administration and rule [EGT] in his work as a bishop and evangelist [El], the ability to preach, teach, admonish, and supervise [Lns], the power, love, and self-mastery described in the next verse [TG, TNTC]. The singular form refers to the whole of the gifts needed for ministry [Alf, EGT].

which is in you through^a the laying-on^b of my hands.

LEXICON—a. διά with genitive object (LN 90.4): 'through' [Herm, LN, NTC; NASB, NIV, NJB, NRSV, REB], 'by' [ICC, LN, Lns; KJV], 'when' [NAB, TEV, TNT], 'as a result of' [HNTC].

b. ἐπίθεσις (LN 85.51) (BAGD p. 293): 'laying on' [BAGD, Herm, HNTC, ICC, Lns, NTC; NAB, NASB, NIV, NJB, NRSV, REB], 'putting on' [KJV]. This noun is also translated as a verb: 'to lay on' [LN; NAB, TEV, TNT].

QUESTION—When did this laying on of hands occur?

This happened at Timothy's ordination (at Ephesus, 1 Tim. 4:14) [Alf, Brd, EBC, HNTC, ICC, Lns, MNTC, My, NCBC, TG]. Other writers, referring to the same event, designate it as his 'call' or 'public ceremony to enter ministry' or 'commissioning' or 'consecration' [Brd, GNC, LSA, TNTC]. Some relate this to the laying of hands on Timothy at Lystra on Paul's 2nd journey (Acts 14:23) [NTC]. Paul's hands were a medium through which the gift was imparted [El].

1:7 For^a God did not give^b to-us (a/the) spirit^c of-cowardice,^d

LEXICON—a. γάρ (LN 89.23): 'for' [Herm, HNTC, ICC, Lns, NTC; all versions except NAB, NJB], not explicit [NAB, NJB].

b. aorist act. indic. of δίδωμι (LN 90.51): 'to give' [Herm, ICC, Lns, NTC; all versions except TEV, TNT], 'to make someone something' [TEV, TNT].

c. πνεῦμα (LN 12.18; 26.9) (BAGD 5.e. p. 677): 'spirit' [Herm, HNTC, ICC, Lns, NTC; all versions except NAB, TEV, TNT], 'Spirit' [BAGD; NAB, TEV], not explicit [TNT].

d. δειλία (LN **25.266**) (BAGD p. 173): 'cowardice' [BAGD, HNTC, ICC, LN, Lns; NAB, NRSV, TNT], 'fear' [Herm; KJV], 'timidity' [LN, NTC; NASB, NIV, NJB]. This noun is also translated as an adjective: 'cowardly' [NAB, REB]; or as a verb phrase: 'to make someone a coward' [TNT] 'to make timid' [TEV].

QUESTION—What relationship is indicated by γάρ 'for'?

1. It indicates another grounds for the preceding exhortation [Alf, Lns, LSA, My, TG]: fan into flame God's gift, since God gave us a spirit of power, love, and self-control. There is a need for such an exhortation since Timothy has not fully drawn on these gifts [Alf].
2. It explains what is meant by 'gift' [EGT, GNC, TNTC]: fan into flame God's gift, specifically, his gift of power, love, and self-control.

QUESTION—To whom does the pronoun ἡμῖν 'us' refer?

1. It refers to Timothy and Paul [Brd, HNTC, ICC, Lns, TG, TNTC]: you and me. Some think that this three-fold gift was for all active office-bearing ministers [Brd, HNTC, ICC].
2. It refers to Christians in general [EGT, LSA, My, NTC].

QUESTION—What is meant by πνεῦμα 'spirit'?
1. It refers to an inner quality of a person [Brd, EBC, EGT, Herm, HNTC, ICC, Lns, MNTC, NCBC, TNTC; all versions except NAB, TEV]: God did not give us a cowardly spirit. God did not infuse fear into us [EGT], he did not make us cowards [TNT].
2. It refers to the Holy Spirit [Alf, BAGD, El, GNC, LSA, NTC, TG; NAB, TEV]: God did not give us the Spirit as one who causes us to be cowardly. The Spirit does not cause us to be terrified of difficulties [GNC]. The Spirit does not make us timid [TG] nor cause us to be afraid [LSA].

but of-power[a] and of-love[b] and of-self-control/prudence/discipline.[c]
LEXICON—a. δύναμις (LN 76.1) (BAGD 1. p. 207): 'power' [BAGD, HNTC, LN, Lns, NTC; KJV, NASB, NIV, NJB, NRSV, REB, TEV, TNT], 'strength' [BAGD, Herm, ICC], '(to be made) strong' [NAB].
b. ἀγάπη (LN 25.43) (BAGD I.1.a. p, 5): 'love' [BAGD, Herm, HNTC, ICC, LN, Lns, NTC; all versions].
c. σωφρονισμός (LN **32.34, 88.93**) (BAGD 1. p. 802): 'self-control' [NJB, TEV], 'self-restraint' [TNT], 'self-discipline' [HNTC, ICC, NTC], 'moderation' [LN], 'discipline' [NASB], 'sound mind' [KJV], 'prudence' [BAGD, Herm, LN], 'ability to understand how to make wise decisions' [LN], '(to be) sensibly-minded' [Lns], 'wise' [NAB].

QUESTION—What is meant by δυνάμεως 'power'?
It is the limitless power of endurance to fulfill his arduous work for God [Brd, Lns, LSA, NTC, TG]. It refers to force of character in general [EGT], and more specifically, strength to boldly dominate any difficult situation with moral authority [HNTC, MNTC; and probably Herm]. It is strength of character to be bold in the exercise of authority [TNTC]. It refers to the ability to withstand the attacks of the world [My].

QUESTION—What is the gift of love?
It is an impulse to help those who are in need [ICC], a practical helpfulness [MNTC]. It is self-sacrificing service [HNTC].

QUESTION—What area of meaning is intended by σωφρονισμοῦ 'self-control/prudence/discipline'?
1. It means self-control and moderation [EBC, EGT, El, HNTC, ICC, LSA, NTC, TG, TNTC; NJB, NRSV, REB, TEV, TNT].
2. It means prudence, having a sound mind to make wise decisions [GNC, Herm, Lns; KJV, NAB].
3. It means the ability to discipline others [Brd, MNTC, My].

1:8 Therefore
LEXICON—οὖν (LN 89.50): 'therefore' [LN, NTC; KJV, NAB, NASB], 'so' [HNTC; NIV, NJB, REB, TNT], 'so then' [ICC; NRSV, TEV], 'then' [Lns], 'thus' [Herm].

QUESTION—What relationship is indicated by οὖν therefore?
It indicates that the following exhortation is based on the preceding grounds [Alf, Brd, EBC, El, GNC, HNTC, Lns, LSA, My, NTC, TNTC]: since God

2 TIMOTHY 1:8

has given us such a spirit of power, love, and self-control/prudence, do not, therefore, be ashamed to testify. Some include more than just 1:7 in the grounds for the exhortation, that is, all of Timothy's heritage: the faith of Lois and Eunice, and the examples of Paul and others who have unashamedly suffered hardships for their faith [Lns, NTC].

do not be-ashamed-of[a] the testimony[b] of-our Lord

LEXICON—a. aorist pass. subj. of ἐπαισχύνομαι (LN **25.193**) (BAGD 1. p. 282): 'to be ashamed of' [BAGD, Herm, HNTC, ICC, LN, Lns, NTC; all versions].

b. μαρτύριον (LN 33.262) (BAGD 1.b. p. 494): 'testimony' [BAGD, Lns, NTC; KJV, NAB, NASB, NRSV, REB], 'witness' [Herm, ICC]. This noun is also translated as a verb: 'to testify' [HNTC; NIV], 'to witness' [NJB, TEV], 'to speak out' [TNT].

QUESTION—How are the event noun and the Lord related in the genitive construction τὸ μαρτύριον τοῦ κυρίου 'the testimony of the Lord'?

1. The testimony is about the Lord [Brd, EBC, El, GNC, Herm, HNTC, ICC, Lns, LSA, MNTC, My, NTC, TG, TNTC; NAB, NIV, NJB, NRSV, REB, TEV, TNT]: do not be ashamed to testify about the Lord. Two translations preface 'testimony' with the pronoun 'your' to make clear that this is Timothy's testimony [NAB, REB] and other translations use a verb form for the Greek noun 'testimony' to imply or make explicit the actor, Timothy [HNTC; NIV, NJB, NRSV, TEV, TNT].
2. The testimony is what the Lord testified [EGT]: do not be ashamed of what the Lord testified to. This refers to his words, teaching, etc. (cf. 1 Cor. 1:6; 2:1; 2 Thess. 1:10).

nor (of) me the prisoner[a] of-him,

LEXICON—a. δέσμιος (LN 37.117) (BAGD p. 176): 'prisoner' [BAGD, Herm, HNTC, LN, Lns, NTC; all versions], 'imprisonment' [ICC].

QUESTION—How are the noun and the pronoun related in the genitive construction τὸν δέσμιον αὐτοῦ 'the prisoner of him'?

1. Paul was made a prisoner by people because he believed in and served the Lord [EGT, GNC, My, TG]: nor of me who am a prisoner for the sake of the Lord.
2. Paul was made a prisoner by people as a result of the Lord's providential rule [El, Lns, MNTC, NTC]: nor of me who am a prisoner by the Lord's decree.
3. 'Prisoner' is used figuratively. Paul was made a prisoner by the Lord in a spiritual relationship [HNTC, TNTC]: nor of me who am like the Lord's prisoner. The point of comparison between a prisoner and Paul is being bound to the will of the one who makes them prisoners [TNTC].

but[a] share-in-suffering[b] for-the gospel

LEXICON—a. ἀλλά (LN 89.125): 'but' [Herm, HNTC, Lns, NTC; all versions except TEV, TNT], 'instead' [TEV], 'nay' [ICC], not explicit [TNT].

b. aorist act. impera. of συγκακοπαθέω (LN 24.84) (BAGD p. 773): 'to share in suffering' [ICC], 'to accept one's share of suffering' [REB], 'to take part in suffering' [TEV], 'to take one's share of hardships' [TNT], 'to bear one's share of the hardships' [NAB], 'to join with someone in suffering' [Herm, HNTC; NASB, NIV, NRSV], 'to share in another's hardships' [NJB], 'to suffer hardship in fellowship with someone' [NTC], 'to join with someone in suffering' [BAGD, LN], 'to join in suffering disgrace' [Lns] 'to be partaker of afflictions' [KJV].

QUESTION—In what sense was Timothy to share in suffering?

Timothy was to be ready to suffer for the gospel along with Paul [Brd, EBC, EGT, El, Herm, HNTC, ICC, LSA, My, NTC, TG], with other Christian leaders [NCBC, TNTC], with Christ [EGT], or with all martyrs [Brd].

QUESTION—What relationship is indicated by the use of the dative case of τῷ εὐαγγελίῳ 'the gospel'?

It means to suffer for the gospel [HNTC, NTC; NASB, NIV, NJB, NRSV, TEV], that is, for the sake of the gospel [Brd, EBC, GNC, Herm, ICC, LSA; TNT], in the interest of the gospel [Lns].

according-to[a] (the) power[b] of-God,

LEXICON—a. κατά with accusative object (LN 89.8): 'according to' [NTC; KJV, NASB], 'in accord with' [Lns], 'with' [NAB], 'in' [Herm, HNTC], 'by' [NIV], 'through' [REB], 'relying on' [NJB, NRSV]. This preposition is also translated 'rely on' [ICC; TNT], 'as (God) gives' [TEV].

b. δύναμις: 'power'. See this word at 1:7.

QUESTION—What relationship is indicated by κατά 'according to'?

1. It indicates the standard by which he is to share the suffering [Brd, El, GNC, Lns; KJV, NASB]: share in suffering according to the power of God. He is to share as God gives him strength to do so [GNC; TEV]. Strength will be given in proportion to what must be endured [MNTC].
2. It indicates the means by which he is to share the suffering [EBC, Herm, ICC; NAB, NIV, NJB, NRSV, TNT]: share in suffering by relying on God's power.

QUESTION—How are the attribute word and God related in the genitive construction δύναμιν θεοῦ 'power of God'

1. Power is an attribute Timothy has which God imparts [Brd, EGT, GNC, HNTC, ICC, LSA, MNTC, TG, TNTC]: take your share of suffering according to the power that God gives you. This refers to the power mentioned in 1:7.
2. Power is an attribute God has by which God enables Timothy to endure suffering [El, Lns, LSA, NTC]: take your share of suffering in accordance with the help God gives you by his power.

1:9 the (one) having-saved[a] us and having-called[b] (us) with-a-holy[c] calling,[d]

LEXICON—a. aorist act. participle of σῴζω (LN 21.27) (BAGD 2.a.α. p. 798): 'to save' [Herm, HNTC, ICC, LN, Lns, NTC; all versions except REB],

'to bring salvation' [REB], 'to save or preserve (from eternal death)' [BAGD].
   b. aorist act. participle of καλέω (LN 33.312) (BAGD 2. p. 399): 'to call' [BAGD, Herm, HNTC, ICC, LN, Lns, NTC; all versions except TNT], not explicit [TNT].
   c. ἅγιος (LN 88.24) (BAGD 1.a.α. p. 9): 'holy' [BAGD, Herm, HNTC, ICC, LN, Lns, NTC; KJV, NAB, NASB, NIV, NRSV], 'dedicated' [REB], 'dedicated to God' [BAGD]. This adjective is also translated as a substantive: 'his own people' [TEV, TNT].
   d. κλῆσις (LN 33.313) (BAGD 1. p. 435): 'a calling' [BAGD, Herm, HNTC, ICC, LN, Lns, NTC; KJV, NASB, NRSV], not explicit [NAB, NIV, NJB, REB, TEV, TNT]. The noun form refers not to the act of calling, but to the condition or state into which we have been called [Alf, EGT].
QUESTION—What relationship is indicated by the use of the participles σώσαντος 'having saved' and καλέσαντος 'having called'?
   1. These give proof that God's power is exercised toward believers [Alf, EGT, GNC, HNTC, MNTC]: share in suffering according to God's power, since he has the power that saved and called us. We can rely on God's powerful help because God has already saved us [HNTC]. It strengthens our faith for the continuation of future gifts of power to us [EGT].
   2. These indicate the grounds for not being ashamed [LSA, My]: do not be ashamed since God has saved and called us. It strengthens the exhortation by detailing God's saving work of grace [My].
QUESTION—How are the participles σώσαντος 'having saved' and καλέσαντος 'having called' connected?
The operation of divine power manifests its nature in saving us from sin and its purpose in calling us to holy living [EGT, NTC, TG, TNTC]. Salvation is given to man by God through the call [My]. The call is the first stage of salvation [HNTC]. Salvation constitutes our calling [GNC]. There are two sides of divine assistance: God effected salvation and he enabled us to receive it [HNTC, MNTC].
QUESTION—To whom does he refer by the pronoun ἡμᾶς 'us'?
   1. He refers primarily to Paul and Timothy [Brd, Lns]: he saved and called you and me. However, what is true for them is true for all Christians [Brd, Lns].
   2. He refers to all Christians [Alf, El, LSA, My, TG]: he saved and called us all.
QUESTION—What is the meaning of κλήσει ἁγίᾳ 'holy calling'?
   1. 'Holy' is an attribute of the life to which they were called [EBC, EGT, GNC, HNTC, ICC, LSA, NCBC, TG; TEV, TNT]: God called us to live in a holy manner. God called us to belong to himself [TEV].
   2. 'Holy' is an attribute of the one who called them and thus it gives the event of calling a holy character [El, Herm, Lns, My, NTC, TNTC]: God called us with a calling that is holy in origin and character. What God

does takes on his character. Since God has called them 'in' holiness they are holy, having received his effective call unto holiness of life [El, Herm, NTC].

not according-to/because-of[a] our works[b]
LEXICON—a. κατά with accusative object (LN 89.8) (BAGD II.5.a.δ. p. 407): 'according to' [Herm, NTC; KJV, NASB, NRSV], 'in accord with' [BAGD, LN, Lns], 'because of' [BAGD; NAB, NIV, NJB, TEV, TNT], 'for' [REB], 'in virtue of' [HNTC, ICC].
  b. ἔργον (LN 42.11): 'work' [Herm, Lns, NTC; KJV, NASB, NRSV], 'deed' [LN], 'effort' [ICC], 'merit' [NAB, REB], 'anything done' [HNTC; NIV, NJB, TNT], 'what's done' [TEV].
QUESTION—What relation is indicated by the preposition κατά 'according to/because' here and in the following clause?
  1. It indicates correspondence [Alf, El, Herm, Lns, My, NTC; KJV, NASB]: God did not save and call us in accordance with what we have done. It gives the principle used in God's activity [My].
  2. It indicates the reason for God's acts [HNTC, ICC, TG; NAB, NIV, NJB, NRSV, TEV, TNT]: God did not save and call us because of what we have done.
QUESTION—What is implied in the phrase τὰ ἔργα ἡμῶν 'our works'?
This refers to righteous acts they have done (as in Titus 3:5, Rom. 4:5; Gal. 2:9) [Brd, EGT, El, GNC, Herm, HNTC, Lns, LSA, MNTC, My, NTC, TNTC]: not because we have done good deeds.

but[a] according-to/because-of[b] his-own purpose[c] and grace,[d]
LEXICON—a. ἀλλά (LN 89.125): 'but' [Herm, ICC, Lns, NTC; all versions].
  b. κατά with accusative object: 'according to', 'because of'. See this word in the preceding clause.
  c. πρόθεσις (LN 30.63) (BAGD 2.b. p. 706): 'purpose' [BAGD, HNTC, ICC, LN, NTC; KJV, NASB, NIV, NJB, NRSV, REB, TEV, TNT], 'plan' [BAGD, LN], 'design' [Herm; NAB].
  d. χάρις (LN 88.66) (BAGD 2.a. p. 877): 'grace' [BAGD, Herm, HNTC, LN, Lns, NTC; all versions except TNT], 'a gift freely given' [ICC]. This noun is also translated as an adjective: 'gracious' [TNT].
QUESTION—What is the relationship between the event noun πρόθεσις 'purpose' and the attribute noun χάρις 'grace'?
  1. The construction is a hendiadys in which the second noun modifies the first [HNTC, LSA; TNT]: he saved and called us because he graciously purposed to do so, or according to what he graciously purposed.
  2. Both nouns refer to what God did: he saved and called us because he purposed to do so and then acted in grace to bring it about [EGT, Lns, NTC, TG], or he called and saved us because he purposed to do so by acting in grace [El], or he saved and called us because he purposed to do so since he is a God of grace [GNC].

QUESTION—What is indicated by the use of the adjective ἰδίαν 'his own'?
It is emphatic, indicating the freedom of divine purpose [Brd], and the grounds of his purpose is in himself alone [El, LSA, My].

the (one) given^a us in^b Christ Jesus before^c times^d eternal,

LEXICON—a. aorist pass. participle of δίδωμι (LN 57.71): 'to give' [ICC, LN, Lns, NTC; KJV, NIV, NRSV, TEV, TNT], 'to grant' [Herm; NASB, NJB, REB], 'to bestow' [HNTC], 'to hold out (to us)' [NAB].
   b. ἐν with dative object (LN 89.119): 'in' [HNTC, Lns, NTC; all versions except TEV, TNT], 'by means of' [TEV], 'through our union with' [TNT], 'as embodied in' [ICC], not explicit [Herm].
   c. πρό with genitive object (LN **67.133**) (BAGD 2. p. 701): 'before' [BAGD, Herm, ICC, Lns, NTC; KJV, NAB, NIV, NJB, NRSV, TEV, TNT], 'from' [LN; NASB, REB], not explicit [HNTC].
   d. χρόνος (LN 67.133) (BAGD p. 888): 'time'. The phrase πρὸ χρόνων αἰωνίων 'before times eternal' is translated 'before times everlasting' [NTC], 'before eon-long times' [Lns], 'before the beginning of time' [NIV, NJB, TEV], 'before time began' [Herm, ICC; TNT], 'before the ages began' [NRSV], 'before the world began' [KJV, NAB], 'from all ages past' [LN], 'from all eternity' [NASB, REB], 'ages ago' [HNTC].

QUESTION—What is the antecedent of τήν 'the (one which was given)'?
   1. It refers to χάριν 'grace' [EBC, EGT, ICC, Lns, LSA, MNTC, My, NTC, TG, TNTC; NAB, NASB, NIV, NJB, NRSV, TEV, TNT]: the grace which was given to us. 'Purpose' does not collocate with 'given' [Lns].
   2. It refers to both πρόθεσιν 'purpose' and χάριν 'grace' [GNC]. Both found expression in Christ [GNC].

QUESTION—In what sense was this given to us before times eternal?
What God has determined in eternity is as good as accomplished in time [Alf, Brd, My]. It was given from the beginning, but manifested later in time [El]. Another view is that it was given to Christ for imparting to us [HNTC, ICC, TG, TNTC].

QUESTION—What relationship is indicated by the preposition ἐν 'in (Christ Jesus)'?
   1. It indicates a spiritual union with Christ Jesus [Brd, EBC, EGT, El, HNTC, ICC, TNTC]: it is given to us who are in union with Christ Jesus. Some are quite emphatic that it is not through Christ that we are given grace [Brd, El].
   2. It indicates agent or means [Lns, LSA]: given us by means of or through Christ.

QUESTION—To what time does this phrase relate?
It refers to pre-time eternity [Brd, EBC, El, Lns, LSA, MNTC, My, TNTC]. The meaning of the expression here is stronger than that in Eph. 1:4 'before the foundation of the world' [El], and even than that in Titus 1:2 where the same phrase is used [MNTC]. It is before the most remote time a person can imagine [EGT].

1:10 but having-been-revealed[a] now through[b] the appearance[c] of our Savior Christ Jesus,

LEXICON—aorist pass. participle of φανερόω (LN 28.36) (BAGD 1.b. p. 852): 'to be revealed' [BAGD, Herm, HNTC, LN; NASB, NIV, NJB, NRSV, TEV], 'to be shown' [ICC], 'to be manifested' [NTC; KJV, NAB], 'to be made known' [LN], 'to be disclosed' [REB], 'to be published' [Lns], 'to be brought to light' [LN; TNT].
- b. διά with genitive object (LN 89.76): 'through' [Herm, HNTC, Lns, NTC; NAB, NIV, NRSV, TEV, TNT], 'by' [ICC; KJV, NASB, NJB, REB], 'in' [MNTC].
- c. ἐπιφάνεια (LN 24.21) (BAGD 2. p. 304): 'appearance/ appearing' [BAGD, Herm, ICC, LN, NTC; all versions except TEV], 'coming' [TEV], 'manifestation' [HNTC], 'epiphany' [Lns].

QUESTION—What relationship is indicated by διά 'through'?
This indicates the means by which grace was revealed [LSA, MNTC, My]: it has been revealed by means of our Savior's appearance.

QUESTION—What is meant by ἐπιφάνεια 'appearance'?
1. It refers to the incarnation [GNC, HNTC, ICC, NCBC, TG].
2. It refers to the whole manifestation of Christ in human form on earth: his incarnation, birth, life, redemptive work, and ascension [Alf, Brd, EBC, El, Herm, Lns, My, NTC].
3. It refers to the manifestation of Christ from his incarnation and continues to his second coming [EGT].

QUESTION—What is indicated by the addition of 'our Savior' before 'Christ Jesus'?
'Savior' reflects back to 'who saved us' and 'by his grace' in 1:9 [Lns, My, NTC]. It refers back to 'the promise of life' in 1:1, and here Christ was now the fulfiller of the promise, bringing to light incorruptible life [Herm]. The word 'Savior' also looks forward to where his saving work is most clearly delineated in the succeeding two clauses: defeated death and brought incorruptible life to light [HNTC, Lns, MNTC, NTC].

having-abolished[a] the death[b]

LEXICON—a. aorist act. participle of καταργέω (LN **13.163**, 76.26) (BAGD 2. p. 417): 'to abolish' [BAGD, LN, Lns; KJV, NASB, NJB, NRSV], 'to rob of power' [NAB], 'to break the power of' [BAGD; REB], 'to destroy the power of' [ICC], 'to end the power of' [TEV], 'to put an end to' [LN; TNT], 'to destroy' [HNTC; NIV], 'to dethrone' [Herm], 'to utterly defeat' [NTC].
- b. θάνατος (LN 23.99): 'death' [LN]. The phrase τὸν θάνατον 'the death' is translated 'death' [Herm, HNTC, NTC; all versions], 'the death' [Lns], 'the dread tyrant death' [ICC]. The presence of the article refers to 'that death' or 'the well-known death' we all dread [Brd, EGT, GNC, HNTC, ICC, Lns, LSA, TG, TNTC].

2 TIMOTHY 1:10

QUESTION—What relationship is indicated by the use of the participial form καταργήσαντος 'having abolished'?
It explains 'having saved us' in 1:9 [ICC]: God saved us, that is, he nullified death. It summarizes Christ's saving work [HNTC].

QUESTION—What is meant by 'having abolished death'?
1. It means that the effects of physical death have been nullified [Alf, Brd, EGT, GNC, HNTC, ICC, LSA, TG, TNTC]. It does not mean that people no longer will physically die [EGT, TG], but that death has lost its sting (1 Cor. 15:55) [Alf, Brd, EGT, HNTC, TNTC]. Death can be treated as of no account [Alf]. It no longer means the end of life [TG].
2. It means that spiritual death has been changed to life [El, Lns]. We were once dead in sin, but now have life [Lns]. The power and principle of death have been made of none effect [El].
3. It means that both physical and spiritual death are defeated [My, NTC]. Eternal death no longer exists and physical death has been robbed of its curse [NTC]. Both physical and eternal death are one in their inner relation to one another and are brought to nothing [My].

and having-brought-to-light^a life^b and immortality^c through^d the gospel^e

LEXICON—a. aorist act. participle of φωτίζω (LN 28.36) (BAGD 2.c. p. 873): 'to bring to light' [BAGD, Herm, HNTC, LN, Lns, NTC; all versions except NAB, TEV], 'to bring into clear light' [NAB], 'to bring to clear view' [ICC], 'to reveal' [BAGD, LN; TEV].
b. ζωή (LN 23.88): 'life' [Herm, HNTC, ICC, LN, Lns, NTC; all versions].
c. ἀφθαρσία (LN **23.127**) (BAGD p. 125): 'immortality' [BAGD, HNTC, LN], 'incorruption' [Lns], 'incorruptibility' [BAGD, NTC; all versions except TEV]. This noun is also translated as an adjective: 'immortal' [Herm, ICC, LN; TEV].
d. διά with genitive object (LN 89.76): 'through' [Herm, HNTC, ICC, LN, NTC; all versions], 'by means of' [Lns].
e. εὐαγγέλιον (LN 33.217) (BAGD 1.a. p. 318): 'gospel' [BAGD, Herm, HNTC, LN, Lns, NTC; all versions except TNT], 'good news' [BAGD, LN; TNT], 'good tidings' [ICC].

QUESTION—What is meant by φωτίσαντος 'having brought to light'?
The word means 'to illuminate or flood with light', hence to bring into clear sight [Brd; TNT]. Without the figure, it means 'to reveal' [GNC, Herm, HNTC, LSA, My]. Various synonyms are given: to display [EGT], to make known by teaching, action, or example, to give clearness and distinctness, to make positive, to bring out of implicit into explicit position [ICC], to make real and available [TG].

QUESTION—What kind of life is meant by ζωή 'life', and how is it related to ἀφθαρσίαν 'immortality'?
It refers to a life for human beings which is more than the natural physical life in quality and duration, and is characterized by the noun which follows, 'immortality' [ICC, NTC]: immortal life. Or it is epexegetical, the second

defining the first [EGT, HNTC, ICC, My]: life, an immortal life. It is a future life [Brd], an unending eternal life [EBC, LSA, My, TNTC], an immortal life [El, GNC, HNTC, TG], an incorruptible life [EGT, El, Lns, MNTC, NTC], the life of the resurrection body [HNTC, Lns].

QUESTION—What relationship is indicated by διά 'through'?

The gospel is the means by which life is made known [Alf, Brd, EBC, EGT, LSA, MNTC, My, TG]. These things are made known by preaching the gospel [Alf]. The message includes all that God had revealed through the life, teaching, and death of Christ [GNC, HNTC, Lns, TNTC]. The gospel is the means by which we know that death has been defeated and that eternal life is possible [TG].

1:11 for[a] **which I was-appointed**[b]

LEXICON—a. εἰς with accusative object (LN 89.57): 'for' [Herm, HNTC, Lns, NTC; NASB, NRSV], 'in the service of' [NAB, NJB], 'of' [MNTC; NIV, REB], '(I was appointed) to (proclaim)' [ICC; TEV, TNT]. The phrase εἰς ὅ 'for which' is also translated 'whereunto' [KJV].

b. aorist pass. indic. of τίθημι (LN 37.96) (BAGD I.2.a.α. p. 816): 'to be appointed' [Herm, HNTC, ICC, LN, Lns, NTC; KJV, NAB, NASB, NIV, NRSV, REB, TNT], 'to be made' [BAGD; NJB]. This verb is also translated in the active voice with God as the subject: 'to appoint' [TEV].

QUESTION—To what does the relative pronoun ὅ 'which' refer?

1. It refers to the gospel (1:10) [Alf, Brd, EBC, EGT, El, GNC, Herm, HNTC, ICC, Lns, LSA, MNTC, My, NTC, TG, TNTC; NAB, NIV, NRSV, REB]: for which gospel I was appointed to be a preacher. Specifically, he was appointed to proclaim the gospel [Alf, Brd, EBC, LSA, My].
2. It refers to our Savior Christ Jesus [NJB]: in whose service I was appointed to be a preacher.

QUESTION—What relationship is indicated by εἰς 'for'?

This indicates the purpose for which Paul was appointed [Alf, Brd, EBC, HNTC, ICC, LSA; TEV, TNT]: I was appointed a herald, apostle, and teacher in order to (make known) the gospel. The implied verb is variously supplied: in order to proclaim the gospel [Alf, Brd, EBC, LSA, My, TG; TEV, TNT], in order to promulgate the gospel [HNTC], in order to serve the gospel [NAB].

preacher[a] **and apostle**[b] **and teacher;**[c]

TEXT—Some manuscripts add ἐθνῶν 'of the Gentiles' after διδάσκαλος 'teacher'. GNT omits it with a C rating, indicating a considerable degree of doubt. It is included by only [KJV].

LEXICON—a. κῆρυξ (LN **33.259**) (BAGD 2. p. 431): 'preacher' [BAGD, LN; KJV, NAB, NASB, NRSV], 'herald' [Herm, HNTC, Lns, NTC; NIV, NJB, REB]. This noun is also translated as a verb: 'to proclaim' [ICC; TEV, TNT].

b. ἀπόστολος (LN 53.74) (BAGD 3. p. 99): 'apostle' [BAGD, Herm, HNTC, LN, Lns, NTC; all versions]. This noun is also translated as a verb phrase: 'to carry with authority throughout the whole world' [ICC].

c. διδάσκαλος (LN 33.243) (BAGD p. 191): 'teacher' [BAGD, Herm, HNTC, LN, Lns, NTC; all versions except KJV]. This noun is also translated as a verb: 'to teach (its truths)' [ICC].

QUESTION—What is the relationship between the three designations of his work named here?

1. There are three different functions [EBC, El, GNC, HNTC, Lns, LSA, MNTC, NCBC, NTC, TNTC; all versions except TEV, TNT]: I was appointed to be a herald, an apostle, and a teacher. 'Preacher' relates to public proclamation of the gospel [EBC, HNTC, Lns, NTC]. 'Apostle' relates to fulfilling his commissioned church leadership [EBC, HNTC, Lns]. 'Teacher' relates to teaching the gospel [EBC] as a pastoral obligation [HNTC] and admonishing people to believe and obey it [NTC]. The three titles are listed in order to enhance his authority [NCBC]. The three designations do not refer to distinct offices; rather they enforce the idea that Paul had unique authority as teacher of the gospel [MNTC]. See these three terms in 1 Tim. 2:7.

2. The first designation is a general term specified by the two following offices [My; TEV, TNT]: I was appointed to be a preacher, specifically to be an apostle and a teacher to proclaim the gospel.

1:12 for[a] which reason[b] also/even[c] these (things) I-suffer.[d]

LEXICON—a. διά with accusative object (LN 90.44): 'for' [Herm, Lns, NTC; KJV, NAB, NASB, NRSV, TEV]. The phrase διὰ ἣν αἰτίαν 'for which reason' is translated 'that is the reason' [REB], 'that/this is why' [NIV, NJB, TNT], 'it is because' [ICC].

b. αἰτία (LN 89.15) (BAGD 1. p. 26): 'reason' [BAGD, LN; NASB, NRSV, REB, TEV], 'cause' [BAGD, LN; KJV], 'sake' [NAB]. See this word at 1:6.

c. καί (LN 89.92; 89.93): 'also' [Herm, Lns, NTC; KJV, NASB], 'and' [NAB, NRSV, TEV], not explicit [HNTC, ICC; NAB, NIV, NJB, NRSV, REB, TEV, TNT].

d. πάσχω (LN 24.78) (BAGD 3.b. p. 634): 'to suffer' [BAGD, Herm, LN, Lns, NTC; KJV, NASB, NIV, NRSV, TEV, TNT], 'to undergo hardships' [HNTC; NAB], 'to experience suffering' [NJB], 'to endure' [ICC]. This verb is also translated as a noun: '(my) plight' [REB].

QUESTION—What relationship is indicated by διά 'for'?

This indicates the reason he is suffering [Herm, HNTC, ICC, NTC; NASB, NIV, NJB, REB, TEV, TNT]: I suffer because of that reason.

QUESTION—What is the reason he is suffering?

1. It refers to his appointment as a preacher of the gospel [Alf, EBC, El, HNTC, LSA, My]: I suffer these things because I was appointed to be a preacher.

2. It refers to his activity as a preacher of the gospel [EGT, GNC, ICC, MNTC, NTC, TNTC]: I suffer these things because I am a preacher.

QUESTION—To what does οὗτος 'these things' refer?

It refers to what he is suffering [HNTC; NJB]. Specifically, it means hardships [NAB], and being a prisoner [Alf, ICC].

QUESTION—What relationship is indicated by καί 'also, even'?

1. It indicates addition [Herm, Lns, NTC; KJV, NASB]: I also suffer these things. He has suffered many previous hardships, and in addition he now is suffering imprisonment [Lns].
2. It emphasizes his present hardships [Brd, El, LSA]: I suffer even these things.

But[a] (I am) not ashamed,[b]

LEXICON—a. ἀλλά (LN 89.125): 'but' [Herm, HNTC, ICC, NTC; all versions except KJV, NIV], 'nevertheless' [Lns; KJV], 'yet' [NIV].

b. ἐπαισχύνομαι (LN 25.193) (BAGD 4. p. 282): 'to be ashamed' [BAGD, Herm, HNTC, ICC, LN, Lns, NTC; all versions except TEV]. The negative statement is also translated positively: 'to be full of confidence' [TEV].

QUESTION—What is the implied object of ἐπαισχύνομαι 'I am not ashamed'?

Paul is not ashamed of being subjected to suffering for Christ [HNTC LSA]. Specifically, he is not ashamed of being a prisoner [GNC, Lns, My, NCBC, NTC, TNTC].

for[a] I-know[b] whom I-have-believed[c]

LEXICON—a. γάρ (LN 89.23): 'for' [HNTC, ICC, LN, Lns, NTC; KJV, NRSV, TNT], 'because' [Herm, LN; NIV, NJB, REB, TEV].

b. perf. (= present) act. indic. of οἶδα (LN 28.1) (BAGD 1.g. p. 556): 'to know' [BAGD, Herm, HNTC, ICC, LN, Lns, NTC; all versions].

c. perf. act. indic. of πιστεύω (LN 31.85) (BAGD 2.a.α. p. 661): 'to believe' [BAGD, HNTC, LN; KJV, NAB, NASB, NIV] 'to trust' [ICC, Lns; REB, TEV, TNT], 'to put one's trust in' [Herm, NTC; NJB, NRSV]. The perfect tense marks it as a settled matter [Brd, EBC, El, HNTC, Lns, LSA, NTC, TNTC].

QUESTION—What relationship is indicated by the word γάρ 'for'?

1. It indicates the reason he is not ashamed [EBC, GNC, HNTC, LN, Lns, LSA, NTC].
2. It indicates the reason suffering doesn't prevent him from proclaiming Christ [MNTC, My].

QUESTION—What is meant by οἶδα 'to know'?

It indicates the close/intimate relation of the object to the subject [Brd, Lns, My]. Here it appears to signify less than γινώσκω but really says more by understatement [My].

2 TIMOTHY 1:12

QUESTION—Who is the antecedent of the relative pronoun ᾧ 'whom'?
1. It refers to God (1:8) [Alf, EGT, El, GNC, HNTC, ICC, MNTC, My, NTC, TNTC].
2. It refers to Christ Jesus (1:10) [Lns, TG].

andᵃ I-am-convincedᵇ that he-is ableᶜ to guardᵈ the depositᵉ of-me
LEXICON—a. καί (LN 89.93): 'and' [Herm, HNTC, ICC, Lns, NTC; all versions].
  b. perf. pass. indic. of πείθω (LN 33.301) (BAGD 4. p. 640): 'to be convinced' [BAGD, Herm, LN, NTC; NASB, NIV], 'to be persuaded' [LN, Lns; KJV], 'to be confident' [HNTC; NAB, REB], 'to feel confident' [ICC], 'to be sure' [NRSV, TEV, TNT], 'to be certain' [BAGD], 'to have no doubt at all' [NJB]. See this word at 1:5.
  c. δυνατός (LN 74.2) (BAGD 1.a.β. p. 208): 'able' [BAGD, LN]. The phrase δυνατός ἐστιν 'able is he' is translated 'he is able' [HNTC Lns, NTC; all versions except REB, TNT], 'he can' [TNT], 'he has power' [Herm], 'he has strength' [ICC], '(of) his power' [REB].
  d. aorist act. infin. of φυλάσσω (LN 37.120) (BAGD 1.c. p. 868): 'to guard' [BAGD, Herm, LN, Lns, NTC; NAB, NASB, NIV, NRSV], 'to guard safely' [ICC], 'to safeguard' [NJB], 'to keep' [HNTC; KJV], 'to keep safe' [REB, TEV], 'to take care of' [TNT].
  e. παραθήκη (LN 35.48) (BAGD p. 616): 'deposit' [BAGD, Herm, Lns]. The phrase τὴν παραθήκην μου 'my deposit' is translated 'that which I've committed unto him' [KJV], 'what I've entrusted to him' [LN, NTC; NASB, NIV, NJB, NRSV, TNT], 'all that I've entrusted to his keeping' [ICC], 'the deposit entrusted to me' [Herm], 'what has been entrusted to me' [BAGD, HNTC; NAB], 'what he has entrusted to me' [LN; TEV], 'what he has put into my charge' [REB].

QUESTION—What relationship is indicated by καί 'and'?
1. It coordinates two reason clauses [LSA]: because I know him and I have been persuaded.
2. It explains what trusting in God means in the present connection [Lns, My]: because I know him and thus I have been persuaded.

QUESTION—What is meant by φυλάξαι 'to guard'?
The primary sense is to take care of in a secure manner a precious thing which has been entrusted to someone. It means to keep safe [Brd, EGT, GNC, HNTC, ICC, MNTC], to preserve [Herm], to guard [NTC], to take under one's own protection [MNTC].

QUESTION—How are the noun and pronoun related in the genitive construction τὴν παραθήκην μου 'the deposit of me'?
1. The deposit is made by Paul [Alf, EBC, EGT, GNC, ICC, NTC; KJV, NASB, NIV, NJB, NRSV, TNT]: he will guard what I have entrusted to him. The deposit Paul entrusted to God is Paul's own being or soul [Alf, EBC, EGT, GNC, ICC, NTC], Paul's commitment to Christ and the gospel [GNC], Paul's work, teaching, and his converts [EBC, ICC].

2. The deposit is given to Paul [Brd, El, Herm, HNTC, Lns, LSA, MNTC, My, NCBC, TG, TNTC; NAB, REB, TEV]: he will guard what he has entrusted to me. The deposit God entrusted to Paul is the gospel [HNTC, Lns, LSA, MNTC, TG], the Christian doctrine [Brd, Herm, NCBC, TG, TNTC], the work of preaching [El, My]. In the matter of Christian doctrine, the deposit entrusted to Paul is also entrusted to the church in general [Herm, MNTC]. Even though Paul might be put to death, yet the Christian faith will be preserved to the end [TG]. The work of the gospel will not end with the death of Paul, but it will be entrusted to others [Lns].

until[a] that day.[b]
LEXICON—a. εἰς with accusative object (LN 67.119) (BAGD 2.a.α. p. 228): 'until' [BAGD, Herm, ICC, LN; NAB, NASB, NJB, NRSV, REB, TEV], 'against' [HNTC, Lns; KJV], 'for' [NIV], 'up to' [TNT], 'with a view to' [NTC].
b. ἡμέρα (LN 67.178) (BAGD 3.b.β. p. 347): 'day' [BAGD]. The phrase ἐκείνην τὴν ἡμέραν is translated 'that day' [Herm, HNTC, Lns, NTC; all versions except REB], 'that great day' [ICC], 'the great Day' [REB].
QUESTION—To what does ἐκείνην τὴν ἡμέραν 'that day' refer?
It refers to the time of the final judgment [Brd, EGT, El, HNTC, MNTC], when Christ comes again [Alf, ICC, LSA, My, NCBC, TNTC]. It is also experienced on the day a person dies [EBC, NCBC].

1:13 **Take/Hold-to[a] the pattern[b] of-being-sound[c] words[d] which you-heard[e] from me,**
LEXICON—a. pres. act. impera. of ἔχω (LN 18.6) (BAGD I.1.c.β. p. 332): 'to take' [Herm, HNTC, ICC; NAB], 'to have' [Lns], 'to hold to' [NRSV, REB], 'to hold on to' [LN, NTC], 'to hold fast' [KJV], 'to hold firmly' [TEV], 'to retain' [NASB], 'to keep' [BAGD; NIV, NJB], 'to keep before oneself' [TNT]. The present tense indicates that Timothy is presently doing this and the imperative form encourages him to keep doing it [LSA].
b. ὑποτύπωσις (LN **58.59**) (BAGD p. 848): 'pattern' [ICC, NTC; NIV, NJB, NRSV], 'form' [KJV], 'standard' [NASB, NRSV], 'outline' [REB], 'model' [BAGD, HNTC, LN, Lns; NAB, TNT], 'example' [BAGD, Herm, **LN**], 'the example for you to follow' [TEV].
c. pres. act. participle of ὑγιαίνω (LN 72.15) (BAGD 2. p. 832): 'to be sound' [LN], 'to be healthy' [BAGD] 'to be correct' [LN], 'to be accurate' [LN]. This participle is also translated as an adjective: 'sound' [Herm, HNTC, ICC, LN (58.59), NTC; all versions except TEV], 'true' [TEV], 'healthy' [GNT, Lns].
d. λόγος (LN 33.98) (BAGD 1.b.β. p. 478): 'word' [GNT, Lns, NTC; KJV, NASB, TEV], 'teaching' [EBC, EGT, GNC, HNTC, TNTC; NAB, NIV, NJB, NRSV, REB, TNT]. 'preaching' [Herm], 'doctrine' [Brd, El, ICC, MNTC], 'message' [BAGD, Herm, HNTC, LN, LSA], 'instruction' [MNTC].

e. aorist act. indic. of ἀκούω (LN 24.52) (BAGD 1.b.β. p. 32): 'to hear' [BAGD, Herm, HNTC, LN, Lns, NTC; all versions except TEV, TNT]. It is also translated 'that I taught you' [ICC; TEV], 'which I gave you' [TNT].

QUESTION—What is meant by ἔχε 'take, hold to'?
1. This means to hold on to something so that it will not be changed. There are variations in the way the grammar is taken.
   1.1 Hold on to what you heard from me as a pattern of sound words. [EBC, MNTC, My, NTC, TNTC; NIV, NJB, TNT]. Timothy is to ever use these words as his example and never depart from them [NTC].
   1.2 Hold firmly to the sound words you heard from me as a pattern [TEV].
   1.3 Hold on to the pattern of the sound words you have heard from me [Brd; KJV, NASB, NRSV, REB].
2. This means to take or accept what Paul has taught him as an example. There are variations in the way the grammar is taken.
   2.1 Take what you heard from me as a pattern of sound words [EGT, GNC, Herm, ICC, Lns, NCBC, TG; NAB].
   2.2 Take the sound words you heard from me as a pattern [El, HNTC].
   2.3 Take for a pattern the sound words you heard from me [Alf].

QUESTION—What is meant by ὑποτύπωσιν 'pattern'?
Literally it means 'outline sketch' [Brd, HNTC, MNTC], which implies it is not the finished product nor the entirety of detail of that which it portrays [HNTC, ICC, MNTC, NCBC, NTC, TNTC]; details can be filled in and more can be expounded and built on the framework of sound words Timothy has heard from Paul [HNTC, MNTC]. Others take the word to indicate, in a more complete sense, a 'pattern' to follow in all Timothy's teaching [Brd, EBC, EGT, El, Lns, LSA, NTC]. 'To model' as a verb is used in one translation: 'Model yourself on the sound instruction you heard from me' [MNTC], but that leans more to right living than to doctrinal orthodoxy which is Paul's primary focus here [NCBC].

QUESTION—What is meant by ὑγιαινόντων λόγων 'sound words'?
Various terms have been used to carry over some aspects of the metaphor to its present application: 'wholesome' [Brd, EGT, HNTC, LSA, TNTC], 'healthy' [EGT, El, GNC, Herm, HNTC, Lns, MNTC, TNTC], 'sound' [Brd, EBC, El, GNC, Herm, HNTC, ICC, MNTC, NCBC, NTC], but many of these writers are using one or all of these terms to redefine the more general one. Some writers hold more to the 'uncontaminated' aspect of the metaphor and use 'pure' [My], 'free from' foreign admixture (other beliefs) or infection of error, or unclean/sickly quibbles or arrogance [EGT, MNTC, My]. Other writers use non-metaphorical terms: 'true' [Brd, GNC, Herm, TNTC], 'authentic' [HNTC], 'correct' [LSA], 'orthodox' [NCBC], 'sound' (not 'wholesome') [ICC].

in[a] faith[b] and love,[c] the (one) in[d] Christ Jesus.
LEXICON—a. ἐν with dative object (LN 89.84; 89.80): 'in' [HNTC, Lns; KJV, NAB, NASB, NJB, NRSV], 'with' [NIV]. It is also translated by the phrases 'live in' [TNT], 'remain in' [TEV], '(and thus remain) in' [Herm], 'living by' [REB], 'in a spirit of' [ICC, NTC].
  b. πίστις (LN 31.85; 31.88) (BAGD 2.d.γ. p. 663): 'faith' [BAGD, Herm, HNTC, ICC, LN, NTC; all versions].
  c. ἀγάπη (LN 25.43) (BAGD I.1.a. p. 5): 'love' [BAGD, Herm, HNTC, LN, Lns, NTC; all versions], 'true love' [ICC].
  d. ἐν with dative object (LN 89.119): 'in' [Herm, HNTC, Lns, NTC; KJV, NAB, NASB, NIV, NJB, NRSV, REB], 'in union with' [ICC; TEV, TNT].
QUESTION—To what is this phrase related?
  1. It indicates the manner in which Timothy is to take/hold the pattern of healthy words [Brd, EGT, El, GNC, ICC, Lns, LSA, MNTC, My, NTC; KJV, REB, TNT]. He is to take and use the model in faith and love [Lns]. He is to let what he heard serve as a model for sound teaching, but to do so as he models faith and love [GNC].
  2. It indicates the manner in which Timothy heard the words [Alf]. He is to remember those sound words he had heard with such receptivity and ardor [Alf].
  3. It indicates an addition [Herm, TG; TEV, TNT]. It is an additional instruction [TG]. The result of taking such an example is to remain in faith and love [Herm].
QUESTION—What relationship is indicated by ἐν 'in' in the phrase 'in Christ Jesus'?
  1. It is connected with both 'faith' and 'love' [Alf, Brd, GNC, Herm, HNTC, Lns, LSA, MNTC, NTC, TG, TNTC; NASB, NRSV, TEV]. Faith and love are ours in union with Christ [TG, TNTC; TEV]. They result from our union with Christ [GNC, HNTC]. They are exercised by us who are Christians [Alf]. They are contained in Christ [Herm]. They mark the servant of Christ [MNTC]. They center in Christ because apart from Christ's merits, Spirit, and example they cannot exist [NTC].
  2. It is connected with only 'love' [ICC, My; TNT]. Love is ours only when we are in union with Christ [ICC; TNT]. It is grounded in Christ [My].

1:14 Guard[a] the good[b] deposit[c]
LEXICON—a. aorist act. impera. of φυλάσσω (LN 37.120) (BAGD 1.c. p. 868): 'to guard' [BAGD, Herm, ICC, Lns, NTC; NAB, NASB, NIV, NRSV], 'to guard closely' [LN], 'to keep' [KJV, TEV], 'to keep safe' [HNTC; REB, TNT], 'to look after' [NJB], 'to protect' [BAGD].
  b. καλός (LN 88.4, 65.22) (BAGD 2.c.β. p. 400): 'good' [BAGD, LN; KJV, NIV, NRSV, TEV], 'rich' [NAB], 'noble' [Lns; TNT], 'wonderful' [Herm], 'splendid' [HNTC], 'precious' [NTC; NJB], 'most precious of all' [ICC], not explicit [NASB, REB].

c. παραθήκη (LN **35.48**) (BAGD p. 616): 'deposit' [BAGD, Lns; NAB], 'trust' [HNTC], 'a thing entrusted to someone' [NTC; TEV], 'a gift entrusted to someone' [TNT], 'a deposit entrusted to someone' [Herm; NIV], 'a treasure entrusted to someone' [NASB, NRSV], 'what has been entrusted to one's care' [LN], 'a thing given in trust' [NJB], 'a thing committed to someone' [KJV], 'a treasure put into one's charge' [REB]. See this word at 1:12.

QUESTION—What is meant by φύλαξον 'guard'?

It is usually a military term 'to hold in close custody/guard closely' [LN], 'to protect' [LSA]. Timothy is to defend the gospel when it is attacked [NTC], and he is not to let it be changed [GNC, HNTC, LSA, NTC].

QUESTION—What is the significance of using the adjective καλός 'good' rather than ἀγαθός 'good'?

The word καλός expresses a union between 'goodness' and 'beauty' (even outward visible beauty) which ἀγαθός does not [Brd]; hence the various heightened terms: 'precious' [EGT, MNTC, NTC, TG], 'splendid' [HNTC], 'noble' or 'excellent' [Lns]. Others just use the basic term 'good' and relate it to parallel terms using καλός: 'good teaching' (1 Tim. 4:6), 'good fight' 1 Tim. 6:12, thus indicating its augmented nature [El, My]. Here καλός is used to distinguish this 'good trust (precious faith)' from 'my trust (deposit)' of v. 12 [EGT].

QUESTION—What is the deposit?

The deposit is the sound words Timothy heard from Paul (1:13) [GNC, HNTC, NTC]. It is the gospel [EBC, Lns, LSA, My, TG], the whole Christian doctrine [EGT, El, NCBC], the faith [NAB]. It was entrusted to Timothy by God [LSA], or Christ [ICC, Lns]. Paul was the human instrument for this commission [EBC, GNC, LSA, NCBC].

through[a] the Holy Spirit the (one) dwelling[b] in[c] us.

LEXICON—a. διά with genitive object (LN 89.76): 'through' [Herm, Lns, NTC; NASB], 'by' [KJV]. It is also translated by a phrase: 'through the power of' [TEV, TNT], 'with the help of' [HNTC, ICC; NAB, NIV, NJB, NRSV, REB].

b. pres. act. participle of ἐνοικέω (LN 85.73) (BAGD p. 267): 'to dwell' [BAGD, Herm, HNTC, ICC, LN, Lns, NTC; KJV, NAB, NASB, NIV, REB, TNT], 'to live' [NIV, NRSV, TEV].

c. ἐν with dative object (LN 89.119) (BAGD I.5.a. p. 259): 'in' [Herm, HNTC, ICC, Lns; KJV, NASB, NIV, NJB, NRSV, TEV, TNT], 'within' [NTC; NAB, REB].

QUESTION—What relationship is indicated by διά 'through'?

It indicates the means by which he is to guard the deposit [EGT, El, GNC, ICC, LSA, My, NTC, TG, TNTC]: guard the deposit by means of the Holy Spirit. The means is made more specific by some: guard the deposit by means of the Holy Spirit helping you [EBC, GNC, HNTC, LSA, MNTC, NCBC].

DISCOURSE UNIT: 1:15–2:2 [LSA, TNTC]. The topic is Paul and his associates [TNTC], receiving God's power and entrusting the message to others [LSA].

DISCOURSE UNIT: 1:15–18 [Brd, GNC, Herm, HNTC, ICC, Lns, MNTC, NCBC, NTC]. The topic is loneliness and faithfulness [Brd], apostasy or authentication [Herm], living examples of disloyalty and loyalty [GNC], examples of warning and encouragement [ICC], instances of perversion and fidelity [MNTC], the example of Paul's associates [HNTC], details of Paul's situation in Rome [NCBC], Onesiphorus being unashamed [Lns].

1:15 **You know**[a] **this, that**[b] **all**[c] **the-ones in Asia turned-away-from**[d] **me,**
LEXICON—a. perf. act. indic. of οἶδα (LN 28.1) (BAGD 1.e. p. 556): 'to know' [BAGD, Herm, ICC, LN, Lns; KJV, NAB, NIV, NJB, TEV, TNT], 'to be aware of' [HNTC, NTC; NASB, NRSV, REB].
  b. ὅτι (LN 90.21): 'that' [Herm, HNTC, ICC, Lns, NTC; all versions except NJB, REB, TNT], not explicit [NJB, REB, TNT].
  c. πᾶς (LN 59.23): 'all' [Herm, HNTC, ICC, Lns, NTC; KJV, NAB, NASB, NRSV], 'all the others' [NJB], 'everyone' [NIV, REB, TEV, TNT].
  d. aorist pass. indic. of ἀποστρέφω (LN **35.18**; 34.26) (BAGD 3.a. p. 100): 'to be turned away from' [Lns; KJV]. This passive form is also translated actively: 'to turn away from' [BAGD, Herm, ICC, LN, NTC; NASB, NRSV], 'to turn one's back on' [NAB], 'to desert' [HNTC; NIV, NJB, REB, TEV, TNT], 'to refuse to help' [**LN**]. The aorist passive form of the verb has here the force of the middle voice [EGT, El, My]. The Greek aorist is at times translated by the English perfect tense 'have turned away' [LSA].
QUESTION—What is meant by οἶδας 'you know'?
  With the presence of the demonstrative pronoun τοῦτο 'this', there is an emphatic tone that indicates the certainty of knowledge of the matter by Timothy [GNC, HNTC, Lns, My]. The statement may be taken as a reminder and an appeal to Timothy for loyalty [My]. This word indicates a general hearsay knowledge vs. γινώσκω 'personal knowledge of', as in 1:18 [Brd, EGT].
QUESTION—In what sense is πᾶς 'all' to be taken?
  It is not to be taken literally [Alf, EGT, HNTC, LSA, My, TG, TNTC]. 'All' is used as a hyperbole [LSA, TNTC]. It refers to a very large number of people [GNC] and means 'almost all' or 'very many' [LSA]. He refers to all the Christians from Asia who were in Rome [ICC] or to all his key friends who had deserted him [HNTC]. It is a sweeping exaggeration of depression [EGT, GNC, HNTC] and indicates the intensity of his disappointment [LSA].
QUESTION—In what way did they turn away from Paul?
  Basically the verb means to turn one's countenance away from someone [My], and a variety of terms are found to express the disavowal of personal relations: 'repudiate' [Alf, Brd, TG], 'desert' [EBC, NCBC, NTC], 'defect'

[EGT, TNTC], 'neglect' [EGT, El], 'failure/refusal to help' [ICC, Lns], 'forsake/abandon personally' [Herm, HNTC, TG], 'show indifference, coldness, disloyalty' [HNTC]. They deserted Paul because he was in prison [Brd, EBC, LSA]. They failed to support Paul at his trial [ICC]. Some commentators think that this refers to Christians from Asia who had visited Rome while Paul was in prison and had not gone to visit him [Alf, Brd, EBC, El]. They were ashamed of having a prisoner for a friend [Alf]. Other commentators think that this refers to Christians in Asia who abandoned their loyalty to Paul [EGT, Lns, MNTC, NCBC, NTC]. They would not respond to a letter from Paul asking them to come to Rome and testify on his behalf [EGT, Lns, MNTC, NTC]. A couple of commentators think that besides personal neglect of Paul there may have been a turning away from Paul's gospel [EGT, GNC].

of-whom is Phygelus and Hermogenes.
QUESTION—Why are Phygelus and Hermogenes singled out for mention?
They were probably inhabitants of Ephesus and personally known to Timothy [Brd, EBC, NTC]. They were men known to have abandoned Paul and are here cited as warning examples of turning away through fear, or possibly of being ashamed of Paul as a prisoner [Herm, LSA, MNTC, NCBC]. Of the defecting friends these were the most outspoken [Lns], or conspicuous [My], or main causes of the trouble [TNTC]. Perhaps they were leaders in the defection [GNC, TG].

1:16 (May) the Lord give[a] mercy[b] to-the household[c] of-Onesiphorus,
LEXICON—a. aorist act. opt. of δίδωμι (LN 57.71) (BAGD p. 192): 'to give' [Herm, LN, Lns; KJV], 'to grant' [NTC; NASB, NRSV], 'to have' [NAB], 'to show' [HNTC; NIV, TEV]. The phrase 'to give mercy' is translated 'to be kind' [NJB, TNT], 'to be merciful' [ICC], '(may the Lord's) mercy rest on' [REB]. The optative shows an emotional involvement of the author [LSA].
   b. ἔλεος (LN 88.76): 'mercy' [Herm, HNTC, LN, Lns, NTC; all versions except NJB, TNT].
   c. οἶκος (LN 10.8) (BAGD 2. p. 560): 'household' [BAGD, HNTC, LN, NTC; NIV, NRSV, TNT], 'house' [Lns; KJV, NASB, REB], 'family' [BAGD, Herm, ICC, LN; NAB, NJB, TEV].
QUESTION—To whom does 'Lord' refer?
The Lord is Christ, as shown by 1:8 and 18 [Brd, TG].
QUESTION—What is implied by the mention of Onesiphorus's οἴκῳ 'household'?
The mention of Onesiphorus' household without naming him personally implies that he has died [Alf, Brd, EGT, El, GNC, Herm, HNTC, ICC, MNTC, My], but most commentators recognize that there is no proof. Some definitely reject his being dead, holding that 'household' means all who belong to it and they refer to 1 Cor. 16:15 where the term is used of a living man [Lns, TG, TNTC].

2 TIMOTHY 1:16

QUESTION—What is meant by the Lord's giving them mercy?

To 'give mercy' is an idiomatic expression for 'to be merciful or kind' [LSA, TG]. Some consider that 'to give mercy' as well as 'to find mercy' (1:18) are Hebraisms [EGT]. This is a prayer [El, GNC, Lns, My, TNTC]. Many take the wish that God would give mercy to reciprocate the mercy and kindness Onesiphorus had shown Paul [El, Lns, My, NTC], as well as for the work he had done for the church in Ephesus [My]. The 'mercy' requested is not for any special sin [EGT], but that they might experience God's favor and kindness [LSA, TG].

because[a] often[b] he-refreshed[c] me

LEXICON—a. ὅτι (LN 89.33): 'because' [Lns; NAB, NIV, NJB, TEV], 'for' [Herm, HNTC, ICC, NTC; KJV, NASB, NRSV], not explicit [REB, TNT].

b. πολλάκις (LN 67.11) (BAGD p. 686): 'often' [BAGD, Herm, HNTC, LN, Lns, NTC; all versions except TEV, TNT], 'many a time' [ICC], 'many times' [BAGD, LN; TEV], 'again and again' [TNT].

c. aorist act. indic. of ἀναψύχω (LN **25.149**) (BAGD 1. p. 63): 'to refresh' [BAGD, Herm, ICC, Lns, NTC; KJV, NASB, NIV, NRSV], 'to give a new heart' [NAB], 'to relieve in troubles' [REB], 'to be a comfort to' [NJB], 'to cheer up' [LN; TEV, TNT], 'to cheer one's spirits' [HNTC].

QUESTION—What relationship is indicated by ὅτι 'because'?

The ὅτι clause is grammatically subordinate as the grounds for the optative verb 'may he give'. However, it is considered as more thematic since it carries on the idea of 'not ashamed' in 1:8, 12 [LSA].

QUESTION—In what way did Onesiphorus refresh Paul?

He demonstrated his friendship to Paul [Brd, HNTC] by visiting him in prison [Lns, MNTC] and fellowshipping with him [TNTC]. This includes all the proofs of love [My], including gifts to relieve Paul's hardships in prison [ICC] such as food and reading material [NTC]. This cheered Paul [TG] and caused him to relax [LSA].

and (was) not ashamed-of[a] my chain,[b]

LEXICON—a. aorist pass. indic. of ἐπαισχύνομαι (LN 25.193) (BAGD 1. p. 282): 'to be ashamed of' [BAGD, Herm, HNTC, ICC, LN, Lns, NTC; all versions except REB, TEV], 'to be ashamed to' [REB], 'to be ashamed that' [TEV].

b. ἅλυσις (LN 6.16, 37.115) (BAGD 2. p. 41): 'chain' [HNTC, Lns, NTC; KJV, NRSV], 'chains' [Herm; NAB, NASB, NIV, NJB], 'fetters' [ICC], 'imprisonment' [BAGD, LN]. The phrase 'of my chain' is translated 'to visit a prisoner' [REB], 'that I am in prison' [TEV], 'my being a prisoner' [TNT].

QUESTION—To what does τὴν ἅλυσίν μου 'my chain' refer?

Paul was actually chained as a prisoner [El, ICC, Lns, My, NTC, TNTC]. Some commentators think that there was a single chain attaching Paul to his guard [Brd, El, MNTC]. The phrase is metonymy for the fact of being a prisoner [Brd]. It is marked as prominent by being forefronted, and it has an implied concessive relation [LSA].

1:17 but being^a in Rome diligently^b he-sought^c me and found^d (me).

LEXICON—a. aorist mid. participle of γίνομαι (LN 85.6) (BAGD II.4.a. p. 160): 'to be' [BAGD, LN, Lns, NTC; KJV, NAB, NASB, NIV], 'to come' [Herm; REB, TNT], 'to arrive' [HNTC; NRSV, TEV], 'to reach' [NJB]. It is also translated by an expanded clause: 'when in Rome on a visit' [ICC].
  b. σπουδαίως (LN 68.65, 25.75) (BAGD 2. 763): 'diligently' [BAGD, GNT, Herm, Lns, NTC], 'earnestly' [BAGD, LN; NAB], 'eagerly' [HNTC, LN; NASB, NRSV], 'hard' [NIV, NJB], 'very diligently' [KJV]. This is also translated 'took pains to' [REB], 'took great pains to' [ICC].
  c. aorist act. indic. of ζητέω (LN 27.41) (BAGD 1.a.β. p. 338): 'to seek' [BAGD, Herm, Lns], 'to seek out' [KJV, NAB], 'to search for' [HNTC, NTC; NASB, NIV, NJB, NRSV, TNT], 'to search out' [REB], 'to look for' [BAGD; TEV], 'to enquire where (I was imprisoned)' [ICC].
  d. aorist act. indic. of εὑρίσκω (LN 27.27) (BAGD 1.a. p. 324): 'to find' [BAGD, Herm, HNTC, ICC, Lns, NTC; all versions].

QUESTION—What relationship is indicated by the use of the participial form γενόμενος 'coming'?

This indicates the time of the following verbs [Herm, HNTC, ICC, Lns, NTC; all versions]: when ('as soon as' [TEV, TNT]) he was in Rome, he sought me and found me.

1:18 (May) the Lord grant^a to-him to-find^b mercy^c from^d (the) Lord in that day.^e

LEXICON—a. aorist act. opt. of δίδωμι (LN 13.142) (BAGD p. 192): 'to grant' [BAGD, LN; all versions], 'to give' [BAGD, GNT, Lns], 'to allow' [LN].
  b. aorist act. infin. of εὑρίσκω (LN 13.17; 90.70) (BAGD 3. p. 325): 'to find' [BAGD, Herm, HNTC, ICC, Lns; all versions except NAB, TEV, TNT], 'to obtain' [BAGD], not explicit [NAB, TEV, TNT].
  c. ἔλεος: 'mercy'. See this word at 1:16.
  d. παρά with genitive object (LN 90.14) (BAGD I.3.b. p. 610): 'from' [BAGD, HNTC, ICC, LN, NTC; NASB, NIV, NRSV, REB], 'of' [KJV], 'with' [Herm, Lns], not explicit [NAB, NJB, TEV, TNT].
  e. ἡμέρα (LN 67.142) (BAGD 3.b.β. p. 347): 'day' [BAGD, Herm, HNTC, Lns, NTC; KJV, NASB, NIV, NJB, NRSV, TEV, TNT], 'the great day' [NAB, REB], 'the last great day' [ICC].

QUESTION—To whom does the double reference to the Lord refer?
  1. Both references to the Lord are to Christ [Alf, EGT, El, Herm, ICC, Lns, My]. The somewhat awkward double use of 'Lord' is probably a conflation of two stereotyped formulae: 'May the Lord grant him to find mercy' and 'May he find mercy from the Lord' [Alf, EGT, Herm] and the recurrence would not be noticed [Alf, EGT]. Another explanation is that it is necessary to use 'Lord' twice to avoid ambiguity; one pronoun 'to him'

is already used, so to add 'from him' here would be unclear as to antecedent [Lns].
2. Both references are to God [MNTC, TG].

QUESTION—What is referred to by ἐκείνῃ τῇ ἡμέρᾳ 'that day'?

It refers to the day of judgment [Brd, EBC, El, HNTC, ICC, LSA, MNTC, My, NTC, TG]. The judge will be Christ [El, ICC, Lns, My, TNTC] or God [Brd, HNTC, LSA, MNTC, NCBC, NTC, TG].

And how-much[a] in EPHESUS he served,[b] you very-well/better[c] know.[d]

TEXT—Some manuscripts add μοί 'to me' as modifying the verb 'he served'. Only KJV, NIV, NJB, TEV include this, either because of the variant text or in order to supply what is implied.

LEXICON—a. ὅσος (LN 59.19) (BAGD 2. p. 586): 'how much' [BAGD, LN; NJB, NRSV, TEV], 'in how many things' [Lns; KJV] 'in how many ways' [NIV], 'what (services)' [NTC; NASB], 'all (the services)' [HNTC], 'all the many (services)' [ICC; REB], 'the many (services)' [TNT], 'the many (services for Christ)' [NAB], 'what (his service has accomplished)' [Herm].

b. aorist act. indic. of διακονέω (LN 35.19) (BAGD 2. p. 184): 'to serve' [BAGD, LN], 'to minister' [Lns; KJV], 'to perform' [NAB], 'to render service' [BAGD, HNTC, ICC, LN, NTC; NASB, NRSV, REB, TNT], 'to help' [LN; NIV, NJB], 'to do' [TEV], 'to accomplish' [Herm].

c. βέλτιον (LN **65.23**) (BAGD p. 139): 'very well' [BAGD, LN; KJV, NASB, NIV, NRSV, TEV, TNT], 'best' [Herm, ICC]. It is also translated by a comparative phrase: 'better than I' [NTC], 'even better than I' [NAB], 'thou on thy part better (than I)' [Lns], 'better than anyone else' [NJB], 'as well as anyone' [HNTC; REB].

d. pres. act. indic. of γινώσκω (LN 28.1): 'to know' [Herm, HNTC, NTC; all versions], 'to realize' [Lns]. It is also translated by a clause: 'to have the means of knowing' [ICC].

QUESTION—What relationship is indicated by καί 'and'?

1. It is an afterthought, recalling Onesiphorus' prior service in Ephesus [EGT, GNT].
2. It is not an afterthought, but still ties in, keeping the order already indicated in 1:16, 17 by going back to the earlier services already rendered in Ephesus [Lns].

QUESTION—What is the intended relationship of the form βέλτιον 'very well, better'?

1. Though grammatically a comparative form, (but without a standard of comparison given [LSA]), it is here equivalent to a weak superlative [Brd], an elative [EGT, Herm, HNTC, NCBC], or an intensifier [EGT, LSA].
2. It is an implied comparison: 'better than I do' [Lns, MNTC, NTC], or 'better than I can tell you' [Alf, El, HNTC, My, NTC; NAB, NJB].

QUESTION—What is implied by the use of the word γινώσκω 'know' in place of οἶδα 'know' as in 1:15?
It indicates the service mentioned was from Timothy's own personal knowledge [Brd], or in Timothy's sight, under his own eyes [Lns, NTC]; so well known/familiar personally to Timothy, Paul didn't want to speak in detail [My, TNTC], and a perfectly general use of the word as in Heb. 6:10.
QUESTION—Whom did he serve?
1. He rendered service to people in general [El, Herm HNTC, ICC, LSA, My, TNTC].
2. He rendered service to Paul [GNC, TG; KJV, NIV, NJB, TEV].
QUESTION—Whom did he serve?
1. He rendered service to people in general [El, Herm HNTC, ICC, LSA, My, TNTC].
2. He rendered service to Paul [GNC, TG; KJV, NIV, NJB, TEV].

DISCOURSE UNIT: 2:1–26 [TNTC; NAB]. The topic is instructions for Timothy [TNTC], the true gospel versus false doctrine [NAB].

DISCOURSE UNIT: 2:1–13 [Herm, HNTC, ICC, NTC, TG; NASB, NIV, NJB, TEV]. The topic is enduring hardships and sufferings [Herm, HNTC, NTC; NJB], an appeal for loyalty and faithfulness in guarding the faith [EGT, TG; TEV], encouragement and exhortation to be strong in service [HNTC, ICC, MNTC; NASB, NIV].

DISCOURSE UNIT: 2:1–7 [EBC, GNC, MNTC, NCBC]. The topic is a renewed appeal [GNC], being strong [MNTC], guarding the faith [NCBC], three symbols of the Christian [EBC].

2:1 You therefore,a my child,b be-empoweredc ind the gracee the-(grace which is) inf Christ Jesus,
LEXICON—a. οὖν (LN 89.50): 'therefore' [LN; KJV, NASB], 'so' [LN; NAB], 'then' [HNTC, LN, Lns, NTC; NIV, NRSV], 'so then' [ICC], not explicit [Herm; NJB, REB, TEV, TNT].
b. τέκνον: 'child'. See this word at 1:2.
c. pres. mid./pass. impera. of ἐνδυναμόω (LN 74.6) (BAGD 2.b. p. 263): 'to be empowered' [LN], 'to be strong' [BAGD, Herm, HNTC; KJV, NAB, NASB, NIV, NRSV, TEV, TNT], 'to take strength' [LN; NJB, REB], 'to be strengthened' [LN, NTC], 'to realize constantly the strength' [ICC], 'to be ever made strong' [Lns]. The present tense indicates an abiding state [Alf, Brd, Lns].
d. ἐν with dative object (LN 89.76; 90.10): 'in' [Herm, HNTC, Lns, NTC; KJV, NAB, NASB, NIV, NRSV], 'in virtue of' [Lns], 'through' [TEV, TNT], 'from' [NJB, REB].
e. χάρις (LN 25.89; 88.66) (BAGD 3.b. p. 878): 'grace' [BAGD, Herm, HNTC, ICC, LN, Lns, NTC; all versions], 'favor' [LN], 'kindness' [LN].
f. ἐν with dative object (LN 89.119): 'in' [Herm, HNTC, Lns, NTC; all versions except TEV, TNT], 'in union with' [ICC, LN; TEV, TNT].

QUESTION—What relationship is indicated by οὖν 'therefore'?
1. It indicates an exhortation based on the fact of the general defection [Brd, El, TNTC], on the past exhortations in 1:13–14 [GNC, ICC, My], on the examples of Paul (1:12) and Onesiphorus (1:16–17) [Alf, El], on section 1:15–18 [LSA], or on all of chapter 1 [NTC].
2. It is transitional, introducing a new admonition [Lns]. Nothing precedes on which this exhortation is based [Lns]. It indicates a resumption of the exhortations [El, GNC, ICC, My]: now you be strong to make up for the failure of others.

QUESTION—What is the voice of the imperative ἐνδυναμοῦ 'be empowered'?
1. It is the middle voice [Herm, HNTC, ICC, MNTC, My, NCBC, TNTC; all versions]: strengthen yourself, or be strong.
2. It is the passive voice [Alf, Brd, EGT, El, GNC, Lns, LSA, NTC]: be strengthened, or be made strong. He is to let God strengthen him [EGT, GNC, LSA].

QUESTION—What relationship is indicated by ἐν 'in (the grace)'?
1. It indicates the means by which they are to become strong [GNC, HNTC, Lns, LSA, My, TG]: be strong by means of the grace coming to you from Christ.
2. It indicates the circumstance in which true strength is found for living the Christian life [Brd, El, GNC, NTC; and probably Lns who uses 'in connection with']: be strong or be strengthened by God as you abide in all of God's grace you have received.

QUESTION—What is meant by χάρις 'grace'?
This is grace in its broadest yet simplest theological sense [EGT, HNTC, ICC, Lns, TNTC]: unmerited divine help. It may refer specifically to the χάρισμα 'gift' in 1:6 [ICC, Lns, MNTC] or the grace bestowed on Christians before the world began (1:9) [NTC]. This grace is specifically Christ's help to live a sanctified life [El].

QUESTION—What relationship is indicated by the second ἐν 'in (Christ Jesus)'?
Christ is the mediator of grace to those who are in union with him [El]. It is the grace found by those in union with Christ [GNC, ICC, TG]. Christ imparts the grace [HNTC, LSA, TNTC].

2:2 and what you-heard[a] from[b] me through/with[c] many witnesses,[d]
LEXICON—a. aorist act. indic. of ἀκούω (LN 24.52) (BAGD 1.b.β. p. 32): 'to hear' [BAGD, Herm, HNTC, ICC, LN, Lns, NTC; all versions].
b. παρά with genitive object (LN 90.14): 'from' [Herm, HNTC, ICC, LN, Lns, NTC; NAB, NASB, NJB, NRSV], 'of' [KJV]. The phrase ἃ ἤκουσας παρ' ἐμοῦ 'what you heard from me' is translated 'the thing you heard me say' [NIV], 'the teachings that you heard me proclaim' [TEV], 'you have heard what I taught' [TNT], 'you heard my teaching' [REB].

c. διά with genitive object (LN 90.4) (BAGD A.III.2.a. p. 180): 'through' [BAGD, LN; NAB, NJB, NRSV], 'with' [HNTC], 'among' [NTC; KJV], 'before' [Herm], 'in the presence of' [ICC; NASB, NIV, REB, TEV, TNT], 'supported by' [Lns].

d. μάρτυς (LN 33.270) (BAGD 2.b. p. 494): 'a witness' [BAGD, Herm, HNTC, ICC, LN, Lns, NTC; all versions].

QUESTION—What is the antecedent of the relative pronoun in the phrase 'what you heard'?

It refers to the 'sound words' in 1:13 [Brd, EBC, EGT, El, GNC, HNTC, Lns, LSA, NCBC, NTC, TG, TNTC]. Besides the term 'healthy/sound words/teaching' [Brd, EGT, GNC, Lns, LSA], others describe it more explicitly: tradition of truth [EBC], tradition and doctrine [TNTC], true doctrine [El], true gospel [Lns], gospel of salvation and redemptive truth [NTC], apostolic gospel [HNTC], correct message [LSA], fundamental Christian truths [MNTC], orthodox teaching [NCBC], Paul's teaching [TG], or the deposit of 1 Tim. 6:20 and 2 Tim. 1:12 [EBC]. Timothy heard them at a specific time [TG], probably at his ordination [El, Herm, ICC, MNTC, NCBC], or he heard them during all of Paul's ministry to/with Timothy [ICC, NTC]. It refers to a formulated summary of the Christian teaching heard at his ordination [Herm]. It refers to the instructions given Timothy for the discharge of his office [MNTC, My].

QUESTION—What relationship is indicated by the preposition διά 'through, with'?

1. It indicates the means by which Timothy heard the message [Alf, BAGD, Brd, GNC, LSA, TNTC; NAB, NJB, NRSV]: through many witnesses. One commentator thinks that this means Timothy received Paul's teaching indirectly through reports from many others [Brd]. However, others think that Paul directly taught Timothy and they explain 'through' in various ways. What Paul taught Timothy was also attested to by many others [GNC]. Timothy heard the message not only from Paul, but from many others who testified to the same message [LSA]. Paul's teaching was reinforced by many others who testified that it was the true gospel [Lns]. They could testify to what Paul had taught Timothy [TNTC]. Timothy heard from Paul what Paul had received from the testimony of many others, including Jesus' personal disciples [MNTC]. The witnesses are the believers at large [Brd, EGT, GNC, Lns, NTC]. They are all the people throughout Timothy's life who impressed the gospel truth upon him, including his mother and grandmother [HNTC, LSA, TNTC]. They may include the faithful transmitters of basic Christian truths, even the many who had attested them to Paul [MNTC].

2. It indicates an accompanying circumstance to Paul's direct instructions to Timothy [EGT, El, Herm, HNTC, ICC, Lns, My, NCBC, NTC, TG; KJV, NASB, NIV, REB, TEV, TNT]: you heard from me in the presence of many witnesses. This locative sense frequently refers to Timothy's ordination [Herm, My, NCBC], or, in particular, to the presbyters/elders

[El, ICC, TG]. Another view is that this refers to a public action in the presence of the church [EGT].

these-(things) commit[a] to-faithful[b] men,

LEXICON—a. aorist mid. impera. of παρατίθημι (LN 57.116) (BAGD 2.b.α. p. 623): 'to commit' [LN; KJV], 'to entrust' [BAGD, Herm, HNTC, NTC; NASB, NIV, NRSV, TEV], 'to deposit' [Lns], 'to hand on' [NAB, REB], 'to hand over' [ICC], 'to pass on' [LN (31.87); NJB], 'to pass on to the care of' [TNT].

b. πιστός (LN **31.87**) (BAGD 1.a.α. p. 664): 'faithful' [BAGD, LN, Lns; KJV, NASB, NRSV], 'trustworthy' [BAGD, LN; NAB, TNT], 'reliable' [Herm, HNTC, **LN**, NTC; NIV, NJB, REB, TEV], 'dependable' [BAGD, LN]. The phrase 'faithful men' is translated 'men on whom you can rely' [ICC].

QUESTION—Who are the 'faithful men'?

They are faithful [El, LSA, My, NCBC, TNTC], reliable [EBC, GNC, HNTC, TG], trustworthy [EGT, Lns, MNTC, NTC]. They are faithful guardians of the truth [El, MNTC] or faithful transmitters of the truth [HNTC, My, TG]. Both preservation and transmission of the truth are involved [TNTC]. The term refers to the elders of the church [GNC], to the future leaders of the church [Herm], or to the other ministers Timothy was to prepare and appoint to possibly cover his absence or even replace him at Ephesus [ICC].

who will-be competent[a] to-teach[b] others also.[c]

LEXICON—a. ἱκανός (LN 75.2) (BAGD 2. p. 374): 'competent' [BAGD, Lns; REB, TNT], 'able' [BAGD, HNTC; KJV, NAB, NASB, NJB, NRSV, TEV], 'qualified' [BAGD, LN, NTC; NIV, REB], 'capable' [Herm]. This adjective is also translated as a noun: 'ability' [ICC].

b. aorist act. infin. of διδάσκω (LN 33.224): 'to teach' [Herm, LN, Lns, NTC; all versions], 'to instruct' [HNTC], 'to train' [ICC].

c. καί (LN 89.93): 'also' [HNTC, Lns; KJV, NASB, NIV, TEV, TNT], 'in turn' [Herm; NJB, REB], 'in their turn' [ICC], 'as well' [NTC; NRSV], not explicit [NAB, REB].

QUESTION—How is this clause related to the preceding one?

1. It gives a second qualification of those whom Timothy is to select [Brd, EBC, Lns, NTC, TNTC]: commit these things to men who are faithful and who will be competent to teach others.
2. It states the anticipated result of committing the teaching to faithful men [El, LSA, MNTC; NJB]: commit these things to faithful men so that they will be competent to teach others.
3. It explains in what sense they are faithful [ICC]: commit these things to men on whom you can rely as having the ability to teach others.

QUESTION—What relationship is indicated by καί 'also'?
1. It adds the actions of the faithful men to the action of Timothy [Alf, GNC, HNTC, LSA, My]: commit (by teaching) these things to faithful men who, in turn, will also teach others.
2. It adds the quality of competence in teaching to the quality of faithfulness [NTC]: commit these things to faithful men who, besides being faithful, are also competent to teach others.

DISCOURSE UNIT: 2:3–13 [LSA, TNTC]. The topic is enduring for Christ [LSA], the basis of encouragement and exhortation [TNTC].

2:3 Join-in-suffering[a] as[b] (a) good[c] soldier[d] of-Christ Jesus.

LEXICON—a. aorist act. impera. of συγκακοπαθέω (LN **24.84**) (BAGD p. 773): 'to join in suffering' [**LN**, Lns], 'to share in suffering' [NRSV], 'to take one's part in suffering' [TEV], 'to accept one's share in suffering' [Herm], 'to take one's share of suffering' [ICC], 'to take one's share of hardship' [REB, TNT], 'to take one's share of rough treatment' [HNTC], 'to bear hardships along with someone' [NAB], 'to suffer hardships with someone' [BAGD; NASB], 'to suffer hardship along with someone' [Lns], 'to endure hardship with someone' [NIV], 'to bear with one's share of difficulties' [NJB], 'to endure hardness' [KJV]. Also see this word at 1:8.
   b. ὡς (LN 64.12): 'as' [Herm, ICC, LN, Lns, NTC; KJV, NAB, NASB, TEV, TNT], 'like' [HNTC, LN; NIV, NJB, NRSV, REB].
   c. καλός (LN 88.4; 65.22) (BAGD 2.c.α. p. 400): 'good' [Herm, LN; all versions except TEV], 'loyal' [TEV], 'noble' [Lns, NTC], 'brave' [HNTC], 'true' [ICC], 'blameless' [BAGD].
   d. στρατιώτης (LN 55.17) (BAGD 2. p. 770): 'soldier' [BAGD, Herm, HNTC, ICC, LN, Lns, NTC; all versions].

QUESTION—With whom is Timothy to join in suffering?
   He is to join in suffering with Paul [El, ICC, LSA, My; NAB, NASB], with 'us' [NTC; NIV], with other Christian leaders [NCBC], and with all Christians who suffer [EGT, ICC, Lns, MNTC, TNTC].

QUESTION—In what way would he suffer?
   The very nature of soldiering involves suffering [GNC], and the lot of a Christian evangelist or leader was one of suffering [HNTC]. Suffering involved hardships and privations [EGT, El, HNTC, Lns, LSA, MNTC]. In addition it included persecution and imprisonment [GNC, Herm, My, NCBC, NTC, TNTC].

QUESTION—How is a soldier related to Christ Jesus in the genitive construction 'a soldier of Christ Jesus'?
   The soldier is in the army of Jesus Christ [ICC], who is his general [Lns]. The soldier fights on the side of Christ [TG], serving under him [LSA]. The Christian soldier aids Christ in his warfare against the forces of evil [MNTC].

2:4 No-one serving-as-a-soldier[a] gets-involved[b] with-the affairs[c] of-life,[d]
LEXICON—a. pres. mid. participle of στρατεύω (LN 55.18) (BAGD 1. p. 770): 'to serve as a soldier' [BAGD, LN; NIV], 'to soldier' [Lns], 'to war' [KJV], 'to go forth into the battlefield' [Herm], 'to be a soldier' [LN], 'to serve in the army' [NRSV]. This verb is also translated as a noun phrase: 'a soldier' [NAB], 'a soldier on active service' [Herm, HNTC, ICC; NASB, NJB, REB, TEV, TNT]
  b. pres. mid. indic. of ἐμπλέκω (LN **90.81**) (BAGD 2. p. 256): 'to become involved' [HNTC, LN; NIV, NJB, REB, TNT], 'to become entangled' [BAGD; NRSV], 'to entangle oneself' [Herm, Lns, NTC; KJV, NAB, NASB], 'to get mixed up in' [TEV], 'to tie oneself up with' [ICC].
  c. πραγματεία (LN **41.23**) (BAGD p. 697): 'affair' [BAGD, Herm, ICC, LN, Lns; KJV, NAB, NASB, NJB, NRSV, TEV, TNT], 'preoccupation' [HNTC], 'pursuit' [NTC], 'undertaking' [BAGD, LN].
  d. βίος (LN 41.18) (BAGD 1. p. 141): 'life' [BAGD], 'everyday life' [BAGD; NASB, REB], 'daily life' [LN], 'this life' [KJV], 'the common course of life' [Lns], 'civilian life' [HNTC, NTC; NAB, NJB, TEV, TNT]. This noun is also translated as an adjective modifying 'affairs': 'civilian' [NIV], or 'business' [Herm, ICC], 'everyday' [NRSV].
QUESTION—What is meant by 'not getting involved in the affairs of life'?
  He is not to have ties of home or business [EGT], nor be involved in all the ordinary callings and occupations of life which would be inconsistent with the special duties of a soldier [El], and is to hold aloof from all occupations not directly concerned with his service which might hinder his proper calling [MNTC]. He is to lay aside all secular pursuits so as to serve without distraction [EBC] and not be involved with a side business [NTC].
QUESTION—What is meant by τοῦ βίου πραγματείαις 'the affairs of life'?
  Πραγματεία 'affair' has a general reference to any matter or affair, and a more specific reference to business for a livelihood [NTC]. In the context of soldiering, it means civilian life, affairs, or pursuits [GNC, LSA, MNTC, NTC, TG], preoccupations of civilian life [HNTC], worldly business [Brd], business affairs [Herm], business or occupations by which men earn livelihood [ICC, My], making one's livelihood [NCBC], all secular pursuits [EBC], all the ordinary callings and occupations of life [El], the ordinary course of life [Lns], or any detracting interests [MNTC].

so-that[a] he-may-please[b] the (one) having-enlisted[c] (him).
LEXICON—a. ἵνα (LN 89.59): 'so that' [HNTC; NASB], 'that' [KJV], 'in order to' [NAB], 'in order that' [Lns], not explicit [ICC; NIV, REB, TEV]. This is also translated 'he wants to' [TEV, TNT], 'he only wishes to' [Herm], 'he hopes to' [ICC], '(since) his aim is to' [NTC; NRSV], '(because) he must' [NJB].
  b. aorist act. subj. of ἀρέσκω (LN 25.90) (BAGD 2.a. p. 105): 'to please' [BAGD, Herm, ICC, LN, Lns, NTC; KJV, NAB, NASB, NIV, TEV], 'to

satisfy' [HNTC; NRSV], 'to be wholly at the disposal of' [REB], 'to win the approval of' [NJB], 'to keep in favor with' [TNT].
   c. aorist act. participle of στρατολογέω (LN **55.19; 55.20**) (BAGD p. 770): 'to enlist' [BAGD, Herm, ICC, LN; NAB, NIV, REB, TEV, TNT], 'to choose to be a soldier' [HNTC, LN, Lns, NTC; KJV, NASB, NJB, NRSV], 'to be an army officer' [LN].
QUESTION—What relationship is indicated by ἵνα 'so that'?
   It indicates the purpose for not getting involved [Brd, HNTC, Lns, LSA, TNTC]: he doesn't get involved in order that he may please his commanding officer. All soldiers want to please the one who recruited them and therefore must not get involved [TEV, TNT, ICC].
QUESTION—Who is the implied actor of the participle στρατολογήσαντι 'having enlisted'?
   It is the general or superior officer who has the authority to conscript men for the army and hence the man under whom the soldiers served [EBC, GNC, Herm, ICC, MNTC, My, NTC, TG, TNTC], the enlisting officer [HNTC], the captain who enlisted him [LSA]. The problem is mainly with our present military concepts wherein the conscriptor is usually someone quite removed from the commanding or superior officer under whom a soldier serves and whom he endeavors to please [TG].

2:5 **And also^a if^b anyone competes,^c**
LEXICON—a. καί (LN 89.93): 'also' [Herm, Lns; KJV, NASB], not explicit [TEV]. The phrase ἐὰν δὲ καί 'and also if' is translated 'and' [TNT], 'so too' [ICC], 'similarly' [NAB, NIV], 'again' [HNTC, NTC; NJB, REB], 'or again' [NJB], 'and in the case of' [NRSV].
   b. ἐάν (LN 67.32): 'if' [Herm, Lns, NTC; KJV, NAB, NASB, NIV, NJB], not explicit [HNTC, ICC; NRSV, REB, TEV, TNT].
   c. pres. act. subj. of ἀθλέω (LN **50.2**) (BAGD p. 21): 'to compete' [LN], 'to compete as an athlete' [NASB, NIV], 'to compete in the sport' [NJB], 'to compete in a contest' [BAGD], 'to compete in an athletic game' [**LN**], 'to compete in an athletic event' [NTC], 'to take part in an athletic contest' [Herm; NAB], 'to strive for masteries' [KJV] The phrase 'anyone competes' is also translated as a noun phrase: 'an athlete' [HNTC, ICC; NRSV, REB, TNT], 'an athlete who runs in a race' [TEV].
QUESTION—What relationship is indicated by δὲ καί 'and also'?
   It adds a new comparison to the previous one about a soldier [Alf, El]. The καί 'also' means that what applies in the case of the soldier also applies in the case of an athlete [El]. Δέ 'and' marks the new thought of reward, and καί 'also' adds it to 1:4: 'moreover also' [Lns, My]. This is more individualized than soldiers [El].
QUESTION—What relationship is indicated by ἐάν 'if'?
   It indicates a hypothetical condition [LSA], though very real in Graeco-Roman life at the time [HNTC].

QUESTION—In what way does one compete?
This refers to competing in an athletic event [BAGD, Herm, LN, NTC; NAB, NASB, NIV, NJB]. It refers to competing against others in unspecified athletic events [Alf, Brd, HNTC, ICC, Lns, LSA, MNTC, NTC, TG], or in a race [Brd, My]. Another view is that it is of an individual athlete trying to set a record [Lns]. The present tense refers to the event as it is in progress [NTC].

(he is) not crowned[a] unless[b] lawfully[c] he-competes.[d]
LEXICON—a. pres. pass. indic. of στεφανόω (LN **57.122**) (BAGD 1. p. 767): 'to be crowned' [BAGD, HNTC, Lns; KJV, NRSV], 'to receive the winner's/victor's crown' [NAB, NIV], 'to wear the victor's laurels' [TNT], 'to receive the wreath' [Herm, NTC], 'to win the/a prize' [ICC; NASB, NJB, REB, TEV], 'to receive the prize' [LN].
- b. ἐάν (LN **89.67**): 'unless' [Herm, HNTC, ICC, LN, Lns, NTC; NAB, NASB, NIV, REB, TEV, TNT], 'except' [KJV], 'only if' [NJB], '(no one) without' [NRSV].
- c. νομίμως (LN 72.18) (BAGD p. 541): 'lawfully' [Lns; KJV], 'according to the rules' [BAGD, Herm, HNTC, LN; NASB, NIV, NJB, NRSV], 'in compliance with the rules' [NTC]. This adverb is also conflated with the verb 'to compete' and translated 'to keep/obey the rules' [NAB, REB, TEV, TNT], or 'to observe to the end the rules (of the contest)' [ICC].
- d. aorist act. subj. of ἀθλέω (LN **50.2**) (BAGD p. 21): 'to compete' [BAGD, Herm, HNTC, LN, NTC; NASB, NIV, NJB, NRSV], 'to strive' [KJV], 'to finish the contest' [Lns], not explicit [ICC; NAB, REB, TEV, TNT].

QUESTION—What is meant by στεφανοῦται 'he is crowned'?
This word is from the Olympian games [Brd] and refers to the athletic victor's wreath [EBC, Lns, NTC], in contrast to the διάδημα 'royal crown' (Rev. 12:3; 13:1; 19:12) [EBC]. It was composed of a garland of evergreen leaves or leaf-like gold [NTC]. The 'crowning' indicates the custom [LSA], but is frequently more generally translated 'win or gain the prize' [HNTC, LSA, My, TG; NASB, NJB, REB, TEV].

QUESTION—What is the non-figurative significance of the picture of being crowned?
The application for Timothy was that he was to so discipline his life and ministry proclaiming the true gospel that he would receive the 'wreath of righteousness' (1 Tim. 4:8) and the 'wreath of glory' (1 Thess. 2:19; cf. 1 Peter 5:4; James 1:12; Rev. 2:10) [NTC]. It has also been noted that whereas in the metaphor only one is crowned, in the Christian life every truly devoted Christian will receive the crown [TNTC].

QUESTION—What is meant by the qualification 'lawfully'?
1. It refers to the rules of the event itself [GNC, Lns, LSA, My, NTC, TG]. The emphasis is on disciplining oneself to strictly obey the rules [NTC, TG]. Timothy must do all Jesus has commanded [LSA], and the specific rules in focus are the rules of his evangelistic office [My], the command to

preach the truth in love [NTC], not deviating from faith and love (2:13) [Lns]. It concerns taking one's share of suffering [GNC].
2. It refers to the regulations about training and preparation for qualifying the athlete to enter the event [HNTC, MNTC]. There are hardships involved, but also rewards to devoted Christian service [HNTC].
3. It refers to all the rules both for qualification and the rules of the event [Alf, Brd, EGT, El, ICC, TNTC]. The training is that of 1 Timothy 4:7 and the regulations are the law of Christ as in 2:10–12 [ICC]. It requires self-discipline to follow the rules fixed by the life and teachings of Christ [TNTC].

2:6 The hardworking[a] farmer[b] ought[c] first[d] to-have-a-share[e] of-the crop.[f]

LEXICON—a. pres. act. participle of κοπιάω (LN 42.47) (BAGD 2. p. 443): 'to work hard' [BAGD, HNTC, ICC, LN, NTC; NAB, NASB, NIV, NJB], 'to toil' [BAGD, LN, Lns], 'to labor' [LN; KJV], 'to give one's labor' [REB], 'to do work' [Herm; NRSV, TNT], 'to do hard work' [TEV].
  b. γεωργός (LN 43.2) (BAGD 1. p. 157): 'farmer' [BAGD, Herm, HNTC, LN, Lns, NTC; all versions except KJV], 'husbandman' [ICC; KJV].
  c. pres. act. indic. of δεῖ (LN 71.34) (BAGD: 6. p. 172): 'to be necessary' [LN, Lns], 'must' [ICC; KJV, TNT], 'should' [Herm, NTC; NAB, NIV, TEV], 'ought' [NASB, NRSV], not explicit [HNTC; NJB, REB].
  d. πρῶτον (LN 60.46): 'first' [Herm, HNTC, ICC, Lns; all versions].
  e. pres. act. infin. of μεταλαμβάνω (LN **57.129**) (BAGD 1. p. 511): 'to have a share of' [**LN**; NAB, NRSV, TEV, TNT], 'to receive a share of' [BAGD, LN; NASB, NIV], 'to take a share of' [ICC, Lns, NTC], 'to have a claim on' [HNTC; NJB, REB], 'to be a partaker' [KJV], 'to be the one to enjoy' [Herm].
  f. καρπός (LN 43.15) (BAGD 1.a. p. 404): 'crop' [BAGD, HNTC, LN, NTC; NAB, NASB, NIV, NRSV, REB], 'fruit' [Herm, LN, Lns; KJV], 'harvest' [LN; TEV, TNT], 'crop that is harvested' [NJB], 'fruits of the ground' [ICC].

QUESTION—What is meant by πρῶτον 'first'?

The hardworking farmer should receive his share of the crop first, before others do [Brd, EBC, EGT, El, ICC, Lns, MNTC]. His wages are the first charge against the crop [EGT]. Another way of stating this is that the hardworking farmer should receive the first share of the crop [EGT, GNC, LN, NCBC, TG; NAB, NRSV, TEV, TNT]. Some commentators say that the participle κοπιῶντα 'hardworking' is emphatic and points to the type of farmer [Brd, EBC, EGT, El, GNC, Herm, HNTC, My, TNTC]. He is first before all others, no matter how much they deserve a share [Lns], or he is first before others who are lazy or not hardworking [Brd, El, HNTC, MNTC, My].

QUESTION—What is the non-figurative significance of the 'hard-working farmer'?

In a broad general sense, it means that hard work brings reward [Alf, Brd, EBC, El, Herm]. Some commentators narrow the principle to the religious sphere of working hard for Christ [LSA], or complete devotion to Christ's work [MNTC]. Its significance is primarily the work of the ministry of teaching, preaching, and pastoring [El, HNTC, Lns, NCBC]. 'Laboring' is a term used by Paul to refer to pastoral work and the like [HNTC, NCBC]. Furthermore, the farmer allegory is also used of Christian work, including the derivative γεώργιον 'place/field which is farmed' (cf. 1 Cor. 3:9 and context) [ICC].

QUESTION—What is the non-figurative significance of 'receive his share of the crop'?

1. It signifies the Christian's final reward in the world to come for faithful service [Brd, EGT, El, GNC, NCBC], and parallels the 'well done' said to a soldier who has pleased his commander, and the 'crown' won by an athlete [EGT].
2. It refers to the present rewards in serving Christ, whether spiritual, i.e., approval and/or blessings on oneself, and his work [HNTC, ICC, Lns, NCBC, NTC, TNTC], or material rewards in the way of remuneration or material support [HNTC, ICC, NCBC, TNTC].

QUESTION—What kind of obligation is implied by the verb δεῖ 'to be necessary'?

1. It implies what of necessity must happen (not that which from duty ought to happen) [My]: the toiling farmer in the very nature of things must, without fail, get his part from the crop first.
2. It refers to some rule which Timothy was to see was carried out [ICC]: the farmer must work hard if he hopes to take his share first.

2:7 Consider[a] what I-say;

LEXICON—a. pres. act. impera. of νοέω (LN **30.3**) (BAGD 2. p. 540): 'to consider' [BAGD, Herm; KJV, NASB], 'to reflect on' [NAB, NIV, REB], 'to think over' [BAGD, ICC; NJB, NRSV], 'to think out' [HNTC], 'to think about' [TEV, TNT], 'to think carefully about' [LN], 'to be understanding' [Lns], 'to put one's mind on' [NTC]. It is a command to grasp the meaning of what was said [Brd, EGT, El, HNTC, ICC, Lns, MNTC, My, TNTC].

QUESTION—To what does 'what I say' refer?

It refers to the three allegories he has just given [EBC, EGT, GNC, HNTC, Lns, MNTC, TG, TNTC]. One commentator refers this to only the last allegory, interpreting it to mean that remuneration for the minister was to be expected; so Timothy was to think about how and when to ask for financial help [NCBC].

2 TIMOTHY 2:7

because[a] the Lord will-give[b] to-you understanding[c] in all.[d]

TEXT—Instead of the indicative mood, δώσει 'he will give', some manuscripts have the optative mood, δῴη 'may he give'. GNT does not mention the alternative. The optative mood is taken only by KJV.

LEXICON—a. γάρ (LN 89.23): 'because' [TEV], 'for' [HNTC, ICC, Lns, NTC; NAB, NASB, NIV, NRSV, REB], 'and' [KJV, NJB], not explicit [Herm; TNT].

b. fut. act. indic. of δίδωμι (LN 13.142): 'to give' [Herm, HNTC, ICC, Lns, NTC; KJV, NASB, NIV, NJB, NRSV], 'to grant' [LN], 'to help (you to understand)' [REB, TNT], 'to enable (you to understand)' [TEV], 'to make (the meaning clear)' [NAB].

c. σύνεσις (LN **32.26**): 'understanding' [Herm, HNTC, Lns, NTC; KJV, NASB, NJB, NRSV, REB], 'full understanding' [REB], 'insight' [NIV], 'discernment' [ICC], 'ability to understand' [LN]. This noun is also translated as a verb: 'to understand' [REB, TEV, TNT]. The phrase 'to give understanding' is translated 'to make the meaning clear' [NAB].

d. πᾶς (LN 59.23) (BAGD 2.a.δ. p. 633): 'all'. The phrase ἐν πᾶσιν 'in all' is translated 'in all things' [Herm, ICC; KJV, NRSV], 'in all matters' [NTC], 'in all respects' [Lns], 'in everything' [HNTC; NASB], 'into all this' [NIV]. The phrase is also translated as an adverb: 'fully' [NAB], 'completely' [TNT], or as an adjective: 'full' [NJB, REB], or as a noun phrase: 'it all' [TEV].

QUESTION—What relationship is indicated by γάρ 'because'?

It indicates the grounds for the preceding exhortation [GNC, HNTC, Lns, My, NTC]: consider what I say because the Lord will enable you to understand it. This implies a condition [EBC, EGT, LSA, TG, TNTC]: 'consider what I say, because if you do, the Lord will enable you to understand'.

QUESTION—What is meant by σύνεσις 'understanding'?

Basically the Greek word carries the idea of bringing things together and thus understanding them [Lns]. It is to have the ability to grasp mentally and make discerning judgment [El]. It means understanding [EBC, GNC, Lns, LSA, My, TG], intelligence [MNTC], enlightenment [HNTC, Lns], comprehension and insight [NTC], right judgment [Brd], discerning judgment [El], discretion [NCBC], wisdom [EGT, TNTC].

QUESTION—What is the non-figurative significance of the hyperbole ἐν πᾶσιν 'in all (things)'?

Some commentators take it rather inclusively: the Lord will give understanding in this, as well as in all other weighty matters [HNTC, My], 'in all or every respect', but not meaning that Timothy is to understand all things [Lns]. Others delimit the hyperbole by a qualifying phrase: 'all that is needed for the task' [NTC], 'all he needs to understand' [LSA], 'all the wisdom that is needed' regarding self-discipline and material matters [TNTC]. Others think it refers only to understanding the truths and implications of the three figures just given [TG] and it means 'understand it all' [GNC], or 'understand it perfectly' [MNTC]. He is to understand that he needs to share in suffering and hardships [Brd, GNC], or that he must have an intense devotion and firm self-discipline [EBC].

DISCOURSE UNIT: 2:8–13 [EBC, GNC, Lns, MNTC, NCBC]. The topic is suffering and glory [EBC], the basis for an appeal [GNC, Lns], Christ, the motive to Christian service [MNTC], the content of faith and a hymn of hope and warning [NCBC].

DISCOURSE UNIT: 2:8–10 [ICC]. The topic is the risen Christ.

DISCOURSE UNIT: 2:8 [LSA]. The topic is the means of enduring.

2:8 Remember[a] Jesus Christ having-been-raised[b] from[c] (the) dead,[d]
LEXICON—a. pres. act. impera. of μνημονεύω (LN 29.7, 29.8, 29.16) (BAGD 1.b. p. 525): 'to remember' [BAGD, Herm, LN, Lns; all versions], 'to keep in memory' [NTC], 'to bear in mind' [HNTC], 'to keep ever in your memory' [ICC], 'to think of' [BAGD].
  b. perf. pass. participle of ἐγείρω (LN 23.94) (BAGD 2.c. p. 215): 'to be raised' [BAGD, Herm, ICC, Lns, NTC; KJV, NAB, NIV, NRSV, TEV], 'to rise' [HNTC; NASB, NJB, REB], 'to be raised to life' [LN]. This verb is also translated as a noun: '(his) resurrection' [TNT].
  c. ἐκ with genitive object (LN 84.4): 'from' [Herm, HNTC, ICC, Lns, NTC; all versions].
  d. νέκρωσις (LN 23.99): 'the dead' [Herm, HNTC, ICC, Lns, NTC; all versions except TEV, TNT], 'death' [LN; TEV, TNT].
QUESTION—What relationship is indicated by the use of the participle ἐγηγερμένον 'having been raised'?
  It indicates the state or condition of Jesus Christ and, being in the perfect tense, indicates a present state resulting from a past event [LSA]. They are to remember him as one raised from the dead [El, Lns, My, NTC], the living, risen Lord [ICC]. It keeps the idea of the permanent significance of his personal experience [EGT, El]. The passive implies that God raised him [Lns, LSA, TG].
QUESTION—Why should he remember this?
  Paul presses home the point of the preceding example by the great example of suffering followed by glory [EGT, GNC]. This should console and encourage Timothy as he thinks about the Lord's victory over death and subsequent glory [El]. This will inspire Timothy to courage and faithfulness [Brd], to fulfill his Christian service [MNTC]. It will give him strength to discharge his duties [My].

of[a] the-seed[b] of-David,
LEXICON—a. ἐκ with genitive object (LN 89.3): 'of' [HNTC, NTC; KJV], 'from' [Herm, LN, Lns], 'descended from' [NIV, NRSV], 'sprung from' [NJB], 'born of' [REB], not explicit [NAB, NASB].

b. σπέρμα (LN 10.29) (BAGD 1.b., 2.b. p. 761, 762): 'seed' [BAGD, Herm, Lns, NTC; KJV], 'descendant' [BAGD; NAB, NASB, NRSV, TEV], 'descent' [TNT], 'line' [REB], 'race' [NJB], 'stock' [HNTC], 'offspring' [ICC]. This noun is also translated as a participle: 'descended' [NIV].

QUESTION—Why is this phrase mentioned?

It points out the reality of the Lord's humanity [EBC, EGT, El, ICC, LSA] and shows the Lord's Davidic descent [HNTC, ICC, Lns, MNTC, NTC], verifying that Christ was the Davidic Messiah [NCBC]. It was the prime qualification to recognize and equate Christ with the Messiah [ICC, Lns, MNTC, My, NCBC, TG]. It indicates that Christ was the fulfillment of the hopes and promises of the OT [Brd, El, GNC, Lns, NCBC, NTC]. Along with the preceding clause, it is part of an early creedal formula being quoted here [Alf, GNC, Herm, HNTC, ICC, NCBC, TNTC]. Jesus, himself a man, is the ideal soldier, athlete, and farmer as an example to us [EGT].

according-to[a] **the-gospel**[b] **of-me;**

LEXICON—a. κατά with accusative object (LN 89.8): 'according to' [NTC; KJV, NASB], 'in accord with' [Lns], 'as' [TEV], 'thus' [Herm], 'for' [ICC], not explicit [NIV, NJB, NRSV, TNT].

b. εὐαγγέλιον (LN 33.217) (BAGD 2.b.β. p. 318): 'gospel' [Herm HNTC, Lns, NTC; all versions except TEV, TNT], 'Good News' [TEV, TNT].

QUESTION—What relationship is indicated by the genitive construction τὸ εὐαγγέλιόν μου 'the gospel of me'?

1. It means the gospel Paul preached [EGT, GNC, LSA, TG, TNTC]: the gospel that I preach.
2. It means the gospel Paul was commissioned to preach [Alf, Brd, El, HNTC, ICC]: the gospel which is entrusted to me.

QUESTION—What relationship is indicated by the preposition κατά 'according to'?

It indicates agreement of the preceding statement with what Paul preached: 'in harmony with' [NTC], 'in agreement with' [LSA], 'keeping true to' [MNTC], 'be the heart of' [HNTC], 'according to' [Brd], and 'as' [NCBC, TG]. It is used here to verify or establish a truth [My] by indicating where certain facts are explicitly made known [Lns]. The gospel emphasized the truth of both Christ's humanity and his resurrection [EGT].

2:9 because-of/in[a] **which I-suffer**[b] **to-the-point-of**[c] **bonds**[d] **as**[e] **(an) evildoer,**[f]

LEXICON—a. ἐν with dative object (LN 89.5; 89.26): 'because of' [TEV, TNT], 'on account of' [NJB], 'for' [NTC; NASB, NIV, NRSV, REB], 'in' [Herm, HNTC, ICC; NAB], 'in connection with' [Lns]. The phrase ἐν ᾧ 'in which' is translated 'wherein' [KJV].

b. pres. act. indic. of κακοπαθέω (LN 24.89) (BAGD 1. p. 397): 'to suffer' [ICC, **LN**; NAB, NIV, TEV, TNT], 'to suffer what is bad' [Lns], 'to suffer trouble' [KJV], 'to suffer distress' [LN], 'to suffer misfortune' [BAGD], 'to suffer hardship' [Herm, LN, NTC; NASB, NRSV], 'to be

exposed to hardship' [REB], 'to have to put up with suffering' [NJB], 'to put up with rough treatment' [HNTC].
c. μέχρι with genitive object (LN **78.51**) (BAGD 1.c. p. 515): 'to the point of' [HNTC, LN; NAB], 'even' [Herm; TEV, TNT], 'even to' [Lns; KJV, NASB, NJB] 'even to the point of' [BAGD; NIV, NRSV, REB], 'to the extent of' [Lns].
d. δεσμός (LN 37.115) (BAGD 1. p. 176): 'bonds' [BAGD, Herm, LN, NTC; KJV], 'imprisonment' [Lns; NASB]. This is also translated as a verbal phrase: 'to be chained' [HNTC; NIV, NJB, TEV], 'to be in chains' [TNT], 'to be thrown into chains' [NAB], 'to wear fetters' [NRSV], 'to be shut up' [REB], 'to be in prison' [LN], 'to be imprisoned and fettered' [ICC].
e. ὡς (LN 64.12): 'as' [HNTC, LN, Lns, NTC; KJV, NAB, NASB], 'as though' [ICC], 'like' [Herm, LN; NIV, NJB, NRSV, REB, TEV, TNT].
f. κακοῦργος (LN 88.114) (BAGD p. 398): 'evildoer' [BAGD, HNTC, ICC, LN, NTC; KJV], 'wrongdoer' [LN], 'criminal' [BAGD, Herm; NAB, NASB, NIV, NJB, NRSV, TEV, TNT], 'common criminal' [REB], 'bad person' [LN], 'one who is suffering what is bad' [Lns]. It means a criminal [EBC, EGT, HNTC, MNTC, My, NTC, TG, TNTC], a lawbreaker [TG] convicted of a disgraceful crime [Brd, Lns]. It was used for burglars, murderers, traitors, and the like [HNTC].

QUESTION—What relationship is indicated by ἐν 'in'?
1. It indicates the reason for the following clause [GNC, LSA, My, TG; NJB, TEV, TNT]: because of this, I suffer. Several use the preposition 'for', probably meaning reason (instead of 'for the sake of') [EBC, MNTC, NTC, TNTC; NASB, NIV, NRSV, REB].
2. It indicates the sphere of his suffering [EGT, El, HNTC, Lns, TNTC]: in this I suffer.

QUESTION—What is referred to by ᾧ 'which'?
It refers to the preaching of the gospel [Brd, EBC, GNC, Herm, HNTC, LSA, My], in the service of the gospel [ICC].

QUESTION—What relationship is indicated by μέχρι 'to the point of'?
This preposition indicates the degree of suffering [El, Herm, My]. The bonds were the worst indignities an innocent Roman citizen could suffer [Brd, GNC, Lns]. The extreme measure of degree is most commonly expressed by including 'even' [Alf, Brd, El, GNC, Herm, My, NTC, TG].

but[a] the word[b] of-God (has) not been-bound.[c]
LEXICON—a. ἀλλά (LN 89.125): 'but' [Herm, Lns, NTC; all versions], 'not that' [HNTC], 'yet' [ICC].
b. λόγος (LN 33.260) (BAGD 1.b.β. p. 478): 'word' [Herm, HNTC, ICC, Lns, NTC; all versions except NJB, TNT], 'message' [NJB, TNT], 'what is preached' [LN]. The 'word of God' ('the word from God' [LSA]) is a term used to refer to the gospel [Alf, BAGD, Brd, EGT, El, GNC, Herm, HNTC, My, NCBC, NTC].

c. perf. pass. indic. of δέω (LN 37.114) (BAGD 1.b. p. 177): 'to be bound' [BAGD, NTC; KJV], 'to be chained' [HNTC; NAB, NIV, NJB, NRSV], 'to be in chains' [TEV, TNT], 'to be fettered' [Herm, ICC], 'to be imprisoned' [LN, Lns; NASB], 'to be shut up' [REB].

QUESTION—What is meant by saying that the word of God has not been bound?

This picks up the idea of 'bonds' in the preceding clause [Brd, El, LSA] and personifies 'word' by saying it has not been bound [Herm, HNTC, ICC]. The meaning is that Paul's imprisonment has not weakened the power of the gospel [Alf]. Others carried on Paul's work [Brd] and continued to preach the gospel [ICC, LSA, My, NTC, TG, TNTC]. Paul himself still witnessed to the gospel in prison and by letter [Brd].

2:10 Because-of^a this all-things I-endure^b for-the-sake-of^c the chosen-(ones),^d

LEXICON—a. διά with accusative object (LN 89.26): 'because of' [LN; TNT], 'on account of' [LN, NTC], 'for (this) reason' [Lns; NASB], 'with (this) in view' [REB]. The phrase διά τοῦτο 'because of this' is translated 'therefore' [Herm, ICC; KJV, NAB, NIV, NRSV], 'so' [NJB], 'and so' [TEV], 'it is with this object' [HNTC].

b. ὑπομένω (LN **25.175**) (BAGD 2. p. 846): 'to endure' [BAGD, Herm, LN, Lns, NTC; KJV, NASB, NIV, NRSV, REB, TEV, TNT], 'to be ready to endure' [ICC], 'to bear with' [NAB], 'to bear patiently' [HNTC]. The phrase 'all things I endure' is translated 'I persevere' [NJB].

c. διά with accusative object (LN 90.38): 'for the sake of' [Herm, HNTC, LN, Lns, NTC; all versions]. This preposition is also translated as a verb: 'to help' [ICC].

d. ἐκλεκτός (LN 30.93) (BAGD 1.b. p. 242): 'chosen' [BAGD, LN]. The phrase 'the chosen (ones)' is translated 'the elect' [Lns, NTC; KJV, NIV, NRSV], 'those whom God has chosen' [NAB], 'those who are chosen' [Herm; NASB, NJB], 'God's chosen ones' [ICC; REB, TNT], 'God's chosen people' [TEV], 'God's chosen' [HNTC].

QUESTION—To what does τοῦτο 'this' refer?

1. It refers to what precedes [Brd, ICC, Lns, LSA, My, NTC, TG; and probably translations using 'therefore' (Herm; KJV, NAB, NIV, NRSV) and 'so' (NJB, TEV, TNT)]. He endures all things because the word is not bound [Lns, LSA, My, NTC], the gospel is spreading everywhere [TG], and the work is going on [Brd].
2. It refers to what follows [Alf, EGT, HNTC, TNTC]: I endure all things for the sake of the chosen ones that they may obtain salvation.

QUESTION—To whom does the term 'the chosen ones' refer?

1. It is a general unlimited term without regard to time, referring to people selected by God [Alf, EBC, EGT, El, ICC, LSA, NTC]. It includes those who have already believed and those yet to do so [Alf, EBC, El, ICC, NCBC, NTC, TG].

2. It refers to those chosen but who have not yet obtained salvation [HNTC, MNTC, TNTC].

in-order-that^a they also may-obtain^b salvation^c

LEXICON—a. ἵνα (LN 89.59): 'in order that' [Lns, NTC; NAB], 'that' [HNTC, ICC; KJV, NASB, NIV, REB, TEV, TNT], 'so that' [Herm; NJB, NRSV].
  b. aorist act. subj. of τυγχάνω (LN **90.61**) (BAGD 1. p. 829): 'to obtain' [Herm, HNTC, ICC, Lns, NTC; all versions except REB, TNT], 'to attain' [BAGD; REB], 'to find' [BAGD; TNT], 'to experience' [BAGD, LN].
  c. σωτηρία (LN 21.25) (BAGD 2. p. 829): 'salvation' [Herm, HNTC, LN, Lns; all versions].

QUESTION—Who is the implied referent in the word 'also'?

This refers to Paul [Alf, Brd, El, ICC, Lns, My]: in order that they, along with me, may obtain salvation. It might also include Timothy as well [GNC]: they, along with us. 'Also' is added to show Paul's selflessness [EGT] and his assurance of the salvation he had [Alf, El, HNTC].

QUESTION—What is meant by 'obtaining salvation'?

'Obtain salvation' is a circumlocution for 'be saved' [TG] and highlights the idea of salvation itself [LSA]. Some refer it to attaining final salvation in the final state [GNC, NTC].

the (one that is) in^a Christ Jesus with^b eternal^c glory.^d

LEXICON—a. ἐν with dative object (LN 89.119; 90.6): 'in' [Herm, HNTC, NTC; all versions except TEV], 'through' [TEV], 'by union with' [ICC], 'in connection with' [Lns].
  b. μετά with genitive object (LN 89.123): 'with' [HNTC, ICC, NTC; KJV, NAB, NASB, NIV, NJB, NRSV], 'in company with' [Lns], 'and' [Herm].
  c. δόξα (LN 79.18) (BAGD 1.b.β. p. 203)): 'glory' [BAGD, Herm, HNTC, ICC, LN, Lns, NTC; all versions except REB, TNT], 'praise' [LN]. It is also translated as an adjective: 'glorious (salvation)' [REB, TNT].
  d. αἰώνιος (LN 67.96) (BAGD 3. p. 28): 'eternal' [Herm, HNTC, ICC, LN, Lns; all versions], 'everlasting' [NTC], 'without end' [BAGD].

QUESTION—What relationship is indicated by the word ἐν 'in'?

1. It indicates salvation as being centered in Christ since it was provided by him, declared by him, and realized, on our part, by our communion with him [HNTC]. This expresses the Christian character of salvation and its sphere of operation [TNTC]. Christ is its element and condition of existence [Alf]. It means the salvation that is in connection with Christ [Lns].
2. It indicates the source of salvation: it comes through Christ [GNC], it comes from him [TG], and is found in him who saves us [LSA].
3. It indicates our close communion with Christ [HNTC, ICC, NTC]. Salvation is the result of being united with Christ [HNTC, ICC].

QUESTION—What relationship is indicated by μετά 'with'?

1. Eternal glory accompanies salvation [Brd, EBC, EGT, El, GNC, Herm, ICC, Lns, MNTC, NCBC, TG, TNTC; all versions except REB, TNT]: in

order that they may obtain salvation with eternal glory. Eternal glory goes with salvation [NCBC, TG]. The consummation of this salvation is eternal glory [Brd, EBC, EGT, El, HNTC, LSA, My, TNTC]. The ultimate goal of salvation is eternal glory [EBC].
2. Salvation is described as eternal and glorious [REB, TNT]: in order that they may obtain an eternal and glorious salvation.

2:11 Faithful[a] (is) the saying;[b]

LEXICON—a. πιστός (LN **31.87**) (BAGD 1.b. p. 664): 'faithful' [BAGD, LN, Lns; KJV], 'reliable' [LN, NTC], 'trustworthy' [BAGD, HNTC, LN; NASB, NIV, TNT], 'dependable' [BAGD, LN], 'sure' [NRSV], 'true' [ICC; TEV]. The whole phrase is translated 'you can depend on this' [NAB], 'here is a saying you can rely on' [NJB], 'here are the words you can trust' [REB], 'this word can be trusted' [**LN**], 'the word stands firm' [Herm].

b. λόγος (LN 33.98) (BAGD 1.b.β. p. 478): 'saying' [HNTC, ICC, LN, NTC; KJV, NIV, NJB, NRSV, TEV, TNT], 'word' [BAGD, Herm, LN; REB], 'statement' [LN, Lns; NASB]. This phrase is translated 'you can depend on this' [NAB].

QUESTION—To what does λόγος 'saying' refer?
1. It refers to what follows (2:11b–13) [Alf, EBC, GNC, Herm, HNTC, Lns, LSA, MNTC, My, NCBC, NTC, TG, TNTC]. Many commentators think that this was part of a Christian hymn [Alf, EBC, GNC, Herm, HNTC], but one thinks it is Paul's own prose [Lns].
2. It refers to what precedes [EGT, El]. It refers to 'the word of the cross' which is shown by allegory and personal example in the previous verses [EGT].

for[a] if we-died-with[b] (him),

LEXICON—a. γάρ (LN 89.23; 91.1): 'for' [Herm, HNTC, NTC; KJV, NASB], 'indeed' [Lns], not explicit [ICC; NAB, NIV, NJB, NRSV, REB, TEV, TNT].

b. aorist act. indic. of συναποθνῄσκω (LN 23.118) (BAGD p. 785): 'to die with' [BAGD, Herm, HNTC, Lns, NTC; NAB, NASB, NIV, NJB, NRSV, REB, TEV, TNT], 'to die together with' [LN], 'to be dead with' [KJV], 'to share (Christ's) death' [ICC].

QUESTION—What relationship is indicated by γάρ 'for'?
1. It is part of the quotation and does not have a connection with anything in the text [HNTC, MNTC, NTC, TNTC]. Paul begins the quotation at the point where it is relevant to his subject and disregards the abrupt opening [HNTC].
2. It introduces the saying [LSA]: faithful is the saying, namely, if we died, etc.
3. It indicates the grounds for saying that it is faithful [Alf, EGT]: for the fact is that if we died, etc.

4. It indicates the grounds for the appeal in 2:1–10 [GNC]: take your share of suffering and remember the risen Lord, because if we have died with him, we shall also live with him.

QUESTION—What is meant by dying with him?

1. This refers to a Christian's identification with Christ's death [Alf, EBC, EGT, GNC, HNTC, ICC, Lns, LSA, MNTC, NCBC, TG, TNTC]. This is parallel to Romans 6:8, 11, where we are to count ourselves dead to sin and alive to God [EBC]. It is death to sin as in Romans 6:2–23 [HNTC, Lns] and to self [HNTC]. Christian conversion is a dying and rising with Christ [GNC]. It is a participation in Christ's death which takes place at baptism [Alf, EGT, ICC, MNTC, NCBC, TNTC]. It is a symbolic death at baptism to mark the beginning of a life of self-denial [MNTC]. It is death to worldly confidence, advantages, and honor and a resignation to suffering and martyrdom [NTC]. Implicit is the readiness to meet martyrdom [GNC, ICC].
2. This refers to physical death as a martyr [Brd, My, NTC].

also we-shall-live-with[a] **(him);**

LEXICON—a. fut. act. indic. of συζάω (LN 23.96) (BAGD p. 775): 'to live with' [BAGD, Herm, HNTC, LN, Lns, NTC; all versions], 'to live together with' [LN], 'to share his life' [ICC].

QUESTION—To what kind of life does 'shall live with' refer?

1. It refers to our future life with him in heaven [Alf, Brd, Herm, ICC, Lns, LSA, My, TG].
2. It refers to our present spiritual life in Christ [EBC, EGT, GNC, HNTC, MNTC, NTC, TNTC]. This is the life referred to in Romans 6:8–11 [EBC, GNC]. Our spiritual life is begun in this present life and is fully realized in the resurrection life [EGT, GNC].

2:12 if we-endure,[a] **also we-will-reign-with**[b] **(him);**

LEXICON—a. pres. act. indic. of ὑπομένω (LN **25.175**) (BAGD 2. p. 845): 'to endure' [BAGD, Herm, **LN**, NTC; NASB, NIV, NRSV, REB], 'to persevere' [NJB], 'to suffer' [KJV], 'to hold out to the end' [NAB], 'to continue to endure' [TEV], 'to be enduring' [Lns], 'to be steadfast' [TNT], 'to bear up' [LN], 'to bear patiently' [HNTC], 'to bear one's cross' [ICC], 'to demonstrate endurance' [LN]. The present tense indicates a continuous state [EBC, El, TNTC].

b. fut. act. indic. of συμβασιλεύω (LN 37.66) (BAGD p. 777): 'to reign with' [HNTC, ICC, LN, Lns, NTC; all versions except TEV], 'to rule with' [Herm; TEV], 'to be kings together' [LN].

QUESTION—What is meant by ὑπομένω 'endure'?

It means to endure suffering [GNC, LSA], hardships, and persecution [TG]. It means to remain loyal [GNC], to be steadfast under the threat of martyrdom [NCBC].

QUESTION—What is meant by 'reign with him'?
This pertains to Christ's eternal kingdom [TG]. They will have a part in his kingdom when he returns [MNTC]. They will sit on thrones like kings alongside Christ [HNTC, Lns, NTC], and will judge with him [NTC]. It might be said that they already rule in the world by means of prayer [NTC].

if we-will-deny^a (him), also-that-one will-deny^a us;

LEXICON—a. fut. act. indic. of ἀρνέομαι (LN 33.277; 34.48) (BAGD 3.c. p. 108): 'to deny' [BAGD, Herm, ICC, LN, Lns, NTC; KJV, NAB, NASB, NRSV, TEV], 'to disown' [BAGD, HNTC; NIV, NJB, REB, TNT]. The future tense of the first occurrence is used to show the improbability of denial, its mere contingency [Brd], a condition assumed not yet existing [LSA]. It can reflect more than just a potentiality since it is indicative mode [LSA] and shows the reality of the possibility of denial [EGT, ICC, Lns], and is even prophetic as in 3:1–5 [LSA].

QUESTION—What is meant by denying Christ?
It consists of a refusal to acknowledge Christ as one's own [EBC, My], and is better rendered here as 'disown', since 'deny' strictly means contradicting or declaring untrue [EBC, HNTC, MNTC, NTC]. It is equal to saying 'He is not Lord' [TG]. It is to be unfaithful to him [NTC]. This denial is made through fear of suffering [My]. It is a permanent denial, unlike Peter's [Lns, NTC].

QUESTION—What is meant by the Lord's denying those who deny him?
The Lord's reciprocal denying, not recognizing us as his own [My], will be at the last judgment [HNTC, NCBC, TG], before his Father [Lns].

2:13 if we-are-unfaithful/unbelieving^a that (one) remains^b faithful,^c

LEXICON—a. pres. act. indic. of ἀπιστέω (LN 31.97) (BAGD 2. p. 85): 'to be unfaithful' [BAGD, Herm; NAB], 'to be faithless' [Lns, NTC; all versions except KJV], 'to prove faithless' [HNTC], 'to not believe' [LN; KJV], 'to not be a believer' [LN]. The condition clause is also translated 'though our faith fall' [ICC].

b. πιστός (LN 31.87) (BAGD 1.a.β. p. 664): 'faithful' [BAGD, Herm, HNTC, LN, Lns, NTC; all versions], 'trustworthy, dependable' [BAGD, LN]. It is also translated 'he cannot lie' [ICC].

c. pres. act. indic. of μένω (LN 68.11) (BAGD 1.b. p. 504): 'to remain' [BAGD, Herm, HNTC, LN, Lns, NTC; NAB, NASB, NIV, NRSV, REB, TEV, TNT], 'to continue' [LN], 'to still be' [NJB], 'to abide' [KJV]. It may also simply be implied by a negative statement: 'he cannot (lie)' [ICC].

QUESTION—What is meant by ἀπιστοῦμεν 'we are unfaithful/ unbelieving'?
1. It means to be unfaithful [EGT, GNC, Herm, Lns, LSA, MNTC, My, NCBC, NTC, TG, TNTC; all versions except KJV]: if we are unfaithful. Some commentators take it to mean that believers fail to be faithful [Herm, HNTC, NCBC, NTC]. They are weak in faith [NCBC], they stumble because of sins of the flesh [Herm], they fail to live up to their

profession and they sin [HNTC], they are disloyal by denying Christ [NTC]. Others take it to mean virtually the same as unbelief [EGT, GNC, Lns, My, TG]. It means that they commit apostasy [GNC, TG]. They give up believing [Lns] and lack genuine faith [My].
2. It means that a person does not believe [Alf, Brd, EBC]: if we are unbelieving. It means to distrust God's promises [Brd, El], and Christ's attributes and gospel [El]. It means to break one's pledge and become unbelieving [Alf]. This refers to a settled state of not believing in Christ and not obeying him [EBC].

QUESTION—In what way does Christ remain faithful?

He is faithful to keep his word [Alf, El], and to be true to his nature [El]. He keeps his word concerning both reward and punishment [ICC, Lns, NTC]. His faithfulness in giving salvation to his people is not negated by the faithlessness of some [GNC]. Commentators who have taken unfaithfulness to be less than apostasy understand this to be an encouragement. Christ is faithful to his promise of love [NCBC]. He is faithful to his promise of mercy [ICC]. He is faithful to his covenant and their justification is in the righteousness of God [Herm]. Commentators who have taken unbelief to mean apostasy understand this to be a threat. Christ is faithful to fulfill his threat [LSA], faithful to his word in 2:11 that he will deny those who deny him [Alf, TG, TNTC]. He carries out his decree by rejecting them [My].

for[a] he-is-not-able to-deny[b] himself

LEXICON—a. γάρ (LN 89.23): 'for' [HNTC, Lns, NTC; all versions except KJV, TEV], 'because' [Herm; TEV], 'nay' [ICC], not explicit [KJV].
b. aorist mid. infin. of ἀρνέομαι (LN **88.231**) (BAGD 4. p. 108): 'to deny oneself' [Herm, HNTC, Lns, NTC; KJV, NAB, NASB, NRSV], 'to disown oneself' [NIV, NJB, REB, TNT], 'to be false to one's self' [**LN**; TEV], 'to be untrue to oneself' [BAGD, ICC, LN].

QUESTION—What is meant by Christ's denying himself?

He cannot be self-contradictory by being untrue or false to his own nature [Brd, EGT, El, HNTC, Lns, LSA, MNTC, My, TG, TNTC]. He cannot disown himself or what he was before [EBC, Lns]. He is changeless [Lns]. He cannot break his promise to us of blessing or punishment [Alf, TG].

DISCOURSE UNIT: 2:14–26 [EBC, EGT, GNC, Herm, HNTC, ICC, LSA, MNTC, NCBC, NTC, TG, TNTC; NASB, NIV, NJB, TEV]. The topic is resisting false teaching and teachers [EBC, EGT, GNC, HNTC, LSA, NCBC, TNTC; NJB], an approved worker [TEV], personal authentication as an approved and unashamed worker [Herm, TG; NASB, NIV], the character of the teaching and teachers [ICC], the uselessness of vain dispute [NTC].

DISCOURSE UNIT: 2:14–21 [HNTC, My]. The topic is avoiding false teachers [My], a summons to avoid false teaching [HNTC].

DISCOURSE UNIT: 2:14–19 [EBC, GNC, MNTC]. The topic is true and false teachers [EBC], resisting false teachers [GNC], guarding right doctrine [MNTC].

2:14 Remind[a] (them of) these-things
LEXICON—a. pres. act. impera. of ὑπομιμνῄσκω (LN 29.10) (BAGD 1.b. p. 846): 'to remind' [BAGD, HNTC, ICC, LN, NTC; NAB, NASB, NIV, NJB, NRSV, REB, TEV, TNT], 'to put in remembrance' [Lns; KJV], 'to cause to remember' [LN]. The present imperative indicates that it is to be a regular practice of reminding them [EBC, HNTC, Lns, LSA; NAB, NIV, REB, TNT].
QUESTION—To what does ταῦτα 'these things' refer?
   1. The pronoun refers to what precedes [Brd, EBC, EGT, El, GNC, Herm, HNTC, My, NTC, TNTC]. It refers to the profound truths of the faithful saying expressed by the hymn in 2:11–13 [EGT, El, GNC, HNTC, My, NTC, TNTC]. In the context of false teaching, they must realize their need of persevering and the terrible consequences of rejecting Christ [GNC]. It may include the exhortation from 2:8–13 [Alf, NTC], or all the preceding verses 2:1–13 [NTC], and even to all teaching in the preceding part of the epistle [Lns, TNTC]. It refers to the necessity and recompense of courage and endurance [Brd].
   2. It refers particularly to what Timothy had heard from Paul as referred to in 1:13 and 2:2 [ICC, LSA], but also the truths of 2:3–13 [ICC, LSA], especially 2:2, 8 [LSA].
   3. The pronoun refers forward to the following exhortation about not arguing over words [TG].
QUESTION—Who is Timothy to remind?
He is to remind the faithful men mentioned in 2:2 [ICC, LSA, NTC], who are teachers [LSA]. Some commentators take this reference more generally to faithful believing people, those under him to whom he ministers [Alf, Brd, EBC, El, GNC, TG], his people [TEV, TNT], the church [My], or all the Asian churches [Lns].

charging/warning[a] (them) before[b] God not to-quarrel-about/with-words[c] for nothing useful,[d]
TEXT—Instead of θεοῦ 'God', some manuscripts have κυρίου 'Lord'. 'God' is selected by GNT with a C rating, indicating a considerable degree of doubt. It is also selected by EGT, Herm, HNTC; all versions except KJV and NRSV. 'Lord' is selected by Alf, ICC, NCBC, NTC, TG; KJV, NRSV.
LEXICON—a. pres. mid. participle of διαμαρτύρομαι (LN 33.223; 33.425) (BAGD 1. p. 186): 'to charge' [BAGD, ICC, NTC; KJV, NAB], 'to solemnly charge' [NASB, REB, TNT], 'to tell' [NJB], 'to assert' [LN], 'to adjure' [BAGD, Herm, HNTC], 'to testify' [LN], 'to earnestly testify' [Lns], 'to warn' [BAGD, LN; NIV, NRSV], 'to give a solemn warning' [TEV].

b. ἐνώπιον with genitive object (LN 83.33; 90.20) (BAGD 2.b. p. 270): 'before' [LN; KJV, NAB, NIV, NRSV, REB, TNT], 'in the presence of' [NTC; NASB, TEV], 'in the face of' [Herm], 'in the name of' [NJB], 'in the sight of' [BAGD, HNTC, LN, Lns], 'as in the sight of' [ICC].
c. pres. act. infin. of λογομαχέω (LN **33.454**) (BAGD p. 477): 'to quarrel about words' [NIV], 'to quarrel over words' [LN], 'to strive about words' [KJV], 'to wrangle about words' [NASB, NJB, NRSV, TNT], 'to dispute about words' [BAGD, Herm, HNTC; NAB, REB], 'to fight over words' [TEV], 'to wage word-battles' [NTC], 'to be battling about words' [Lns], 'to split hairs' [BAGD]. It is also translated 'to be word-warriors, constantly arguing and wrangling with words' [ICC].
d. χρήσιμος (LN **65.30**) (BAGD p. 885): 'useful' [BAGD, LN; TNT], 'beneficial' [BAGD]. The phrase 'for nothing useful' is translated 'useless' [NTC], 'this serves no useful purpose' [TNT], 'this/it does no good' [NAB, REB, TEV], 'it is of no value' [NIV], 'it is of no use' [**LN**], 'it is not helpful' [LN], 'it does not help' [LN], 'no good comes of it' [HNTC], 'which are useful for nothing' [Herm], 'which is useless' [NASB], 'which does no good' [NRSV], 'for no useful result' [Lns], 'to no profit' [KJV], not explicit [ICC; NJB].

QUESTION—What is meant by διαμαρτυρόμενος 'charging/warning'?
1. It means to charge them not to fight about words [Alf, Brd, EGT, El, Herm, HNTC, ICC, LSA, MNTC, My, TNTC; KJV, NAB, NASB, NJB, REB, TNT]. It means to adjure [EGT, Herm, HNTC, MNTC, My]. The phrase 'to charge before God' has the same meaning as the identical phrase in 1 Tim. 5:21 [Brd, EGT, El]. Though it is a participle, it has the nature of a command since it depends on the imperative verb 'remind them' [LSA].
2. It means to warn them not to fight about words [EBC, GNC, NTC, TG; KJV, NIV, TEV]. A charge in the presence of the Lord is a warning [NTC]. The Lord is a witness [TG]. It is a warning that they will be called into account by God [GNC]. Or he is to warn them that it is only a waste of time [EBC].

QUESTION—What is the significance of the phrase 'before the Lord'?
It indicates the seriousness of the charge or warning Timothy is to give them [TNTC]. The hearers are to realize that they are liable to be called to account by God himself [GNC], having been charged in the presence of God [NTC, TNTC], with Timothy calling on God as his witness [TG]. This alludes to the final judgment when we shall all stand before God; cf. 1 Tim. 5:21; 2 Tim. 4:1 [HNTC, ICC].

QUESTION—What is meant by λογομαχεῖν 'to quarrel about/with words'?
1. It means to quarrel about words [EBC, EGT, El, Herm, HNTC, Lns, LSA, MNTC, NCBC, NTC, TG; all versions]. They dispute about words without regard to the meaning they are meant to convey [NCBC]. It is disputes about abstract, speculative matters [MNTC]. It is the kind of theological discussion that is verbal, not dealing with the realities of the

Christian religion [HNTC]. It pertains to the myths and genealogies mentioned in 1 Tim. 1:3–4 and to the profane and old wives' tales mentioned in 1 Tim. 4:7 [NTC].
2. It means to quarrel with words [Brd]. It means that they are not to get into controversy [Alf, Brd, ICC].

QUESTION—What does the phrase 'for nothing useful' modify?

It modifies the preceding clause 'don't quarrel about words', being in apposition to it [Alf, Brd, El, Herm, My]. It indicates result [Brd, EGT, ICC, Lns, My]. To fight about words is profitless, [Brd, HNTC], of no value [EBC], purposeless [Alf, GNC], useless [El, Herm, ICC, Lns, LSA, My, NCBC, NTC, TNTC], and does no good [MNTC, TG].

for[a] (the) ruin[b] of-the (ones) hearing.[c]

LEXICON—a. ἐπί with dative object (LN 89.60) (BAGD II.1.b.ε. p. 287): 'for' [BAGD, Lns], 'to' [KJV]. It is also translated '(and) can be (the ruin)' [NAB], '(and) leads to' [NASB, TNT], 'to bring (ruin)' [Herm], 'all this ever achieves' [NJB], '(and/but) only ruins' [NIV, NRSV, REB, TEV], 'it only demoralizes' [HNTC], 'as if they wished to (ruin)' [ICC], 'which upsets' [NTC].
  b. καταστροφή (LN **20.17**) (BAGD p. 419): 'ruin' [BAGD, Herm, LN; NAB, NASB, TNT], 'destruction' [BAGD; NJB]. It is also translated as a verb: 'to ruin' [ICC; NIV, NRSV, REB, TEV], 'to cause harm' [LN], 'to cause ruin' [LN], 'to upset' [Lns, NTC], 'to demoralize' [HNTC], 'to subvert' [KJV].
  c. pres. act. participle of ἀκούω (LN 24.52; 33.212): 'to hear' [LN]. The phrase 'the ones hearing' is translated 'those hearing' [Lns], 'the hearers' [Herm, ICC; KJV, NASB, TNT], 'the listeners' [HNTC, NTC], 'those who listen' [NAB, NIV, NJB, REB], 'the people who listen' [TEV], 'those who are listening' [NRSV].

QUESTION—What relationship is indicated by ἐπί 'for'?

It indicates the result of quarreling about words which are of no use [Brd, EGT, El, ICC, Lns, My, NTC]. It may be used ironically as purpose [ICC]. It is the result of quarreling and also the grounds for the command not to quarrel [LSA].

QUESTION—In what way does it ruin the listeners?

This word refers to the opposite of building them up (as in 2 Cor. 13:10) [Alf, Brd, El, MNTC, My, TNTC]. Quarreling about words demoralizes the listeners [TNTC]. It upsets them [Lns, NTC]. It hurts their faith, causing spiritual damage [TG]. It ruins their faith [ICC]. It destroys their faith by weakening its foundations [MNTC]. It brings catastrophe to them [EBC].

2:15 Be-diligent[a] to-present/show[b] yourself approved[c] to-God,

LEXICON—a. aorist act. impera. of σπουδάζω (LN 68.63) (BAGD 2. p. 763): 'to be diligent' [Lns; NASB], 'to do one's best' [HNTC, LN; NIV, NRSV, TEV, TNT], 'to do one's utmost' [NTC], 'to work hard' [LN], 'to try hard' [NAB, REB], 'to make every effort' [BAGD; NJB], 'to take all

pains' [ICC], 'to be zealous' [BAGD], 'to endeavor' [LN], 'to study' [KJV].
b. aorist act. infin. of παρίστημι (LN 72.4) (BAGD 1.c. p. 628): 'to present' [BAGD, Herm, ICC, Lns, NTC; NASB, NIV, NJB, NRSV, TNT], 'to win (full approval)' [TEV], 'to show' [HNTC; KJV, REB], 'to make oneself (worthy)' [BAGD; NAB].
c. δόκιμος (LN 30.115) (BAGD 1. p. 203): 'approved' [NTC; KJV, NASB, NIV, NRSV, TNT], 'proven' [Herm; NJB], 'worthy of approval' [HNTC; NAB, REB], '(win) full approval' [TEV]. 'tested' [Lns], 'as one who can stand his test' [ICC], 'considered good, regarded as worthy' [LN].

QUESTION—What is meant by παραστῆσαι 'to present/show'?
1. It means to present himself before God as one who is approved by him [Alf, EGT, Herm, HNTC, ICC, Lns, LSA, MNTC, My, NTC, TG; NASB, NIV, NJB, NRSV, TNT]. Timothy is to submit his work to God for his approval [TNTC]. He is to let God see that he is a good workman [MNTC]. He is observed by God and is accountable to him [LSA]. He is to win God's approval [TG; TEV]. He presents himself before God's bar of judgment [NTC]. Another view is that he is to present himself for service [ICC, My].
2. It means to show that he is approved by God [KJV, REB]. Timothy is to show that he is worthy of God's approval [REB].

QUESTION—What is meant by δόκιμος 'approved'?
It includes both testing and approbation [GNC, HNTC, Lns, NTC, TNTC]. It means to be tested by some trial or examination and found to have successfully stood the test [Alf, El, ICC, NTC], to be accepted after testing [Lns, TNTC].

(an) unashamed[a] workman,[b]

LEXICON—a. ἀνεπαίσχυντος (LN **25.192**): 'unashamed, not feeling disgrace' [LN]. This word is also translated 'that needs not to be ashamed' [Herm; KJV, NASB, NIV], 'needing not to be ashamed' [Lns], 'having no need to be/feel ashamed' [HNTC, LN; NJB, NRSV, TNT], 'who is not ashamed of his work' [TEV], 'who has nothing to be ashamed of' [NTC], 'who has no cause to be ashamed' [NAB], 'with no cause for shame' [REB], 'as one who never will be put to shame for bad or scamped work' [ICC].
b. ἐργάτης (LN 42.43) (BAGD 1.b. p. 307): 'worker' [Herm, LN; NJB, NRSV, REB, TEV], 'real worker' [ICC], 'workman' [BAGD, HNTC, Lns, NTC; KJV, NAB, NASB, NIV, TNT].

QUESTION—What is meant by ἀνεπαίσχυντον 'unashamed'?
1. This has an active sense, 'to be ashamed' [GNC, Herm, MNTC, My, NCBC, NTC, TG; all versions]. He is to be a workman who has no cause to be ashamed of his work [GNC, NCBC; NAB, TEV], having nothing to be ashamed of [My, NTC]. He does not fear that he will be ashamed when he hears God's verdict on his work [NTC]. Positively, it means that he should be proud of his work [TG].

2. This has a passive sense, 'to be put to shame' [Alf, Brd, EGT, El, ICC, Lns]. He would be put to shame if his work is found to be unworthy [Alf] because of its poor quality [Brd, ICC]. He would be put to shame by God's disapproval [Lns].

teaching-correctly^a the word^b of-(the)-truth.^c

LEXICON—a. pres. act. participle of ὀρθοτομέω (LN 33.234) (BAGD p. 580): 'to teach correctly' [LN; TEV], 'to teach rightly' [Herm, ICC], 'to teach aright' [BAGD], 'to rightly explain' [NRSV], 'to rightly divide' [KJV], 'to cut straight' [Lns], 'to follow a straight course in preaching' [NAB], 'to handle accurately' [NASB], 'to rightly handle' [NTC], 'to correctly handle' [NIV], 'to dispense in the right way' [HNTC], 'to keep (the message of truth) on a straight path' [NJB], 'to go straight to the point in explaining' [TNT], 'to keep strictly to (the true gospel)' [REB].
   b. λόγος (LN 33.260) (BAGD 1.b.β. p. 478): 'message' [ICC, LN, NTC; NJB, TEV, TNT], 'gospel' [REB], 'the word' [Herm, HNTC, Lns; KJV, NASB, NIV, NRSV], 'preaching' [NAB].
   c. ἀλήθεια (LN 72.2) (BAGD 2.b. p. 36): 'truth' [BAGD, Herm, HNTC, ICC, LN, Lns, NTC; all versions except REB]. It is also translated as an adjective: 'true (gospel)' [REB].

QUESTION—What is meant by ὀρθοτομοῦντα 'teaching correctly'?

Many retain the metaphor of cutting straight: cut the word of truth into its right pattern [Brd], cut straight the word of truth when presenting it to others [Lns], hold a straight course in the word of truth [EBC, EGT], lay out straightly and truly the word of truth [El], follow a straight path in preaching the gospel without being turned aside in vain disputes [HNTC], keep the word on a straight path [NJB]. Others think that the metaphor was no longer a live one and this simply meant to do something correctly [GNC, ICC]. Of these, many give a generic meaning: correctly handle the word of truth [EBC], handle aright or rightly [EGT, NCBC, NTC, TG], rightly administer [Alf, EGT], manage rightly [Alf], treat truthfully so as not to falsify [Alf], deal rightly with it so as not to falsify [My], be scrupulously straightforward in dealing with the word of truth [TNTC]. Others give rather specific meanings: tell correctly the true message, or possibly interpret correctly [LSA], teach correctly [GNC, TG; TEV], interpret or apply correctly [TG], rightly teach [Herm, ICC], truly teach and preach [GNC].

QUESTION—How are the two nouns related in the genitive construction 'word of truth'?

1. This is a genitive of quality, identifying the message as being true [LSA; REB]: the true word.
2. It may be classified as a genitive of substance [El, Lns; NAB, TEV, TNT]: the word concerning the Truth. It is 'the gospel' [Brd, Herm, HNTC, TG, TNTC; REB], the Christian message as a whole [HNTC, MNTC].

2:16 But godless[a] empty-talk[b] avoid;[c]

LEXICON—a. βέβηλος (LN 88.115) (BAGD 1. p. 138): 'godless' [Herm, LN; NIV, NJB], 'irreligious' [ICC; REB], 'worldly' [BAGD, LN; NAB, NASB], 'profane' [BAGD, HNTC, Lns, NTC; KJV, NASB, TEV], 'of worldly people' [TNT].
- b. κενοφωνία (LN **33.376**) (BAGD p. 428): 'empty talk' [BAGD], 'foolish talk' [LN], 'idle talk' [NAB], 'idle chatter' [TNT], 'empty chatter' [BAGD, NTC; NASB], 'chatter' [Herm, HNTC; NIV, NRSV, REB], 'vain babblings' [KJV], 'profane babblings' [Lns], 'frivolous hair-splittings' [ICC], 'foolish discussions' [TEV], 'philosophical discussions' [NJB].
- c. pres. mid. impera. of περιΐστημι (LN 13.157) (BAGD 2. p. 647): 'to avoid' [BAGD, LN; NAB, NASB, NIV, NRSV, REB], 'to shun' [BAGD, NTC; KJV], 'to have nothing to do with' [NJB, TNT], 'to keep away from' [TEV], 'to keep clear of' [HNTC], 'to keep oneself from doing' [LN], 'to flee from' [Herm], 'to give a wide berth to' [ICC], 'to turn one's back on' [Lns].

QUESTION—What is meant by βεβήλους 'godless'?

It indicates separation from spiritual, religious, or holy matters and hence is secular [Brd], profane [Alf, EBC, El, HNTC, Lns, NTC, TG, TNTC; KJV, NRSV, TEV], materialistic [HNTC, MNTC], having nothing to do with true godliness [GNC], radically separate from (and opposed to) the holy [HNTC], contributing nothing to religion [ICC], bearing no moral fruit [El], lacking all relationship or affinity to God [LSA], and worldly [TG]. It also indicates non-godlikeness: godless [NCBC, TNTC], impious [NCBC], unhallowed [EBC, LSA], unholy [NTC], not sacred [LSA]. It also means substituting human speculation for divine revelation [HNTC], contrary to the gospel [TG].

QUESTION—What is meant by κενοφωνίας 'empty talk'?

This emphatic term, which occurs only here and in 1 Tim. 6:20, characterizes heretical teaching as empty talk [Brd, EBC, EGT, El, MNTC], empty sounds [EBC, HNTC, Lns], empty chatter [NTC]; empty utterances which are shallow discussions on useless subjects [LSA], empty discourses [Alf], foolish discussions [GNC, TG], foolish arguments [GNC], babblings [EBC, El], vain babblings [TNTC], chatter [HNTC, NCBC, TG], mere chatter [Herm].

for[a] to[b] more[c] ungodliness[d] will-they-increase,[e]

LEXICON—a. γάρ (LN 89.23): 'for' [HNTC, Lns, NTC; KJV, NAB, NASB, NRSV], 'because' [Herm; NIV], not explicit [ICC; NJB, REB, TEV, TNT].
- b. ἐπί with accusative object (LN 78.51): 'to' [NTC; NASB, TNT], 'unto' [KJV], not explicit [NAB, NIV, NJB]. This phrase is translated 'which only drive people farther away from God' [TEV].

c. πλείων (LN 78.28): 'more' [KJV], 'more and more' [Herm, HNTC; NAB, NIV, NRSV], 'further' [NASB], 'further and further' [NJB], 'farther' [Lns; TEV], 'farther and farther' [REB] 'even worse' [TNT], 'an increase of' [NTC], not explicit [ICC].
d. ἀσέβεια (LN 53.10) (BAGD p. 114): 'ungodliness' [HNTC, Lns, NTC; KJV, NASB], 'godlessness' [BAGD, Herm, LN], 'irreverence' [TNT], 'impiety' [ICC; NRSV], 'godless ways' [REB]. It is also translated as an adjective: 'godless' [NAB], 'ungodly' [NIV], or as a prepositional phrase: 'away from true religion' [NJB], 'away from God' [TEV].
e. fut. act. indic. of προκόπτω (LN **59.64**) (BAGD 2. p. 708): 'to increase' [LN; KJV], 'to become more' [NAB, NIV], 'to make progress' [Herm], 'to progress forward' [Lns], 'to go forward' [ICC], 'to advance' [BAGD, HNTC, NTC], 'to lead' [NASB, NJB, NRSV], 'to drive away' [TEV], 'to stray' [REB], 'to go on to' [TNT]. The future tense indicates that those in the most developed state had not yet appeared [El].

QUESTION—What is the implied subject of the verb 'they will increase'?
1. It is those who indulge in godless empty talk [Alf, Brd, EBC, EGT, El, GNC, Herm, HNTC, ICC, Lns, LSA, MNTC, My, NCBC, NTC; NAB, NIV, REB, TNT]: these people will increase to more ungodliness. These are the people who are referred to by 'they' in the next verse [GNC, Lns, LSA]. They are the false teachers [Alf, Brd, EBC, GNC, MNTC, NTC].
2. The subject is the godless empty talk referred to in the preceding clause [GNC, TG; NASB, NJB, NRSV, TEV]: this godless and empty talk will increase to more ungodliness.

QUESTION—What is meant by προκόψουσιν 'advance'?
Normally it has a positive sense of changing one's state for the better by making progress and in the present context is used in irony [GNC, Herm, HNTC, ICC, MNTC, NTC], paralleling that used in 2 John 9 where the progressives were those who didn't adhere to Christian doctrine [MNTC, NCBC]. So the term as used here in association with the forefronted adverb of degree [LSA] has several synonymous expressions of increased deterioration: advance to a worse pitch of impiety [Alf], proceed, progress or advance further in ungodliness [Brd, EBC, HNTC, Lns, NCBC, NTC, TNTC], make progress on a downward grade [ICC], become even more ungodly [LSA], progress from one degree of irreligion to another [MNTC], cause people to be more godless [LN, TG], become even more ungodly [LSA], lead still further into godlessness [Herm, MNTC, NCBC, TG]. Reciprocally, it may be stated 'drive people further away from God' [TG].

2:17 and their word[a] like[b] gangrene[c] will-have (a) spread.[d]
LEXICON—a. λόγος (LN 33.98): 'word' [LN, Lns, NTC; KJV], 'talk' [HNTC; NASB, NJB, NRSV], 'teaching' [Herm; NIV, TEV, TNT], 'message' [ICC, LN]. It is also translated as a noun phrase: 'the influence of their talk' [NAB], 'the infection of their teaching' [REB]. This refers to their false teachings [TG].

b. ὡς (LN 64.12) (BAGD II.2. p. 897): 'like' [BAGD, Herm, HNTC, ICC, NTC; all versions except KJV], 'as' [Lns; KJV].
c. γάγγραινα (LN **23.165**) (BAGD p. 149): 'gangrene' [BAGD, Herm, HNTC, LN, Lns, NTC; NASB, NIV, NJB, NRSV, REB], 'a gangrenous sore' [TNT], 'cancer' [BAGD, ICC, **LN**], 'canker' [KJV], 'an open sore' [TEV], 'ulcer' [LN], 'the plague' [NAB].
d. νομή (LN **84.1**) (BAGD 2. p. 541): 'spread' [LN], 'spreading' [BAGD]. The phrase νομὴν ἕξει 'to have a spread' is translated: 'to spread' [BAGD, **LN**; NAB, NASB, NIV, NJB, NRSV, REB, TNT], 'to devour' [NTC], 'to eat' [KJV], 'to eat its way' [HNTC], 'to feed upon' [Herm], 'to have pasture' [Lns], 'to eat away' [ICC; TEV].

QUESTION—What is meant by comparing their word to the spreading of gangrene?

This compares the spread of their teaching with the spread of gangrene [Alf, Brd, EBC, El, GNC, Herm, HNTC, Lns, LSA, NCBC, TNTC; NASB, NIV, NJB, NRSV, REB, TNT] or cancer [ICC, LN, My]. The community is compared to a body in which a spreading sore has begun [MNTC, My]. Their teaching will spread like the spread of gangrene [GNC, Herm]. It will eat away at the life of the church [GNC]. Their teaching spreads further into the church and corrupts others [ICC, TG]. Their message will harm others as gangrene harms the body [LSA]. Their teaching finds a 'grazing ground' as easily as a gangrene spreads in a body [TNTC]. Like cancer eats away healthy tissue and aggravates the person's condition, so their heresy will affect an ever increasing part of the church members and tend to destroy the organism of the church [NTC].

Of-whom[a] are Hymenaeus and Philetus,

LEXICON—a. ὧν gen. pl. of ὅς (LN 92.27): 'of whom (is)' [KJV], 'to whom (belong)' [Lns], 'to that class (belongs)' [ICC], 'among them (are)' [Herm, HNTC, NTC; NASB, NIV, NRSV, TNT], 'such (are)' [REB]. It is also restructured and rendered as a clause: 'This is the case with' [NAB], or is imbedded in an explanatory clause: 'Two men who have taught such (are)' [TEV], or an expanded adverbial prepositional phrase: 'as in the case of' [NJB].

QUESTION—What relation did these two men have with the church?

They were, or had been, members of the church at Ephesus where Timothy was in charge (cf. 1 Tim. 1:3) [Alf, El, GNC, HNTC, MNTC, NCBC, NTC]. They were possibly Jews and perhaps even Sadducees [El], and were opponents of Paul [Alf, NCBC], spreading heretical error [Alf, El, MNTC, NTC]. They are included among the ones mentioned in 2:16 [LSA]. Of the two, Hymenaeus was possibly the leader [HNTC, NTC], and is mentioned in 1 Tim. 1:20 [Brd, EBC, EGT, El, GNC, Herm, HNTC, ICC, Lns, MNTC, My, NCBC, NTC, TG, TNTC]. Philetus (whose name means 'beloved' [NTC]) is mentioned only here and nothing more is known of him [Brd, EBC, EGT, El, GNC, HNTC, ICC, Lns, NTC].

2:18 who concerning[a] the-truth[b] went-astray,[c]

LEXICON—a. περί with accusative object (LN 89.6) (BAGD 2.d. p. 645): 'concerning' [LN; KJV], 'as regards' [Lns; TNT], 'with regard to' [BAGD, Herm, LN], 'about' [ICC], not explicit [HNTC, NTC; NAB, NASB, NIV, NJB, NRSV, REB, TEV].
  b. ἀλήθεια (LN 72.2): 'truth' [Herm, HNTC, ICC, LN, NTC; all versions]. It is also translated 'the faith' [Lns].
  c. aorist act. indic. of ἀστοχέω (LN 31.68) (BAGD p. 118): 'to go astray (from)' [NASB, NJB], 'to wander away (from)' [NTC; NIV], 'to swerve (from)' [NRSV], 'to lose one's way' [LN], 'to miss the way' [TNT], 'to leave the way (of)' [TEV], 'to err' [KJV], 'to miss the mark' [BAGD, Herm, Lns], 'to miss one's aim (about)' [ICC], 'to shoot wide (of)' [MNTC], 'to go far wide (of)' [NAB], 'to be wide (of)' [REB].

QUESTION—What is meant by τὴν ἀλήθειαν 'the truth'?
This word is used in an objective sense, meaning the Christian truth and doctrine which is believed [Lns, NTC]. It is the true message [LSA], the true path [TNTC]. It describes 'the faith' [Brd, EGT, Lns, TG].

saying[a] the resurrection[b] already[c] has-happened,[d]

LEXICON—a. pres. act. participle of λέγω (LN 33.69) (BAGD II.1.e. p. 469): 'to say' [Herm, HNTC, ICC, LN, NTC; KJV, NAB, NASB, NIV, REB, TEV, TNT], 'to declare' [BAGD, Lns], 'to claim' [NJB, NRSV].
  b. ἀνάστασις (LN 23.93) (BAGD 2.b. p. 60): 'resurrection' [BAGD, Herm, HNTC, ICC, LN, Lns, NTC; all versions].
  c. ἤδη (LN 67.20): 'already' [Herm, HNTC, Lns, NTC; all versions].
  d. perf. act. infin. of γίνομαι (LN 13.107): 'to happen' [Herm, LN], 'to occur' [LN, Lns, NTC], 'to take place' [HNTC; NAB, NASB, NIV, NJB, NRSV, REB, TEV, TNT], 'to be past' [KJV].

QUESTION—What relationship is indicated by the use of the participle λέγοντες 'saying'?
  1. It explains the previous statement 'they went astray' by specifying what the error was [El, HNTC, LSA; NAB, REB]: they went astray from the truth in saying that the resurrection already had happened.
  2. This tells how they went astray [Lns; NRSV, TEV]: they went astray by saying that the resurrection already had happened.

QUESTION—How did the heretics think the resurrection had already happened?
They taught that the resurrection was only spiritual, not physical [Brd, EBC, El, Herm, ICC, NTC, TG, TNTC]. They referred resurrection to receiving spiritual life when one believed [Brd, EBC, Lns, LSA, NTC]. It was pictured in their baptism [HNTC, ICC, Lns]. It implies that there will be no future resurrection of the body [LSA]. They equated resurrection to what Paul taught about our spiritual dying and rising with Christ in Romans 6:1–11 and Colossians 2:20–3:4 [GNC, TG]. Another view is that the knowledge of divine things is the only "resurrection" people attain to [EGT].

and they-upset^a the faith^b of-some.

LEXICON—a. pres. act. indic. of ἀνατρέπω (LN 31.72) (BAGD 2. p. 62): 'to upset' [BAGD, ICC, LN, NTC; NAB, NASB, NJB, NRSV, TEV, TNT], 'to overthrow' [KJV], 'overturn' [Lns], 'to destroy' [Herm; NIV], 'to undermine' [HNTC; REB].

b. πίστις (LN 31.85) (BAGD 2.d.α. p. 663): 'faith' [BAGD, Herm, HNTC, LN, Lns, NTC; all versions].

QUESTION—What relationship is indicated by καί 'and'?

It indicates the result of what they say [LSA; NASB]: they say that the resurrection has already happened and thus upset the faith of some.

QUESTION—In what way was the faith of some upset?

The terms 'upset' [ICC, NTC; various versions], 'disturb the minds of people' [LSA], and 'damage' [TG] are very mild descriptions, but are brought into true focus by 'cause to believe wrongly' [LSA], 'subvert' [Brd, EBC, El, Lns], 'undermine' [HNTC, MNTC], 'overturn' [Alf, GNC, LSA, MNTC], 'overthrow' or 'completely overthrow' [NTC, TNTC], and 'destroy' [EBC, Lns, My, TG]. Their faith was being subverted and destroyed since belief in the bodily resurrection is the keystone of Christianity, and without it one's faith is in vain (1 Cor. 15:17) [HNTC, Lns, NTC]. In denying a physical resurrection, Christ's physical resurrection was denied and the basis of faith was destroyed [Lns]. Further, since they said that the body wouldn't be resurrected because it was evil, they tried to save themselves by ascetic practices. Since any kind of resurrection was past, the body and its lusts were treated as unimportant, and this led to moral indifference [GNC, HNTC, Lns, MNTC].

2:19 However^a the firm^b foundation^c of God stands,^d

LEXICON—a. μέντοι (LN **89.130**) (BAGD 2. p. 503): 'however' [NJB], 'nevertheless' [BAGD, HNTC, LN, Lns, NTC; KJV, NASB, NIV], 'but' [Herm; NAB, NRSV, REB, TEV, TNT], 'yet' [ICC].

b. στερεός (LN **79.7**) (BAGD 1. p. 766): 'firm' [BAGD, Herm, HNTC, LN, NTC; all versions except KJV, TEV], 'sure' [KJV], 'solid' [BAGD, **LN**, Lns; TEV], 'once for all' [ICC].

c. θεμέλιος (LN 7.41) (BAGD 2.b. p. 356): 'foundation' [BAGD, Herm, HNTC, LN, Lns, NTC; KJV, NAB, NASB, NIV, NRSV, TEV, TNT], 'foundation stone' [ICC; NJB, REB].

d. perf. act. indic. of ἵστημι (LN 13.29) (BAGD II.2.c.α. p. 382): 'to stand' [Herm, HNTC, Lns, NTC; all versions except TEV], 'to stand firm' [BAGD], 'to firmly remain' [LN], 'to not be shaken' [TEV], 'to be fixed' [ICC], 'to continue steadfastly' [LN].

QUESTION—What relationship is indicated by μέντοι 'however'?

It indicates a contrast with the tottering faith and defection of those just mentioned [Alf, Brd, EGT, El, GNC, HNTC, Lns, MNTC, My, NTC].

QUESTION—How are the nouns related in the genitive construction ὁ θεμέλιος τοῦ θεοῦ 'the foundation of God'?

It is part of the figure and means the foundation laid down by God [Alf, El, Lns, TG].

QUESTION—What is meant by this metaphor?

1. The foundation refers to the church [Alf, Brd, EGT, El, HNTC, Lns, MNTC, My, NTC, TG, TNTC]. The beginning church is the foundation of the building that will gradually be constructed [My]. The congregation of the faithful believers is considered to be a foundation of the building referred to in the following verse [Alf]. The figure carries the ideas of firmness, strength, and solidity [El]. The church will endure [TG]. The church will remain firm in spite of the aberrations of individual members [Brd]. Its integrity is unaffected by the defection of those who had seemed to belong to it [EGT].
2. The foundation refers to the true message [LSA]. Faith may rest on the message without being overturned since that message is the dependable and reliable message from God [LSA].
3. The foundation refers to Christ as referred to in Isa. 8:14; 28:16, Rom. 9:33, 1 Cor. 3:11, and Eph. 2:20–21 [NCBC]. Despite the threat posed by the false teachers, Christ will not fail [NCBC].

having[a] this inscription:[b]

LEXICON—a. pres. act. participle of ἔχω (LN 57.1): 'to have' [Lns, NTC; KJV, NASB], 'to bear' [Herm; NAB, NRSV, REB, TNT], 'to be sealed' [NIV], 'to be (the seal) on it' [ICC; NJB], 'to be written on' [TEV]. It is also translated by a prepositional phrase: 'with (this seal) on it' [HNTC].

b. σφραγίς (LN **33.47**; 33.483; 33.484) (BAGD 1.c. p. 796): 'inscription' [BAGD, ICC, LN; NAB, NIV, NRSV, REB, TNT], 'words' [TEV], 'seal' [Herm, HNTC, Lns, NTC; KJV, NASB, NJB], 'the mark or impression of a seal' [BAGD].

QUESTION—What relationship is indicated by the use of the participle ἔχων 'having'?

It indicates the grounds for stating that the foundation stands [Alf, El, LSA].

QUESTION—What is the non-figurative significance of σφραγίς 'inscription'?

In the figure, this refers to an inscription engraved in the foundation [Alf, Brd, EBC, El, ICC, LSA, MNTC, My, NTC, TG; NAB, NIV, NRSV, REB, TNT]. The Greek word normally refers to an impression made by a seal or stamp [LN], and many translate it as 'seal' [Brd, GNC, Herm, HNTC, ICC, Lns, LSA, MNTC, My, NTC; KJV, NASB, NJB]. As a seal, the inscription has a function. It indicates ownership [Alf, EBC, El, GNC, HNTC, NTC] and the purpose for the building [Alf, HNTC, MNTC, TG]. It guarantees that it is permanent [Lns, My], that it is protected [NTC], and certifies that the congregation belongs to God [NTC].

(The) Lord knew[a] the (ones) being his,
LEXICON—a. aorist act. indic. of γινώσκω (LN 28.1) (BAGD 6.a.β. p. 161): 'to know' [BAGD, Herm, HNTC, ICC, LN, Lns, NTC; all versions]. Although it is in the aorist tense, it is translated as a present tense by all versions. The aorist denotes the complete result of a past action [ICC].
QUESTION—What is the significance of this statement?
It is an allusion to the Septuagint wording of Numbers 16:5 where Moses said that God would discriminate between those who were faithful and those who rebelled with Korah [Brd, EGT, GNC, Herm, HNTC, LSA, MNTC, My, NCBC, TG, TNTC]. This is placed here to encourage the faithful members by reminding them that God will discriminate between his loyal and disloyal servants [HNTC]. God knows which people really belong to him [TG]. God knows the characters of each and knows who truly believe in him [ICC, MNTC].

and Let-depart[a] from unrighteousness[b] every one naming[c] the name of-the-Lord.
TEXT—Instead of κυρίου 'Lord', some manuscripts have Χριστοῦ 'Christ'. GNT does not mention this alternative. 'Christ' is selected only by KJV.
LEXICON—a. aorist act. impera. of ἀφίστημι, ἀφίσταμαι (LN 15.51) (BAGD 2.b. p. 127): 'to depart' [ICC, LN; KJV], 'to stand off' [Lns], 'to stand aloof' [NTC], 'to stay away' [Herm], 'to turn away' [NIV, NRSV, TEV, TNT], 'to turn his back on' [HNTC], 'to abandon' [NAB], 'to forsake' [REB], 'to abstain' [BAGD; NASB], 'to avoid' [NJB].
  b. ἀδικία (LN 88.21) (BAGD 2. p. 18): 'unrighteousness' [BAGD, LN, Lns, NTC], 'evil' [NAB, NJB, TNT], 'iniquity' [ICC; KJV], 'injustice' [Herm], 'wickedness' [BAGD, HNTC; NASB, NIV, NRSV, REB], 'wrongdoing' [TEV].
  c. pres. act. participle of ὀνομάζω (LN **53.62**) (BAGD 2. p. 574): part of an idiom 'to name' [BAGD, Herm, HNTC, Lns, NTC; KJV, NASB], 'to profess' [NAB], 'to confess' [NIV], 'to call on' [NJB, NRSV], 'to take upon his lips' [REB], 'to speak' [TNT]. The idiom 'to name the name of the Lord' is translated 'to say that one belongs to the Lord' [**LN**; TEV], 'to worship the Lord' [ICC], 'to declare that one is a worshiper of the Lord' [LN].
QUESTION—What is meant by the phrase 'naming the name of the Lord'?
This is a Hebraism using a verb and noun form of the same word [LSA], and is an idiomatic expression [LN]. It indicates that the person is designating Christ as his Lord [Alf, El, LSA, TG; TEV]. The person embraces the revelation by which the Lord has made himself known [Lns, NTC]. It means that the person says that he belongs to the Lord [GNC, HNTC, ICC, LSA, TG]. It means 'to worship Christ' [ICC, LN, LSA, TG].
QUESTION—What is the significance of this statement?
This defines who the Lord's true people are, since they reveal that they belong to him by forsaking unrighteousness [HNTC]. It is an implied

exhortation to abstain from all unrighteousness in the face of the influence of the heretics [EBC, My].

DISCOURSE UNIT: 2:20–26 [MNTC]. The topic is personal direction.

DISCOURSE UNIT: 2:20–22 [LSA]. The topic is avoiding evil things and being useful by doing good things.

DISCOURSE UNIT: 2:20–21 [EBC, GNC]. The topic is noble and ignoble vessels.

2:20 But/Now^a in a large^b house^c there is not only golden and silver vessels/articles,^{d} but also wooden and earthen^e (ones),
LEXICON—a. δέ (LN 89.94; 89.124): 'but' [NTC; KJV], 'yet' [ICC], 'now' [Lns; NASB, REB], 'admittedly' [HNTC], not explicit [Herm; NAB, NIV, NJB, NRSV, TEV, TNT].
  b. μέγας (LN 79.123) (BAGD 1.b. p. 497): 'large' [BAGD, Herm, LN, Lns, NTC; all versions except KJV, REB], 'big' [ICC, LN], 'great' [BAGD, LN; KJV, REB].
  c. οἶκος (LN 7.3): 'house' [Herm, HNTC, ICC, LN, Lns, NTC; all versions except NAB], 'household' [NAB].
  d. σκεῦος (LN 6.118, cf. 6.1) (BAGD 1.b. p. 754): 'vessel' [Herm, ICC; KJV, NAB, NASB, NRSV, TNT], 'container' [LN], 'dish' [NJB], 'dishes and bowls' [TEV], 'utensils' [HNTC, Lns, NTC; REB], 'articles' [NIV].
  e. ὀστράκινος (LN 2.20) (BAGD p. 587): 'earthen' [NTC], 'earthenware' [BAGD, ICC, LN, Lns; NASB, NJB, TNT], 'of earth' [KJV], 'of clay' [Herm, LN; NAB, NIV, NRSV, TEV].
QUESTION—What relationship is indicated by δέ 'but, now'?
  1. It indicates a contrast [Alf, Brd, EGT, El, HNTC, ICC, LN, My, NTC; KJV]: but. Although the church is holy [Brd] and unaffected by the disloyalty of some of its members [EGT], yet it contains different kinds of members. This answers a possible objection to the suitability of the description of the church in 2:19 [Brd, El].
  2. This indicates a new topic [GNC, Lns, LSA]: now. The connector is used to set off parenthetical matter introducing preliminary thoughts preparatory for the following imperatives [Lns]. This elaborates on the second part of the inscription in 2:19 [GNC].
QUESTION—To what does 'the large house' of the analogy refer?
  It refers to the Church [Alf, Brd, EBC, EGT, El, HNTC, ICC, Lns, MNTC, NCBC, NTC, TG, TNTC]. It is the actual, visible church [Brd, EBC, El, HNTC, Lns, NTC], which is like a drag-net (Matt. 13:47 ff.) [Alf, El], a field with a mixture of tares and wheat (Matt. 13:24 ff.) [NTC].

and some for^a honor^b but others for dishonor.^{c}
LEXICON—a. εἰς with accusative object (LN 89.57) (BAGD 4.d. p. 229): 'for' [BAGD, ICC, Lns, NTC; NAB, NRSV], 'for the purpose of' [LN], 'to' [KJV, NASB]. It is also translated as a verb phrase: 'to be held in (honor)'

[NJB], 'to be (valued/valuable)' [REB, TNT], 'to be for (noble purposes or special occasions)' [NIV, TEV, HNTC], 'to be designated for' [Herm].
   b. τιμή (LN 87.4) (BAGD 2.b. p. 817): 'honor' [BAGD, LN, Lns, NTC; KJV, NASB, NJB], 'honorable use/purposes' [Herm, HNTC, ICC], 'distinguished use' [NAB], 'noble purposes/use' [NIV, NRSV], 'special occasions' [TEV], 'special use' [LN]. It is also translated 'to be valued (or valuable)' [REB, TNT].
   c. ἀτιμία (LN 87.71) (BAGD p. 120): 'dishonor' [BAGD, LN, Lns, NTC; KJV, NASB], 'dishonorable use' [BAGD], 'common use' [NAB], 'ordinary use' [NRSV, TEV], 'mean use' [ICC], 'cheap' [NJB, REB, TNT], 'ignoble/ignominious purposes/use' [HNTC; NIV], 'disreputable use' [Herm].
QUESTION—What is meant by these qualities?
   1. These qualities refer to the use to which the vessels are put [Alf, Brd, El, GNC, Herm, HNTC, ICC; NAB, NIV]. 'Honorable' means the use of vessels at public functions such as meals, and 'dishonorable' means the use of containers for garbage or excrement [GNC].
   2. These qualities refer to how the objects are regarded [Lns, My, NTC]. 'Honorable' means that they are prized and will be kept, while 'dishonorable' means that they are not prized and will be discarded [Lns]. Some articles are kept and displayed, while others are thrown out after serving their purposes [NTC]. They are given honor or shame by the way the owner uses them [My].

2:21 Therefore[a] if anyone cleanses[b] himself from these,
LEXICON—a. οὖν (LN 89.50) (BAGD 5. p. 593): 'therefore' [BAGD, LN; KJV, NASB], 'so' [LN, NTC], 'then' [ICC, LN, Lns], 'the lesson is that' [NAB], not explicit [Herm, HNTC; NIV, NJB, NRSV, REB, TEV, TNT].
   b. aorist act. subj. of ἐκκαθαίρω (LN 79.50) (BAGD 2. p. 240): 'to cleanse' [BAGD, Herm; KJV, NAB, NASB, NIV, NRSV, REB, TNT], 'to effectively cleanse' [NTC], 'to make clean' [TEV], 'to clean out' [BAGD, LN], 'to keep clean' [HNTC, Lns], 'to keep quite clear of' [ICC], 'to hold aloof from' [NJB].
QUESTION—What relationship is indicated by οὖν 'therefore'?
   It indicates the application to be drawn from the illustration in 2:20 [Alf, GNC, TG]. There is an implied exhortation to fulfill the condition [El, TNTC].
QUESTION—To what does τούτων 'these' refer and how are they to be cleansed?
   1. It refers to the dishonorable vessels mentioned at the end of 2:20 [Alf, Brd, EGT, El, HNTC, ICC, Lns, LSA, My, TNTC]. They are to keep from being contaminated by the false teachers [Lns] and separate themselves from their company [EGT, HNTC, ICC, My]. They are to purge the church of these false teachers [EBC].

2. It refers to the false teachings [GNC, TG]. These are the teachings he has been talking about [TG].
3. It refers to the evil thoughts and acts that cause men to be dishonorable [MNTC].

he-will-be (a) vessel[a] for honor, having-been-sanctified,[b] useful[c] for-the master,[d] for[e] all good[f] work[g] having-been-prepared.[h]

LEXICON—a. σκεῦος: 'vessel'. See this word at 2:20.
   b. perf. pass. participle of ἁγιάζω (LN 53.44; 88.26) (BAGD 2. p. 8): 'to be sanctified' [BAGD, Herm, Lns, NTC; KJV, NASB], 'to be dedicated' [NAB, NJB, NRSV, REB, TEV, TNT], 'to be consecrated' [BAGD, HNTC, LN], 'to be set apart for service' [ICC], 'to be made holy' [NIV].
   c. εὔχρηστος (LN 65.31) (BAGD p. 329): 'useful' [BAGD, Herm, LN; all versions except KJV, NJB], 'very useful' [NTC], 'serviceable' [BAGD, HNTC], 'well serviceable' [Lns], 'ready' [ICC], 'fit' [NJB], 'meet' [KJV], 'valuable' [LN].
   d. δεσπότης (LN **57.13**) (BAGD p. 176): 'master' [BAGD, Herm, **LN**, Lns, NTC; KJV, NASB, NIV, NJB], 'his master' [LN; TEV, TNT], 'his Master's hand' [ICC], 'master of the house' [NAB, REB], 'owner of the house' [NRSV], 'householder' [HNTC].
   e. εἰς with accusative object (LN 89.57): 'for' [Herm, HNTC, Lns, NTC; NAB, NASB, NJB, NRSV, REB, TNT], 'unto' [KJV]. It is also translated by an infinitive: 'to do' [NIV], or infinitive phrase: 'to be used for' [TEV], or 'to take part in' [ICC].
   f. ἀγαθός (LN 88.1) (BAGD 1.b.β. p. 3): 'good' [BAGD, Herm, HNTC, ICC, LN, Lns, NTC; all versions except NAB, REB], 'noble' [NAB], 'honorable' [REB].
   g. ἔργον (LN 42.42): 'work' [Herm, HNTC, ICC, LN, Lns, NTC; KJV, NASB, NIV, NJB, NRSV, TNT], 'service' [NAB], 'deed' [TEV], 'purpose' [REB].
   h. perf. pass. participle of ἑτοιμάζω (LN 77.3) (BAGD 1. p. 316): 'to be prepared' [Herm, ICC, Lns, NTC; KJV, NASB, NIV], 'to be ready' [HNTC; NAB, NJB, NRSV, TEV, TNT], 'to be fit' [REB], 'to be kept in readiness' [BAGD].

QUESTION—In what way is a person prepared?
The person has come to a state of readiness to carry out good works [HNTC, ICC, Lns, LSA, TG, TNTC]. Even though he doesn't have opportunity to do every good work, he is fit and ready to do so [EGT, El].

DISCOURSE UNIT: 2:22–26 [EBC, GNC, HNTC, My]. The topic is personal conduct [HNTC, My], responsibility in the light of false teachers [GNC], the kind and the quarrelsome [EBC].

2:22 Now/But^a the youthful^b desires^c flee-from,^d

LEXICON—a. δέ (LN 89.87; 89.124): 'now' [Lns; NASB], 'so' [HNTC; NAB] 'also' [KJV], 'but' [ICC, NTC], not explicit [Herm; NIV, NJB, NRSV, REB, TEV, TNT].
  b. νεωτερικός (LN **67.155**) (BAGD p. 537): 'youthful' [BAGD, HNTC, ICC, LN, Lns; KJV, NAB, NASB, NRSV], 'of youth' [Herm, **LN**, NTC; NIV, NJB, REB, TEV, TNT].
  c. ἐπιθυμία (LN **25.20**) (BAGD 3. p. 293): 'desire' [BAGD, Herm, LN, NTC; TNT], 'evil desire' [NIV], 'lust' [Lns; KJV, NASB], 'passion' [HNTC; NAB, NJB, NRSV, TEV], 'wayward passion' [REB], 'impulses and passions' [ICC].
  d. pres. act. impera. of φεύγω (LN **13.161**) (BAGD 3. p. 856): 'to flee from' [BAGD; NASB], 'to flee' [Herm, Lns; KJV, NIV], 'to flee away from' [NTC], 'to turn from' [NAB, REB], 'to turn away from' [NJB], 'to turn your back on/upon' [ICC; TNT], 'to avoid' [BAGD, HNTC, LN; TEV], 'to shun' [NRSV].

QUESTION—What relationship is indicated by δέ 'now, but'?
  1. It indicates a resumption of 2:15–16 [Herm, HNTC, Lns; NAB, NASB]: now, and. This resumes the personal note that was suspended for the warning against evil people (2:16–21) [HNTC]. It specifies what the good works consist of [Lns].
  2. It indicates a contrast [Alf, EBC, El, ICC, NTC, TNTC]: but. It contrasts every good work with youthful desires [El, TNTC].
  3. It introduces an exhortation based on 2:21 [LSA].

QUESTION—What is meant by νεωτερικὰς ἐπιθυμίας 'youthful desires'?
These are wrong, sinful desires [Alf, EBC, El, GNC, Lns, LSA, NTC]. They include sexual lusts [EGT, El], but are much more [El, GNC, HNTC, My, TG]. They include selfish ambition [TNTC], impatience [ICC, TNTC], giving in to sudden impulses [GNC, HNTC, MNTC, NTC], argumentation [GNC, ICC, TNTC], intolerance [HNTC], and self-indulgence [ICC]. They are traits that yield to novelties, foolish discussions, and arguments [GNC]. They are everything inconsistent with the following virtues [ICC, NTC].

QUESTION—What is implied about Timothy's age?
The word νεωτερικάς 'youthful' is used by an old man writing to his disciple [Brd]. Actually, Timothy was in his early thirties [EBC], or almost forty [MNTC], between thirty-seven and forty [NTC]. According to ancient standards, he was still a young man [HNTC]. The lusts and passions are those especially characterizing youth, but may be felt by one who is not a youth in the strictest sense of the term [El].

but/and^a pursue^b righteousness,^c faith,^d love,^e peace^f

LEXICON—a. δέ (LN 89.87; 89.124): 'but' [Herm, Lns; KJV], 'on the other hand' [LN], 'and' [HNTC, NTC; NAB, NASB, NIV, NRSV, REB, TEV, TNT], not explicit [ICC; NJB].

b. pres. act. impera. of διώκω (LN 68.66) (BAGD 4.b. p. 201): 'to pursue' [BAGD, Herm, Lns; NAB, NASB, NIV, NRSV, REB], 'to run after' [NTC], 'to follow' [KJV], 'to aim at' [HNTC], 'to set one's face toward' [ICC], 'to concentrate on' [NJB], 'to strive toward' [LN], 'to strive for' [BAGD; TEV,], 'to do with effort' [LN].
c. δικαιοσύνη (LN 88.13) (BAGD 2.b. p. 196): 'righteousness' [BAGD, LN, Lns, NTC; KJV, NIV, NRSV, TEV, TNT], 'uprightness' [BAGD, Herm; NJB], 'justice' [REB], 'just dealings with others' [ICC], 'integrity' [HNTC; NAB, NASB], 'doing what is right' [LN].
d. πίστις (LN 31.88; 31.85) (BAGD 2.d.γ. p. 663): 'faith' [BAGD, Herm, HNTC, Lns, NTC; all versions except REB, TNT], 'integrity' [REB], 'faithfulness' [TNT], 'loyalty' [ICC].
e. ἀγάπη (LN 25.43) (BAGD I.1.a. p. 5): 'love' [BAGD, Herm, ICC, LN, Lns, NTC; all versions except KJV], 'charity' [HNTC; KJV].
f. εἰρήνη (LN 22.42) (BAGD 1.b. p. 227): 'peace' [BAGD, Herm, HNTC, ICC, LN, Lns, NTC; all versions], 'tranquility' [LN], 'harmony' [BAGD].

QUESTION—What is meant by δικαιοσύνη 'righteousness'?

It refers in the widest sense to general conformity to God's law, i.e., to what is right towards God and man [Brd, EGT, My, NTC, TNTC]. It is moral rectitude in contrast to ἀδικία 'iniquity' (2:19) [Alf]. It refers to right conduct [El, GNC, Herm, HNTC], doing what is right [LSA], or right behavior [Herm, TG].

QUESTION—What is meant by πίστις 'faith'?

1. It means confidence, belief, and trust in God, Christ, or his doctrines [Alf, EBC, El, Lns, LSA, My, NTC].
2. It refers to the trait of faithfulness and trustworthiness [EBC, ICC, MNTC, TG; TNT]. This trait may be in relation to Christ [TG], to other men [ICC], or to both (indefinite) [EBC, MNTC].

QUESTION—What is meant by εἰρήνη 'peace'?

It means peace and harmony between people [Alf, BAGD, Brd, EBC, EGT, El, HNTC, ICC, LSA, My, NTC, TNTC]. It is the absence of contention [El]. It is spiritual concord [El, HNTC], fellowship and harmony [My].

with[a] the (ones) calling-on[b] the Lord out-of[c] a pure[d] heart.

LEXICON—a. μετά with genitive object (LN 89.108) (BAGD A.II.3.b. p. 509): 'with' [BAGD, HNTC, ICC, LN, NTC; KJV, NASB], 'together with' [LN], 'along with' [NAB, NIV, NRSV], 'in union with' [NJB], 'in company with' [LN, Lns], 'together with' [Herm; REB, TEV]. It is also translated as an imperative phrase: 'join the company of' [TNT].
b. pres. mid. participle of ἐπικαλέω (LN 33.176) (BAGD 2.b. p. 294): 'to call on/upon' [BAGD, Herm, HNTC, LN, Lns, NTC; all versions except REB, TEV, TNT], 'to call out to for help' [TEV], 'to ask for help' [LN], 'to invoke' [TNT], 'to worship' [REB]. The phrase 'the ones calling on the Lord' is translated 'to call the Lord their God' [ICC]. This phrase

refers to prayer [Lns, NCBC] and to worship [NTC; REB]. It is a technical term for 'Christian' [EGT, MNTC, My].
   c. ἐκ with genitive object (LN 90.16) (BAGD 3.g.γ. p. 235): 'out of' [BAGD, HNTC, ICC, NTC; KJV, NIV], 'from' [LN, Lns; NASB, NRSV], 'with' [Herm; NJB, TEV], 'in' [NAB, REB, TNT].
   d. καθαρός (LN 53.29) (BAGD 3.b. p. 388): 'pure' [BAGD, Herm, HNTC, ICC, LN, NTC; KJV, NAB, NASB, NIV, NJB, NRSV, TEV], 'in purity' [NAB], 'clean' [Lns], 'free from sin' [BAGD]. The phrase 'out of a pure heart' is translated 'in singleness of mind' [REB], 'sincerely' [TNT].
QUESTION—To what does this phrase relate?
   1. It relates to the verb δίωκε 'pursue' [GNC, Herm, Lns, MNTC, TG; all versions]: seek, along with those who call on the Lord, to have righteousness, love, and peace. Timothy must strive for peace as do all those who call on the Lord [GNC].
   2. It relates to the word εἰρήνην 'peace' [Alf, Brd, EBC, EGT, El, HNTC, ICC, LSA, My, NTC, TNTC]: seek to have peace with those who call on the Lord. Timothy is to avoid the company of evil men, but he is to cultivate friendly relations with sincere worshipers [EGT]. He would not seek to maintain peaceful relations with the impure [LSA].
QUESTION—What is meant by ἐκ καθαρᾶς καρδίας 'out of a pure heart'?
   1. It means that they are people who have pure lives, free from sin [El, Lns, LSA, NTC]. It means the same as 'sanctified' in 2:21 [Lns].
   2. It means that they are completely sincere in their calling on the Lord [Alf, HNTC, TG; REB, TNT].

DISCOURSE UNIT: 2:23–26 [LSA]. The topic is a command to refuse foolish questions but gently instruct opposers of the true message.

2:23 Now/But[a] foolish[b] and ignorant[c] questionings[d] avoid,[e]
LEXICON—a. δέ (LN 89.87; 89.124): 'now' [Lns], 'and' [REB], 'but' [ICC, NTC; KJV, NASB, TEV], not explicit [Herm, HNTC; NAB, NIV, NJB, NRSV, TNT].
   b. μωρός (LN 32.58) (BAGD 2. p. 531): 'foolish' [BAGD, Herm, HNTC, ICC, LN, NTC; KJV, NASB, NIV, NJB, REB, TEV, TNT], 'senseless' [NAB], 'nonsensical' [LN], 'stupid' [BAGD; NRSV], 'silly' [Lns].
   c. ἀπαίδευτος (LN **27.25**) (BAGD p. 79): 'ignorant' [**LN**, NTC; NAB, NASB, TEV], 'uneducated' [BAGD, LN, Lns], 'uninstructed' [BAGD, Herm], 'unlearned' [KJV], 'undisciplined' [HNTC; NJB], 'wild' [REB], 'senseless' [NRSV], 'stupid' [NIV, TNT], 'foolish' [LN], 'of untrained minds' [ICC]. This word is synonymous with the preceding word μωρός 'foolish' [My].
   d. ζήτησις (LN 33.440) (BAGD 1., 2. p. 339): 'questioning' [Lns], 'QUESTION' [KJV], 'inquiry' [NTC], 'discussion' [ICC], 'disputation' [NAB], 'speculation' [Herm, HNTC; NASB, NJB, REB], 'argument' [NIV, TEV, TNT], 'dispute' [LN], 'controversy' [BAGD; NRSV].

e. pres. mid. impera. of παραιτέομαι (LN 27.60) (BAGD 2.b. p. 616): 'to avoid' [BAGD, LN; KJV, NJB], 'to not pay attention to' [LN], 'to have nothing to do with' [HNTC; NAB, NIV, NRSV, REB, TNT], 'to keep away from' [TEV], 'to refuse' [NASB], 'to reject' [BAGD, Herm, NTC], 'to persistently avoid' [ICC], 'to disdain to be bothered with' [Lns]. The present tense means that he must constantly refuse to have anything to do with them [NTC].

QUESTION—What relationship is indicated by δέ 'now, but'?
  1. It indicates a continuation [HNTC, Lns, LSA, MNTC; REB]: now, and. Along with the warnings of 2:22 it is a further caution [MNTC]. It is a second admonition [NTC], a second specification [Lns].
  2. It indicates a contrast [Alf, ICC, My, NTC; KJV, NASB, TEV]: but. The contrast is with the preceding positive command [Alf, My].

QUESTION—What is meant by ignorant questionings?
  The heretical doctrines generate questions that are either unimportant or insoluble [Brd]. They arise from misunderstanding the matter in dispute [EGT] and show a lack of elementary Christian education [Lns]. The questions are the work and mark of ignorant men, those who have not been properly educated in God's redemptive truth [NTC].

knowing^a that they-cause^b quarrels.^c

LEXICON—a. perf. act. participle of οἶδα (LN 28.1; 32.4): 'to know' [Herm, ICC, Lns, NTC; all versions], 'to understand' [NJB].
  b. pres. act. indic. of γεννάω (LN **13.129**) (BAGD 3. p. 155): 'to cause' [BAGD, LN], 'to engender' [ICC; KJV], 'to produce' [BAGD, LN; NASB, NIV], 'to beget' [Lns], 'to breed' [HNTC, NTC; NAB, NJB, NRSV, TNT], 'to end up in' [TEV], 'to bring forth' [BAGD], 'to give rise to' [LN; NJB], 'to create' [Herm].
  c. μάχη (LN 39.23) (BAGD p. 496): 'quarrel' [BAGD, Herm, HNTC, NTC; all versions except KJV], 'dispute' [BAGD], 'fight' [LN], 'battle' [Lns], 'strife' [BAGD, ICC; KJV].

QUESTION—What relationship is indicated by the use of the participle εἰδώς 'knowing'?
  1. It indicates the grounds for the preceding command [Herm, HNTC, Lns, LSA; NIV]: avoid foolish and ignorant questionings since such questions cause quarrels.
  2. It indicates the circumstance of the preceding command [My]: avoid foolish and ignorant questionings as you consider that they cause quarrels.

2:24 And/But^a (a) servant^b of-(the) Lord must^c-not quarrel^d

LEXICON—a. δέ (LN 89.87; 89.124): 'and' [ICC, NTC; NAB, NASB, NIV, NJB, NRSV, REB], 'now' [Lns], 'but' [Herm, HNTC; KJV], not explicit [TEV, TNT].
  b. δοῦλος (LN 87.76) (BAGD 4. p. 206): 'servant' [Herm, HNTC, NTC; all versions except NASB], 'bondservant' [LN; NASB], 'slave' [BAGD, LN, Lns].

c. pres. act. indic. of δεῖ (LN 71.21, 71.34) (BAGD 6. p. 172): 'must' [BAGD, ICC, LN, Lns, NTC; all versions], 'should' [Herm, HNTC, LN].
d. pres. mid. infin. of μάχομαι (LN 39.23) (BAGD 2. p. 496): 'to quarrel' [BAGD, Herm, NTC; NIV, TEV], 'to be quarrelsome' [HNTC; NAB, NASB, NRSV, REB, TNT], 'to dispute' [BAGD], 'to strive' [ICC; KJV], 'to fight' [BAGD, LN], 'to be battling' [Lns], 'to be engaged in quarrels' [NJB].

QUESTION—What relationship is indicated by δέ 'and, but'?
1. It indicates an additional instruction [EBC, ICC, Lns, NTC; NAB, NASB, NIV, NJB, NRSV, REB]: and. It gives a third specification [Lns].
2. It indicates contrast [Alf, Brd, GNC, Herm, HNTC, LSA; KJV]: but. Timothy's actions are to be in contrast with the quarreling of the false teachers [GNC, HNTC]. Timothy is told what to avoid in the first, but what to do in the second [LSA].

QUESTION—To whom does 'servant of the Lord' refer?
It refers to a minister or Christian leader [Alf, EGT, El, GNC, HNTC, ICC, Lns, MNTC, My, NCBC, NTC, TG, TNTC]. It reflects the Old Testament passages (e.g., Isa. 42:1-3 and Isa. 53) which speak of the Servant of the Lord [HNTC, ICC]. This is a description that could be used for all Christians, but here it is especially appropriate for pastors and those with oversight [Brd, EBC].

but[a] be[b] gentle[c] toward[d] all, skillful-in-teaching,[e] patient,[f]

LEXICON—a. ἀλλά (LN 89.125): 'but' [HNTC, Lns, NTC; KJV, NAB, NASB, NJB, NRSV], 'instead' [NIV], 'rather' [Herm], 'nay' [ICC], not explicit [REB, TEV, TNT].
b. pres. act. infin. of εἰμί (LN 13.1): 'to be' [NTC; KJV, NASB]. It is also translated with the obligatory mode from the verb δεῖ of the previous clause: 'must be' [Lns; NAB, NJB], 'he must be' [ICC; NIV, REB, TEV, TNT], 'he should be' [Herm], not explicit [HNTC; NRSV].
c. ἤπιος (LN **88.61**) (BAGD p. 348): 'gentle' [BAGD, Herm, LN, Lns, NTC; KJV], 'kind' [BAGD; NASB, NIV, NJB, TEV, TNT], 'kindly' [HNTC; NAB, NRSV, REB], 'courteous' [ICC].
d. πρός with accusative object (LN 90.58) (BAGD III.4.b. p. 710): 'toward' [BAGD, Herm, Lns; NAB, REB, TEV], 'to' [BAGD, HNTC, ICC, LN, NTC; NASB, NIV, NJB, NRSV, TNT], 'unto' [KJV], 'with' [BAGD, LN].
e. διδακτικός (LN 33.233) (BAGD p. 191): 'skillful in teaching' [BAGD, Herm], 'able to teach' [LN; NASB, NIV], 'qualified to teach' [NTC], 'apt to teach' [Lns; KJV], 'an apt teacher' [NAB, NRSV], 'a good teacher' [NJB, REB], 'a good and patient teacher' [TEV], 'a skilful teacher' [TNT], 'an understanding teacher' [HNTC], 'skilful to teach' [ICC]. In addition to the capability, this term also includes a willingness to do so [EGT, El, My].

f. ἀνεξίκακος (LN **25.170**) (BAGD p. 65): 'patient' [BAGD, LN, NTC; KJV, NASB, NJB, TEV], 'forbearing' [HNTC; NRSV], 'tolerant' [REB, TNT], 'not resentful' [NIV], 'without resentment' [Herm], 'ready to bear with contradictions' [ICC], 'putting up with what is bad' [Lns]. This adjective is also translated as an adverb modifying the teaching verb of the next clause: 'patiently' [NAB].

QUESTION—In what sense is he to be patient?

It is a general character quality relating to any servant of the Lord, and refers to being patient when wronged [Alf, El], being forbearing [Brd, El, TG], or tolerant [GNC]. It is being ready to put up with evil or wrong treatment and hence he is patient under injuries [MNTC, NTC], holding up under evil [NTC], and tried by persecution [ICC]. It relates to one's reactions to the opponents mentioned in v. 24 and has the sense of bearing evil without resentment [EBC, LSA], being submissive, patient, or forbearing with those who oppose him [EGT, My, TNTC], so that he can correct his opponent [EGT].

2:25 with[a] gentleness[b] instructing[c] the (ones) opposing,[d]

LEXICON—a. ἐν with dative object (LN 89.84): 'with' [HNTC, LN, NTC; NASB, NRSV], 'in' [Herm, ICC, Lns; KJV]. The phrase 'with gentleness' is translated 'gently' [NAB, NIV], 'be gentle' [LN; NJB, REB, TEV, TNT], 'speaking in a gentle tone' [ICC].

b. πραΰτης (LN 88.59) (BAGD p. 699): 'gentleness' [BAGD, Herm, HNTC, LN; NASB, NRSV], 'meekness' [BAGD, LN, Lns; KJV], 'mildness' [NTC].

c. pres. act. participle of παιδεύω (LN **36.10**) (BAGD 2.a. p. 603): 'to instruct' [Herm; KJV, NIV], 'to give guidance' [BAGD], 'to correct' [BAGD, HNTC, NTC; NAB, NASB, NJB, NRSV, TEV, TNT], 'to discipline' [LN; REB], 'to educate' [Lns], 'to train someone's mind' [ICC].

d. pres. mid. participle of ἀντιδιατίθημι (LN **39.1**) (BAGD p. 74): 'to oppose' [BAGD, LN]. The phrase τοὺς ἀντιδιατιθεμένους 'the ones opposing' is translated 'those who are in opposition' [NASB], 'those who oppose him' [NIV, REB], 'people who oppose him' [NJB], 'opponents' [ICC, NTC; NRSV], 'his opponents' [Herm, HNTC; TEV, TNT], 'those who contradict him' [NAB], 'those placing themselves in opposition' [Lns], 'those that oppose themselves' [KJV], 'those who oppose the true message' [LSA].

if-perhaps[a] God may-give[b] them repentance[c] to[d] acknowledgment[e] of-truth,[f]

LEXICON—a. μήποτε (LN 71.18) (BAGD 3.b.β. p. 519): 'if perhaps' [Lns; NASB], 'if peradventure' [KJV], 'whether perhaps' [BAGD, LN], 'but perhaps' [TNT], 'perhaps' [NRSV], 'that perhaps' [Herm], 'in case' [HNTC], 'in the hope that' [NTC; NAB, NIV, NJB], 'for it may be that' [TEV], 'then' [REB].

b. aorist act. opt. of δίδωμι (LN 13.142) (BAGD p. 192): 'to give' [BAGD, ICC; KJV, NJB], 'to give the opportunity' [TEV], 'to grant' [BAGD, Herm, HNTC, LN, NTC; NASB, NIV, NRSV, REB], 'to allow' [LN], 'to enable' [NAB], 'to help' [TNT], 'to get to give' [Lns].
c. μετάνοια (LN 41.52) (BAGD p. 512): 'repentance' [BAGD, Herm, LN; KJV, NASB, NIV], 'a change of mind or heart or attitude' [HNTC, ICC, Lns; NJB, REB], 'conversion' [NTC]. It is also translated as a verb: 'to repent' [NAB, NRSV, TEV, TNT].
d. εἰς with accusative object (LN 89.48; 89.57): 'to' [KJV], 'for' [Herm, Lns], 'leading to' [HNTC, NTC; NASB, NIV, REB], 'come (to know)' [ICC; NRSV, TEV], 'so that (they recognize)' [NJB], not explicit [NAB, TNT].
e. ἐπίγνωσις (LN 28.18; 28.2) (BAGD p. 291): 'acknowledgment' [HNTC, NTC; KJV], 'knowledge' [BAGD, ICC; NASB, NIV], 'recognition' [Herm], 'realization' [Lns]. This is also translated as a verb: 'to know' [NAB, NRSV, TEV, TNT], 'to recognize' [NJB, REB].
f. ἀλήθεια (LN 72.2) (BAGD 2.b. p. 36): 'truth' [Herm, HNTC, ICC, Lns, NTC; all versions].

QUESTION—What is the function of the word μήποτε 'if perhaps'?

It is a subordinating conjunction indicating uncertainty to introduce the purpose for instructing opposers [LSA]. He is to instruct them in the hope that this will happen [EBC, El].

QUESTION—In what sense does God give repentance?

1. Repentance is made possible by God [Herm, LSA, TG]. The term 'give/grant repentance' is Judaistic in origin, is common in other writings, and used without an implication that repentance is necessarily a gift [Herm]. 'Give' is here used figuratively in the sense of 'cause' or 'enable' [LSA], 'make possible', or 'allow' [TG].
2. 'Repentance' is a gift of God [GNC, My, TNTC], not that he ever withholds it but men so frequently refuse it [Lns]. It is wholly the working of God's power by His grace within us [HNTC, MNTC], giving the capacity to repent [TG] and causing a change of heart [EBC, El], a change of view or outlook [NTC], of attitude [HNTC], and mind [MNTC, TNTC]. It is a turning to God from apostate evils [El, My, NCBC], a returning to the truth [Herm]. False doctrine, when believed, gives a moral twist and faulty practice, hence the need for repentance [Alf, EGT]. It is a change of the mind so as to recognize the truth, since the mind was previously ensnared by error [TNTC].

QUESTION—What relationship is indicated by εἰς 'to'?

1. It indicates the purpose for giving them repentance [Alf, GNC, Lns, My]: God may give them repentance in order that they acknowledge the truth.
2. It indicates the result of repentance [EBC, EGT, HNTC, LSA, NTC, TNTC]: God may give them repentance that causes them to acknowledge the truth.
3. It clarifies by amplification the term 'repentance' [Lns].

2:26 and they-may-come-to-their-senses[a] from[b] the devil's[c] snare,[d]

LEXICON—a. aorist act. subj. of ἀνανήφω (LN 30.27) (BAGD p. 58): 'to come to one's senses' [BAGD,; NASB, NIV, NJB, REB, TEV], 'to come back to one's senses' [LN], 'to return to one's senses' [HNTC], 'to return to one's right senses' [LN], 'to come back to one's sober senses' [ICC], 'to return to soberness' [NTC], 'to come back to soberness' [Lns], 'to recover one's self' [KJV]. The man who accepts the truth has returned to his right mind [MNTC].
  b. ἐκ with genitive object (LN 84.4) (BAGD 1.d. p. 234): 'from' [BAGD, Herm, HNTC, ICC, LN; NASB, NIV, NRSV, REB, TEV, TNT], 'out of' [LN, Lns, NTC; KJV], not explicit [NAB, NJB].
  c. διάβολος (LN 12.34) (BAGD 2. 182): 'devil' [BAGD, Herm, HNTC, ICC, Lns, NTC; all versions], 'Devil' [LN; TEV].
  d. παγίς (LN 6.23; 37.15) (BAGD 2. p. 602): 'snare' [BAGD, Herm, HNTC, ICC, LN, Lns, NTC; KJV, NASB, NRSV, REB, TNT], 'trap' [LN; NAB, NIV, NJB, TEV].

QUESTION—To what does the prepositional phrase 'from the devil's snare' relate?

It relates to an implied event: 'to escape' [BAGD, El, GNC, HNTC; NASB, NJB, REB, TEV], 'to get away' [TNT].

QUESTION—What is meant by 'the devil's snare'?

The genitive construction means the snare that is set by the devil to catch others [Alf, Brd, ICC, LSA, NTC]. Some commentators believe that there is a mixing of metaphors: 'returning to soberness' and 'getting out of a snare' [El, HNTC]. Others admit that it is mixed, but consider it to be meaningful [NCBC]. Still others say there is no confusion of metaphor [Alf, Lns]. The figure of a snare or trap means to be entangled in false teachings [GNC], to accept false doctrines [MNTC], which becloud men's wits [My], benumb their consciences and paralyze their wills [TNTC]. Men are misled [Lns], deceived [LSA], deluded [MNTC], and captivated [HNTC], in their minds [TNTC]. They are put into a state of moral and spiritual intoxication [Alf]. Being ensnared in false teachings causes them to stumble and fall into sin [Herm], and they become disgraced by their improper lives [TG]. They are defeated by the devil [TG], and under his power [NTC], doing his will [HNTC, NTC].

having-been-captured[a] by[b] him for[c] the will[d] of-that (one).

LEXICON—a. perf. pass. participle of ζωγρέω (LN 37.1) (BAGD p. 340): 'to be taken captive' [NTC; KJV, NAB, NIV], 'to be held captive' [BAGD; NASB], 'to be made captive and subject' [NJB], 'to be made captive in subjection' [HNTC], 'to be controlled' [LN], 'to be trapped and held' [REB], 'to be captured' [Herm; NRSV], 'to be caught alive' [Lns; TNT], 'to caught and made to obey' [TEV].

> b. ὑπό with genitive object (LN 90.1): 'by' [Herm, HNTC, LN, Lns, NTC; KJV, NAB, NASB, NRSV], not explicit [ICC; NIV, NJB, REB, TEV, TNT].
>
> c. εἰς with accusative object (LN 89.57): 'for' [Lns], 'for the purpose of' [LN], 'to do' [Herm, ICC, NTC; NAB, NASB, NIV, NRSV], 'at' [KJV, REB], 'to' [HNTC; NJB], not explicit [TEV, TNT].
>
> d. θέλημα (LN 25.2; 30.59) (BAGD 1.c.β. p. 354): 'will' [BAGD, Herm, HNTC, ICC, LN, Lns, NTC; all versions except TNT], 'whatever he wants' [TNT].

QUESTION—To whom do the pronouns αὐτοῦ 'him' (the actor of the verb 'to capture'), and ἐκείνου 'that one' (who exercises his will) refer?

> 1. The actor of the verb 'catch' is the devil, and this action is done to accomplish the devil's will [EBC, GNC, Herm, HNTC, LSA, My, NCBC, NTC, TNTC; NIV, NJB, NRSV, REB, TEV, TNT]: having been captured by the devil to do the devil's will.
> 2. The actor of the verb 'catch' is the devil, and this is done according to God's will [Alf, Brd, MNTC]. Taking people captive can take place only as far as God permits [Alf]. They are caught by the devil to do God's will [Brd]. Those who have been captured by the devil may recover themselves out of his snare so as to serve God's will [EGT].
> 3. The actor of the verb 'catch' is the 'servant of the Lord' (2:24), and this is done for the Lord's will [ICC]: having been captured by the servant of the Lord to do the Lord's will.
> 4. The actor of the verb 'catch' is God who captivates men to do his will [Lns]: having been captured by God to do God's will.

DISCOURSE UNIT: 3:1–17 [NASB, NJB]. The topic is the coming difficult times [NASB], the dangers of the last days [NJB].

DISCOURSE UNIT: 3:1–9 [Alf, Brd, EBC, GNC, Herm, HNTC, LSA, MNTC, NTC, TG, TNTC; NAB, NIV, TEV]. The topic is the last days [TEV], characteristics of the last days [EBC], predictions of the last days [TNTC], prediction of a period of moral dissolution [MNTC], disasters of the last days [HNTC], the corruptions of the future [Brd], godlessness in the last days [NIV], the rise of enemies [NTC], final indictment of the false teachers [GNC; NAB], the heretics as the sinners of the last days [Herm].

3:1 Now/But[a] this know,[b] that in (the) last[c] days difficult[d] times[e] will-come;[f]

LEXICON—a. δέ: (LN 89.87; 89.124): 'now' [Lns], 'also' [KJV], 'but' [ICC, NTC; NASB, NIV], 'however' [HNTC], not explicit [NAB, NJB, NRSV, REB, TEV, TNT].

> b. pres. act. impera. of γινώσκω (LN 32.16): 'to know' [Herm; KJV, TNT], 'to understand' [NTC; NRSV], 'to realize' [ICC, Lns; NASB], 'to not forget' [NAB], 'to remember' [REB, TEV], 'to mark' [NIV], 'to take note of' [HNTC], 'to be quite sure' [NJB].

2 TIMOTHY 3:1

c. ἔσχατος (LN 61.13) (BAGD 3.b. p. 314): 'last' [BAGD, Herm, HNTC, ICC, LN, Lns, NTC; all versions except REB], 'final' [REB].
d. χαλεπός (LN **22.29**) (BAGD p. 874): 'difficult' [BAGD; NASB, NJB, TEV, TNT], 'troublous' [LN], 'troublesome' [HNTC], 'perilous' [KJV], 'terrible' [NAB, NIV], 'grievous' [Lns, NTC], 'distressing' [NRSV], 'very difficult to face' [ICC], 'hard' [BAGD, Herm], 'of turmoil' [REB].
e. καιρός (LN 67.78) (BAGD 1. p. 394): 'times' [BAGD, Herm, HNTC; all versions], 'seasons' [Lns, NTC], 'moments' [ICC].
f. fut. mid. indic. of ἐνίστημι (LN **13.109**) (BAGD 2. p. 266): 'to come' [Herm; KJV, NASB, NRSV], 'to come about' [LN], 'to come upon' [TNT], 'to be present' [Lns], 'to set in' [HNTC, NTC], 'to be' [ICC; NAB, NIV, NJB, REB, TEV], 'to be impending' [BAGD].

QUESTION—What relationship is indicated by δέ 'now, but'?
1. It indicates a transition to new material [Lns, LSA, NCBC]: now.
2. It indicates contrast [Alf, El, HNTC, ICC, NTC; NASB, NIV]: but. The dark prophetic announcement is in contrast with the hope just expressed [Alf]. There is a change from the present to the future [El]. Things are not yet at their worst [ICC].

QUESTION—What time is referred to in the phrase 'the last days'?
1. It refers to a definite future period immediately preceding the second coming of the Lord [Alf, Brd, EBC, El, HNTC, ICC, LSA, MNTC, My, TG, TNTC]. It will be the end of the Christian era [El], just before the consummation of the present age [TNTC], at the end of the world [TG].
2. It refers to the lengthy era since Christ came and lasts until he comes again [EGT, GNC, Lns, NTC, TNTC]. This is the age of the fulfillment of the Messianic prophecies and was ushered in by Christ's appearance on earth [NTC].

QUESTION—In what way will the times be difficult?
There will be both spiritual and temporal dangers [El, HNTC]. It will be hard to keep to the path of duty [Brd], difficult to maintain proper conduct [LSA], and difficult, especially for teachers, to keep the spirit of gentleness, etc. (2:24–26) toward all men [ICC, MNTC]. It will be difficult to know how to act and confront all the evil [El] and moral corruption [TNTC]. It will be grievous [EGT, Lns, NTC], hard to endure [EBC, NTC], even painful for Christians [Lns, NTC], because of all the grief that will come from self-loving, indulgent, materialistic people manifesting any or many of the nineteen evil characteristics noted in 3:2–5 [Lns, LSA, MNTC, My, NCBC, NTC, TG]. There will be a new heathendom with a Christian name [My], with vicious men in the church [NCBC], who still claim to be Christian [TG] holding a supposed form of godliness but rejecting in their lives any transforming power [TNT].

3:2 for[a]

LEXICON—a. γάρ (LN 89.23): 'for' [Herm, HNTC, Lns, NTC; KJV, NASB, NRSV], not explicit [ICC; NAB, NIV, NJB, REB, TEV, TNT].

QUESTION—What relationship is indicated by γάρ 'for'?
It indicates the reason why the time will be difficult [Alf, NTC].
QUESTION—Is there any meaningful order, emphasis, or focus in the listing of these nineteen evil traits?
1. There is no premeditated formal order, design, or logical sequence consistent throughout from which any practical inference can be deduced [Alf, Brd, EGT, El, GNC, Herm, HNTC, My, NCBC, NTC, TNTC]. However, the very confusion of the array of terms vividly depicts the moral anarchy and the people in chaos who are tossed about by their lower passions [MNTC], as well as pointing out the extensive and varied manifestations of the evil one in men in the last days [Alf, My]. The total effect of this is what is most important [TG]. The listing does show various pairs, groups, and sets of terms according to their formal features; e.g., the words in the two middle groups each begin with the α- negative prefix, but no central ideas or emphases of such groups can be consistently deciphered [EBC, GNC, Herm, ICC, Lns, NTC].
2. There is a very decided order in the listing of the evil traits, 3:2-4, displaying a chiasmus in the Greek language which possibly highlights the basic roots and results of holding heretical doctrine. It all begins where one sets his affections: the opening two words and the closing two words are compounds of φιλέω 'to love' with negative connotations (as regards godliness). Then the results, first in character then in action, are highlighted by the center two sets of terms, all of which have the α- negative prefix. The sets are separated only by the single term διάβολοι 'slanderers' which links the evil people with ὁ διάβολος 'the devil' [LSA]. For a full display of all the relations see LSA of 2 Timothy, pp. 84-85.

the men[a] will-be self-lovers,[b] money-lovers,[c]

LEXICON—a. ἄνθρωπος (LN 9.1): 'man'. The plural form ἄνθρωποι is translated 'men' [Herm, HNTC, ICC, Lns; KJV, NAB, NASB, TNT], 'people' [LN, NTC; NIV, NJB, NRSV, REB, TEV].
  b. φίλαυτος (LN **25.39**) (BAGD p. 859): 'self-lover' [Lns], 'lover of self' [LN; KJV, NAB, NASB, NIV, NRSV], 'self-loving' [BAGD, HNTC, NTC], 'self-centered' [NJB], 'selfish' [BAGD, Herm; TEV]. This word is also translated as a verb phrase: 'to love nothing but self' [REB], 'to love only themselves' [TNT], 'to set affections on self' [ICC]. They are selfish [Alf].
  c. φιλάργυρος (LN 25.108) (BAGD p. 859): 'money-lover' [Lns], 'lover of money' [NAB, NASB, NIV, NRSV], 'money loving' [HNTC, NTC], 'fond of money' [BAGD], 'loving wealth' [LN], 'lover of riches' [LN], 'covetous' [KJV], 'avaricious' [BAGD; NJB], 'greedy' [Herm; TEV]. This word is also translated as a verb phrase: 'to love nothing but money' [REB], 'to love only money' [TNT], 'to set affections on money' [ICC].

QUESTION—To whom does οἱ ἄνθρωποι 'the men' refer?
1. It is a generic term referring to people in general living in those grievous times [Alf, EGT, Lns, NTC].
2. It refers to men generally but not as an inclusive totality. The article οἱ indicates generality, pointing not merely to those addressed by Paul, but to the majority [El], taking the average, or as a general rule [My], yet not everybody living in those grievous times [TG].
3. It refers to the generality of men of the Christian communities [Brd], people in general who were professing Christians [LSA], at first indirectly but in 3:4–5 obviously the sectaries in and about the church [HNTC].

boasters,[a] arrogant,[b] blasphemers,[c]
LEXICON—a. ἀλαζών (LN **88.220**) (BAGD p. 34): 'boaster' [BAGD, Lns, NTC; KJV, NRSV], 'braggart' [BAGD, ICC, LN]. This word is also translated as an adjective: 'boastful' [Herm, HNTC; NASB, NIV, NJB, REB, TEV, TNT], 'proud' [NAB]. They brag about themselves [Lns].
b. ὑπερήφανος (LN 88.214) (BAGD p. 841): 'arrogant' [BAGD, Herm; NASB, NJB, NRSV, REB, TNT], 'haughty' [BAGD, HNTC, LN, Lns], 'overbearing' [ICC, NTC], 'proud' [KJV, NAB, NIV], 'conceited' [TEV]. They are overbearing toward others [Lns].
c. βλάσφημος (LN 33.403) (BAGD p. 143): 'blasphemer' [BAGD, Herm, LN, Lns, NTC; KJV], 'reviler' [NASB], 'defamer' [LN]. This noun is also translated as an adjective: 'abusive' [HNTC; NAB, NIV, NRSV, REB, TNT], 'rude' [NJB], 'insulting' [TEV], 'quick to rail at both God and man' [ICC]. They say bad things about others [LSA] and are abusive to them [HNTC]. They are slanderous [My]. They rail against both God and men [ICC, Lns, NTC], using scornful language to insult them [NTC]. Another view is that this is in reference to their fellow men rather than to God [Brd, TNTC].

disobedient[a] to-parents, unthankful,[b] unholy,[c]
LEXICON—a. ἀπειθής (LN **36.24**) (BAGD 1. p. 82): 'disobedient' [BAGD, Herm, HNTC, LN, Lns; all versions except TNT]. It is also translated as a verb phrase: 'to have no respect for' [TNT].
b. ἀχάριστος (LN 25.101; 33.353) (BAGD p. 128): 'unthankful' [LN, NTC; KJV], 'ungrateful' [BAGD, Herm, HNTC, LN, Lns; NAB, NASB, NIV, NJB, NRSV, TEV], 'devoid of gratitude' [REB], 'with no sense of gratitude to any' [ICC]. It is also translated as a verb phrase: 'to have no gratitude' [TNT]. They are ungrateful for kindness and benefits they receive [Lns].
c. ἀνόσιος (LN 53.47) (BAGD 1. p. 72): 'unholy' [BAGD, LN, NTC; KJV, NASB, NIV, NRSV], 'profane' [NAB], 'irreligious' [NJB, TEV], 'irreverent' [HNTC], 'impious' [LN, Lns], 'devoid of piety' [REB], 'godless' [LN], 'wicked' [BAGD, Herm], 'with no respect for divine things' [ICC]. It is also translated as a verb phrase: '(to have) no reverence' [TNT].

3:3 without-natural-affection,[a] implacable,[b]

LEXICON—a. ἄστοργος (LN **25.42**) (BAGD p. 118): 'devoid of natural affection' [Lns; REB], 'unloving' [BAGD, HNTC; NASB], 'inhuman' [NAB, NRSV], 'heartless' [NJB], 'unfeeling' [NTC], 'intolerant' [Herm], 'without natural affection' [KJV], 'without love' [NIV], 'with no respect for human affections' [ICC]. This word is also translated as a verb phrase: 'to be unkind' [TEV], 'to lack human affection' [LN], 'to have no natural affection' [TNT].

b. ἄσπονδος (LN **40.7**) (BAGD p. 117): 'implacable' [HNTC; NAB, NRSV], 'implacable in their hatreds' [REB], 'implacable when offended' [ICC], 'irreconcilable' [BAGD, LN; NASB], 'intransigent' [Herm], 'intractable' [NJB], 'merciless' [TEV], 'relentless' [TNT], 'unforgiving' [NTC; NIV], 'held by no truce' [Lns], 'trucebreaker' [KJV].

QUESTION—What is the implied object of 'affection'?

1. The object would be family members [EBC, LSA], the love between parents and children [El, My, NTC], without even the natural attachments observed among animals [Lns].
2. It is a broad term, indicating compassion for others [TG], and in the negative is rendered 'unfeeling, unsympathetic, heartless' [NTC], 'unloving' [GNC, HNTC], 'unkind' [GNC].

slanderers,[a] without-self-control,[b] fierce,[c] haters-of-good,[d]

LEXICON—a. διάβολος (LN 33.397) (BAGD 1. p. 182): 'slanderer' [Herm, LN, Lns, NTC; NJB, NRSV, TEV], 'false accuser' [KJV], 'malicious gossip' [NASB], 'scandalmonger' [REB]. This word is also translated as an adjective: 'slanderous' [BAGD, HNTC; NAB, NIV, TNT], or as an attributive phrase: 'ready to speak evil of others' [ICC].

b. ἀκρατής (LN **88.92**) (BAGD p. 33): 'without self-control' [Herm; NASB, NIV], 'lacking in self-control' [LN], 'uncontrolled' [Lns; REB], 'unrestrained' [NTC], 'violent' [TEV], 'incontinent' [KJV], 'licentious' [NAB], 'profligate' [HNTC; NJB, NRSV], 'dissolute' [TNT], 'with no control over their own passions' [ICC]. Though the word indicates lack of self-control in a broad sense, it especially refers to lacking control of bodily desires [Brd, EBC], one's own drives and impulses [NTC], one's passions [My], and it means to be profligate [NCBC, TG], or dissolute [MNTC]. However, it has far more than just sensual reference and includes lack of control of the tongue, the appetite, and all other aspects of our life [EGT], intemperateness [El]. It means to be unrestrained, uninhibited [NTC], not controlling oneself [LSA].

c. ἀνήμερος (LN **20.5**) (BAGD p. 66): 'fierce' [LN; KJV, NRSV, TEV], 'violent' [REB], 'untamed' [Lns, NTC], 'savage' [BAGD, Herm, HNTC; TNT], 'brutal' [BAGD; NAB, NASB, NIV, NJB], 'with no human tenderness' [ICC].

d. ἀφιλάγαθος (LN **25.106**): 'hating the good' [NAB], 'hating what is good' [HNTC], 'not loving the good' [Herm], 'not loving what is good'

[LN], 'unloving toward the good' [NTC], 'hostile to all goodness' [REB], 'with no love for what is good or for those who are good' [ICC]. This word is also translated as a noun phrase: 'haters of good' [NASB, NRSV], 'not lovers of the good' [NIV], 'no lovers of good' [NTC], 'enemies of everything that is good' [NJB], 'despisers of those that are good' [KJV], or as a verb phrase: 'to hate the good' [TEV], 'to hate whatever is good' [TNT], 'to not love what is good' [LN].

3:4 **betrayers,[a] reckless,[b] having-become-conceited,[c] pleasure-loving[d] rather than God-loving,[e]**
LEXICON—a. προδότης (LN 37.113) (BAGD p. 704): 'betrayer' [BAGD, LN], 'traitor' [BAGD, Herm, Lns, NTC; KJV]. This noun is also translated as an adjective: 'treacherous' [HNTC; NAB, NASB, NIV, NJB, NRSV, TEV, TNT], 'perfidious' [REB], or as a verb: 'to be quite ready to betray' [ICC].
   b. προπετής (LN 88.98) (BAGD p. 709): 'reckless' [BAGD, Herm, HNTC, LN, NTC; NAB, NASB, NJB, NRSV, TEV, TNT], 'reckless in speech and action' [ICC], 'rash' [NIV], 'foolhardy' [REB], 'heady' [KJV], 'headstrong' [Lns], 'thoughtless' [BAGD], 'impetuous' [LN].
   c. pres. pass. participle of τυφόω, τυφόομαι (LN 88.218) (BAGD 1. p. 831): 'to be puffed up' [BAGD, Herm, Lns], 'to be demented by pride' [NJB], 'to be swollen with pride' [TEV], 'to be swollen with self-importance' [REB], 'to be swollen with conceit' [HNTC; NRSV], 'to be blinded with conceit' [NTC], 'to be conceited' [BAGD; NASB, NIV, TNT], 'to be conceited and puffed up' [ICC], 'to be pompous' [NAB], 'to be high-minded' [KJV].
   d. φιλήδονος (LN **25.112**) (BAGD p. 859): 'pleasure-loving' [BAGD, HNTC, NTC], 'preferring one's own pleasure' [NJB], 'devoted to pleasure' [Herm], 'given over to pleasure' [BAGD], not explicit [ICC]. This word is also translated as a noun: 'pleasure lover' [Lns], 'lover of pleasure' [LN; KJV, NAB, NASB, NIV, NRSV], or as a verb: 'to love pleasures' [REB, TEV, TNT].
   e. φιλόθεος (LN **25.40**) (BAGD p. 860): 'God-loving' [HNTC, NTC], 'loving God' [BAGD, LN], 'devout' [BAGD, Herm], 'God-lovers' [Lns], 'lovers of God' [KJV, NAB, NASB, NIV, NRSV].

3:5 **having[a] (a) form[b] of-godliness[c] but the power[d] of-it having-denied.[e]**
LEXICON—a. pres. act. participle of ἔχω (LN 57.1): 'to have' [ICC, Lns, NTC; KJV, NIV], 'to hold to' [NASB, NRSV, TEV], 'to observe' [TNT], 'to keep up' [HNTC; NJB], 'to preserve' [REB]. The phrase 'to have a form of' is translated 'to appear to be' [Herm], 'to make a pretense of' [NAB].
   b. μόρφωσις (LN 58.3) (BAGD 2. p. 528): 'form' [NTC; KJV, NASB, NIV, TNT], 'formation' [Lns], 'essential features' [LN], 'outward appearance' [NJB], 'outward form' [BAGD, HNTC; NRSV, REB, TEV], 'all the externals' [ICC].

c. εὐσέβια (LN 53.1; 53.5) (BAGD p. 326): 'godliness' [BAGD, LN, Lns; KJV, NASB, NIV, NRSV], 'piety' [LN, NTC], 'religion' [BAGD, HNTC, ICC, LN; NAB, NJB, REB, TEV, TNT]. This noun is also translated as an adjective: 'religious' [Herm].
   d. δύναμις (LN 76.1) (BAGD 1. p. 207): 'power' [BAGD, Herm, HNTC, LN, Lns, NTC; KJV, NAB, NASB, NIV, NRSV, REB], 'inner power' [NJB], 'real power' [TEV, TNT], 'power over their lives' [ICC].
   e. perf. pass. participle of ἀρνέομαι (LN 34.48) (BAGD 4. p. 108): 'to deny' [BAGD, Herm, HNTC, LN, Lns, NTC; KJV, NASB, NIV, NRSV], 'to negate' [NAB], 'reject' [NJB, TEV], 'to reject in their lives' [TNT], 'to set at defiance (long ago)' [ICC], 'to be a standing denial of' [REB].

QUESTION—In what way do they deny the power of godliness?

They did not say that they denied it, since outwardly they appeared to be religious. They did not have the gospel's living and renewing influence in their lives [Alf, Brd, HNTC]. They did not let God empower them to live as Christians should live [LSA]. Their actions indicated that their religion did not mean anything to them [TG]. They might have thought themselves to be righteous, but they denied the essential power of godliness since they were engaged in the ungodly attitudes and practices of the pagan world [GNC]. They didn't believe that the gospel had a regenerating force [EGT]. Though their religion made them appear respectable, it didn't have an effective power in their lives [TNTC]. This denial may be once for all [NTC], since it is a perfect tense participle 'having denied' [Alf, Lns, NTC]; but also, though completed, has a continuing force [Lns].

and avoid[a] from these.

LEXICON—a. pres. mid. impera. of ἀποτρέπω, ἀποτρέπομαι (LN 34.41) (BAGD p. 101): 'to avoid' [BAGD, Herm, ICC; NASB, NRSV], 'to keep away from' [BAGD, LN; NJB, TEV], 'to turn away from' [Lns, NTC; KJV], 'to stay clear of' [NAB], 'to keep clear of' [HNTC; REB], 'to have nothing to do with' [NIV, TNT].

QUESTION— What relationship is indicated by καί 'and'?

This word is omitted by most translations [Herm, HNTC; all versions except NASB]. It coordinates this imperative clause with the imperative clause 'know this' in 3:1 [Lns, LSA]. It shows that these corruptions of the gospel were not only to arise in the future, but were also a present danger [Brd]. It specifies the particular people to avoid [El].

QUESTION—Does this list of evil-doers include the opponents of 2:25?
   1. They are of a different group, since in 2:25 there is hope they might repent if they are gently dealt with. These in 3:2–5, though having many evil traits common with the opposing heretics, are far more depraved, and teaching them would be wasted effort [El].
   2. They are the same group of evil opponents to whom Timothy is to be kind (2:24) and not keeping aloof [MNTC]. However, his official attitude is to

keep clear of them [Herm, HNTC] and not to receive such people into the church [MNTC, TNTC].

3:6 For^a from^b these are the (ones) creeping^c into the houses^d and taking-captive^e weak-women^f loaded^g with-sins,^h

LEXICON—a. γάρ (LN 89.23): 'for' [HNTC, ICC, NTC; KJV, NASB, NRSV], not explicit [Herm, Lns; NAB, NIV, NJB, REB, TEV, TNT].
- b. ἐκ with genitive object (LN 89.3): 'from'. The phrase ἐκ τούτων 'from those' is translated 'among them' [Herm; NASB, NRSV, TNT], 'some of them' [TEV], 'from a society like this' [ICC], 'out of these circles' [NTC], 'of this sort' [KJV], 'of the same kind, too' [NJB], 'such as these' [NAB], 'to these belong' [Lns], 'they are the sort' [HNTC; REB], 'they are the kind' [NIV].
- c. pres. act. participle of ἐνδύνω (LN **15.94**) (BAGD 1. p. 263): 'to creep into' [BAGD, ICC; KJV], 'to slip into' [LN], 'to sneak into' [Lns], 'to worm one's way into' [BAGD, HNTC; NAB, NIV], 'to insinuate oneself into' [NJB, REB], 'to make one's way into' [Herm; NRSV, TNT], 'to infiltrate' [NTC], 'to enter' [BAGD; NASB], 'to go into' [BAGD; TEV].
- d. οἰκία (LN 7.3; 10.8): 'house' [LN, Lns; KJV, TEV], 'private house' [ICC; REB], 'home' [NTC; NAB, NIV], 'private home' [TNT], 'household' [Herm, HNTC, LN; NASB, NRSV], 'family' [LN; NJB].
- e. pres. act. participle of αἰχμαλωτίζω (LN **37.29**) (BAGD 3. p. 27): 'to take captive' [ICC, NTC], 'to lead captive' [Lns; KJV], 'to make captives of' [NAB], 'to captivate' [NASB, NRSV], 'to ensnare' [Herm], 'to get into their power/clutches' [HNTC; REB], 'to get/gain control over' [LN; NIV, TEV, TNT], 'to get influence over' [NJB], 'to mislead' [BAGD], 'to deceive' [BAGD].
- f. γυναικάριον (LN **9.35**) (BAGD p. 168): 'weak woman' [NASB, TEV], 'weak-willed woman' [NIV], 'weak-minded woman' [NTC], 'frivolous woman' [LN], 'silly woman' [HNTC, ICC, Lns; KJV, NAB, NJB, NRSV, REB, TNT], 'idle woman' [Herm].
- g. perf. pass. participle of σωρεύω, σωρεύομαι (LN **68.76**) (BAGD 2. p. 800): 'to be loaded' [NTC; NIV], 'to be laden' [KJV], 'to be heaped' [Lns], 'to be burdened' [ICC, LN; NAB, REB, TEV], 'to be weighed down' [HNTC; NASB], 'to be overwhelmed' [BAGD, Herm; NRSV, TNT], 'to be obsessed' [NJB], 'to be given over to' [**LN**].
- h. ἁμαρτία (LN 88.310, 88.289) (BAGD 1. p. 43): 'sin' [BAGD, Herm, HNTC, ICC, LN, Lns, NTC; all versions].

QUESTION—What relationship is indicated by γάρ 'for'?

It indicates the grounds for the preceding command [Alf, Brd, LSA, My, NTC]: avoid such people, because they capture weak women. This explains why they must be avoided [Brd].

QUESTION—In what way did they creep into houses?

This is a figurative expression meaning that the false teachers used great subtlety to persuade people to let them enter their homes [LSA] so they could teach their false doctrines and proselytize [Alf]. The verb is rendered 'creep into' [EBC, El, NCBC], 'sneak into' [Alf, GNC, Lns], 'worm their way into' [EBC, GNC, HNTC, MNTC, NTC, TNTC], 'insinuate themselves into' [EBC, Lns], 'infiltrate' [NTC], and 'get a foothold' [MNTC]. This is done by deceitful and underhanded means [EGT, MNTC, NCBC, TNTC] in order to peddle their strange doctrines [NTC] and religious propaganda [HNTC]. It is a strong word of censure against these religious charlatans [GNC].

QUESTION—In what sense did they capture the women?

This is a figurative use of αἰχμαλωτίζω 'taking captive' [Brd, El, GNC], 'take with the spear' [NTC], 'take as war captive' [Lns], 'make a prisoner of war' [My]. Here it indicates the powerful [TNTC], even complete possession of their minds [Alf, LSA, My, TG], thus 'captivating' them [NTC] and depriving them of freedom of thought [TNTC]. They were deceived into believing what they were told [LSA] and followed the false teachers as if dragged about [Alf]. This concept is also rendered 'to gain control over them' [EBC, TG], but with no sense of physical abuse [TG]. These women have been made deluded converts and dupes of the proselytizers [Lns].

QUESTION—In what way were these women weak?

They were weak-willed [EBC], weak-minded [NTC], weak-natured [NTC], without any firm convictions [TG], having fickle minds [TNTC], even being silly [Alf, Brd, EGT, El, GNC, HNTC, Lns, MNTC, TNTC]. This diminutive term carries with it a contemptuous connotation [Alf, Brd, EBC, El, Lns, MNTC, My, NCBC, NTC]. It is a scornful pejorative [GNC, HNTC]. They are spoken of in this contemptuous way because, without good moral principles, they did not have any real serious purpose in life [MNTC], were easily swayed by spurious doctrines [EBC, TNTC], and became easy prey to the false teachers [GNC, HNTC, Lns, NTC, TG].

QUESTION—What is meant by σεσωρευμένα ἁμαρτίαις 'loaded with sins'?

It is the first of three descriptive participles [My, NTC], further characterizing the 'weak women'. It has an intensifying force, indicating that they were very wicked [LSA, NTC], to the extent of being overwhelmed with their sins [EBC, EGT, LSA, TNTC]. This implies one of the reasons these women were so easily taken in by the false teachers. With burdened consciences [Alf, EGT, NCBC, TG] from the guilt of past sins [Alf, GNC, ICC, TG], and possibly still in such sin [Lns], they were quite vulnerable to any false view to ease their consciences [Alf, Brd]. They were readily giving ear as easy prey [Brd, EBC, HNTC], dabbling in any new idea to make them feel better [GNC], and continuing in their conduct unashamed [NTC]. Their heaped-up culmination of guilt at last becomes so unbearable that they clutch at any solution [TNTC].

being-led[a] by-various[b] desires,[c]

LEXICON—a. pres. pass. participle of ἄγω (LN 15.210) (BAGD 3. p. 14): 'to be led' [BAGD, LN, Lns], 'to be led on' [NASB, TNT], 'to be led away'

[KJV], 'to be carried away' [REB], 'to be swayed' [NTC; NIV, NRSV], 'to be pulled about' [HNTC], 'to be driven' [Herm; NAB, TEV], 'to be at the mercy of' [ICC], 'to follow' [NJB].
  b. ποικίλος (LN 58.45) (BAGD 1. p. 683): 'various' [NTC; NASB], 'of various kinds' [LN], 'of many kinds' [NAB], 'all kinds of' [Herm, HNTC; NIV, NRSV, REB, TEV, TNT], 'of every kind' [ICC], 'diversified' [LN], 'divers' [KJV], 'motley' [Lns], 'one (craze) after another' [NJB].
  c. ἐπιθυμία (LN 25.20) (BAGD 3. p. 293): 'desire' [BAGD, Herm, LN; NAB, NRSV, REB, TEV, TNT], 'evil desire' [NIV], 'lust' [HNTC, LN, Lns; KJV], 'impulse' [NTC; NASB], 'craze' [NJB], 'caprice' [ICC].

QUESTION—What kind of desires is meant by ἐπιθυμίαις 'lusts' in this setting/context?

They are evil desires [EBC, LSA, NTC], or uncontrolled actions of the human spirit [Brd]. These desires are not just sensual [ICC], or fleshly [Alf, Brd], or sexual [Lns]; more probably they are avid desires for change of teaching, for something new or novel, for a new thrill [Alf, ICC, MNTC], or selfish desires to appear learned, [ICC, Lns, NTC], or to be in the favor of, and associated with, the popular teachers [Alf, Lns].

3:7 always learning^a and never being-able to-come^b to (a) knowledge^c of-truth.^d

LEXICON—a. pres. act. participle of μανθάνω (LN 27.12) (BAGD 1. p. 490): 'to learn' [BAGD, HNTC, LN, Lns, NTC; KJV, NAB, NASB, NIV], 'to seek learning' [NJB], 'to try to learn' [TEV, TNT], 'to pretend to learn' [ICC], 'to study' [Herm], 'to be instructed' [NRSV], 'to want to be taught' [REB].
  b. aorist act. infin. of ἔρχομαι (**LN 32.17**, 27.4): 'to come' [Herm, ICC, Lns; KJV, NASB, NJB, TEV], 'to reach' [HNTC; NAB], 'to arrive' [NTC; NRSV], 'to attain' [REB], 'to qualify' [TNT]. The phrase 'to come to a knowledge' is translated 'to acknowledge' [NIV], 'to come to understand' [LN].
  c. ἐπίγνωσις (LN **32.17**) (BAGD p. 291): 'knowledge' [BAGD, HNTC, ICC; all versions except NIV, TEV], 'recognition' [Herm], 'realization' [Lns], 'acknowledgment' [NTC]. This noun is also translated as a verb: 'to know' [TEV].
  d. ἀλήθεια (LN 72.2) (BAGD 2.b. p. 36): 'truth' [BAGD, ICC, LN, Lns, NTC], 'the truth' [Herm, HNTC; all versions].

QUESTION—What kind of learning is referred to since it didn't bring normal results?

It was an intense, morbid curiosity [Brd, El, HNTC, MNTC, My] (rather than a search for information [TNTC]), without ever focusing their minds on spiritual truth [EGT] to find the freedom of the gospel [GNC]. This absorbing curiosity was a love of religious novelty, anything new, and the sensational [Alf, EGT, El, HNTC, My, TNTC], fostered by the desire to pose as wise, learned, having inner wisdom, or being well educated [EBC, Lns, My, NCBC, TNTC].

QUESTION—What relationship is indicated by καί 'and'?

This indicates a close connection with the preceding clause [LSA], and the semantic relationship is contraexpectation [El, Herm, ICC, Lns, LSA; NAB, NIV, NJB]: although they are always learning, they are never able to come to a knowledge of the truth. 'Never able' is not an absolute fact, but a characteristic of this class of women [El].

QUESTION—Why were they not able to learn the truth?

Their inability had its roots in their lack of serious purpose [HNTC], being fickle-minded [TNTC], and not willing to acknowledge and put away evil [El]. As a result, the real truth is unappetizing to them [Lns], and they have no piety or right inner life [ICC, My]. This, then, brings the fruit of warped minds [TNTC], deadening of moral apprehension [Alf], and atrophy of their power of comprehension [EGT].

QUESTION—To what does ἀληθείας 'truth' refer?

This refers to 'the truth' [Herm, HNTC; all versions], meaning orthodox belief [NCBC], the truth revealed in the gospel [MNTC, NTC]. Or it is a more general reference to all that is true [LSA]. See the discussion of this phrase at 2:25. This whole phrase also occurs in 1 Tim. 2:4.

3:8 Now in-which-manner[a] Jannes and Jambres opposed[b] Moses, so[c] also these oppose[b] the truth,[d]

LEXICON—a. τρόπος (LN 89.83) (BAGD 1. p. 827): 'manner' [BAGD, LN], 'way' [BAGD, LN]. The phrase ὃν τρόπον 'in which manner' is translated 'in what manner' [Lns], 'as' [KJV, NRSV, REB, TEV], 'just as' [Herm, HNTC, ICC NTC; NAB, NASB, NIV, NJB, TNT].
- b. aorist act. indic. of ἀνθίστημι (LN 39.1) (BAGD 1. p. 67): 'to oppose' [BAGD, Herm, ICC, LN, NTC; NAB, NASB], 'to withstand' [HNTC, Lns; KJV, NIV, NRSV, REB, TNT], 'to be opposed to' [TEV], 'to defy' [NJB], 'to be hostile toward' [LN]. See this word at 2:25.
- c. οὕτως (LN 61.9) (BAGD 1.a. p. 597): 'so' [BAGD, Herm, HNTC, ICC, NTC; all versions], 'thus' [Lns], not explicit [ICC].
- d. ἀλήθεια: 'truth'. See this word at 2:25.

QUESTION—Who were Jannes and Jambres?

The names of these two men are not mentioned in the Old Testament. However, Jewish tradition names them as two of the Egyptian magicians who opposed Moses and Aaron (Exodus 7:11, 22) [all commentators].

QUESTION—What is the point of comparison between the two magicians and the false teachers mentioned in 3:6?

The similarity is not in the manner in which they acted, but in the act itself: they opposed the truth [EGT, My]. The similarity is in the degree of their hostility [EGT], their opposition to the truth [El, TNTC], the profitless character of their opposition [El, MNTC], and their evil motives [MNTC].

Both groups opposed God's servants [Lns, NTC] and hardened the hearts of others [Lns].

men having-been-corrupted[a] (in) the mind,[b] rejected[c] in-regard-to[d] the faith.[e]
LEXICON—a. perf. pass. participle of καταφθείρω (LN **88.266**) (BAGD 2. p. 420): 'to be corrupted' [BAGD, Herm; TNT], 'to be perverted' [HNTC], 'to be depraved' [BAGD,], 'to be corrupt' [Lns, NTC], 'to be completely debased' [ICC], 'to not function' [TEV]. This word is also translated as an adjective modifying 'mind': 'corrupt' [KJV, NJB, NRSV], 'perverted' [NAB], 'depraved' [LN; NASB, NIV], 'warped' [REB]. The perfect tense indicates that the corruption began in the past and extends into the present [Lns].
b. νοῦς (LN 26.14; 30.5) (BAGD 3.a. p. 544): 'mind' [Herm, HNTC, Lns, NTC; all versions], 'intellect' [ICC], 'way of thinking' [BAGD].
c. ἀδόκιμος (LN 65.13) (BAGD p. 18): 'rejected' [NASB, NIV] 'unqualified' [BAGD; TNT], 'reprobate' [NTC; KJV], 'spurious' [NJB], 'counterfeit' [NRSV]. This word is also translated as a verb: 'to falsify (the faith)' [NAB], 'to disqualify' [REB], 'to fail the test' [HNTC], 'to not pass the test' [Herm], 'to not stand the test' [ICC, Lns], 'to be a failure' [TEV].
d. περί with accusative object (LN 89.6): 'in regard to' [Lns], 'as regards' [NASB], 'as to' [ICC], 'with respect to' [NTC], 'concerning' [KJV], 'as far as (the faith) is concerned' [NIV], 'in (the faith)' [TEV, TNT], not explicit [Herm, HNTC; NAB, NJB, NRSV, REB].
e. πίστις (LN 31.102) (BAGD 2.d.α. p. 663): 'the faith' [BAGD, Lns, NTC; KJV, NAB, NASB, NIV, REB, TEV, TNT], 'their faith' [Herm, ICC; NJB], 'whose faith' [HNTC], '(of counterfeit) faith' [NRSV].
QUESTION—What is meant by καταφθείρω 'to corrupt'?
Their minds have become polluted [El], defiled [NTC], and perverted [HNTC], by letting ungodly, false, and foolish ideas enter their minds through the deception of the devil or demons [Lns, LSA, My]. They became devoid of the truth [TNTC]. Hence, not only were their moral desires, i.e., their willing to do right, destructively corrupted, but their thinking as well [El, MNTC, My, TG], is also distorted, being given over to a base mind; cf. Rom. 1:28 [NCBC]. They think only of what is bad [LSA]. It is most commonly rendered by a term indicating the result of being corrupted, that is, depraved [BAGD, Brd, EBC, El, LN, MNTC, TG, TNTC; NASB, NIV], and shows a type of moral ruin and destruction [LN], a complete moral depravity [El]. All the correcting restraints to wrong have been put away [TNTC], leaving them morally blind [TNTC], and lacking moral reasoning ability [Brd].
QUESTION—What is meant by 'rejected in regard to the faith'?
1. Faith is 'the faith', the doctrines that constitute the Christian faith [Alf, Brd, EBC, El, GNC, Lns, LSA, NTC, TNTC; KJV, NASB, NIV, REB,

TEV, TNT]. When tested in regard to the Christian faith, they are rejected as being unsound in doctrine [EBC, Lns]. They have failed the test [Alf], and are unapproved [El], and rejected [GNC, NTC; NIV]. Some drop the figure and say that they were reprobate concerning the faith [Brd, EGT]. They were rejected by God because they did not believe the true message [LSA]. They could not be trusted to teach the truth [EBC].
2. Faith is the content of what they personally believe or their act of believing [ICC, MNTC, NCBC, TG; NJB, NRSV]. The false teachers could not stand the test as to their faith [ICC]. What they believed failed the test [HNTC]. Some drop the figure and say that they had a corrupted faith [NCBC; NRSV], they were failures as Christians [TG], their faith was spurious [NJB]. They were useless for any purpose of faith since, not having faith themselves, they could not produce faith in others [MNTC].

3:9 But (they will) not progress^a to more:^b

LEXICON—a. fut. act. indic. of προκόπτω (LN **42.18**) (BAGD 2. p. 708): 'to progress' [BAGD]. The phrase 'will not progress to more' is translated 'not make much progress' [LN; NRSV], 'not make further progress' [Herm; NASB], 'not proceed farther' [Lns], 'proceed no further' [KJV], 'not get very far' [LN, NTC; NAB, NIV, TEV], 'not be able to get far' [ICC], 'not go much further' [TNT], 'get no further' [HNTC], 'not go on much longer' [NJB], 'not accomplish much' [LN], 'their success will be short-lived' [REB]. Compare this with the positive use of the verb, rendered 'will increase', in 2 Tim. 2:16 and 3:13.
b. πλεῖον (LN 59.1, 78.28): 'more' [BAGD].

QUESTION—What relationship is indicated by ἀλλά 'but'?

It indicates a contrast between the opposition in 3:8 and its ultimate fate [El]. They will progress in opposing the true message, yet in the end truth will prevail [LSA].

QUESTION—What is meant by 'not progressing more'?
1. It refers to the immediate situation in a literal and local sense; the false teachers will not make any further inroads on true Christianity than what they've already made in getting into homes and persuading some people to believe otherwise [Lns].
2. It implies a longer and less local view. Though false teachers may go on in their opposition [LSA], or increase in degradation and ungodliness [EGT, NTC, TNTC] and deceive people [GNC], as indicated in 2:16–17 and 3:13 [EGT, GNC, My, NCBC, NTC], their apparent success is really very limited [EGT, TNTC] and won't continue long [HNTC, LSA, TG; REB]; their heresy may advance at times, but will not advance without detection and exposure [El]. The phrase 'will not progress much further' also implies that the extension of false teaching would not make any real or ultimate advance [El], but would later come to an end [My] and have its ultimate defeat [Alf]. The progress of its proponents only led to their

destruction [NCBC], as imposters are always exposed ultimately [TNTC]. Truth will prevail and win out [GNC, LSA].

for[a] their folly[b] will-be plain[c] to-all,
LEXICON—a. γάρ (LN **89.23**): 'for' [Herm,, HNTC, ICC, Lns NTC; KJV, NASB, TNT], 'because' [NIV, NRSV, TEV], not explicit [NAB, NJB, REB].
    b. ἄνοια (LN **32.51**) (BAGD p. 70): 'folly' [BAGD, Herm, Lns, NTC; KJV, NASB, NIV, NJB, NRSV], 'utter folly' [ICC], 'lack of understanding' [LN], 'stupidity' [NAB], 'senselessness' [HNTC]. It is also translated by a phrase: 'for the fools they are' [REB], 'how stupid they are' [TEV], 'how foolish they are' [TNT].
    c. ἔκδηλος (LN **28.59**) (BAGD p. 238): 'plain' [BAGD, Herm; NRSV], 'clear' [NIV], 'quite clear' [ICC], 'quite evident' [BAGD], 'manifest' [KJV], 'fully manifest' [Lns], 'obvious' [NTC; NASB, NJB], 'very obvious' [LN], 'plain/exposed (for all) to see' [HNTC; NAB], 'recognized' [REB]. The phrase 'will be plain to all' is translated 'everyone will see' [TEV, TNT].
QUESTION—What is meant by ἡ ἄνοια αὐτῶν 'their folly'?
Folly refers both to the condition of a person and to his resulting actions. The condition is most commonly indicated as a lack of understanding, judgment, or good sense [Lns, My, NTC]. This is reflected in various other terms used: mindless, senseless, senselessness, [El, GNC, HNTC, My, NTC], insensate, unintelligent [Alf, El], stupid, foolish [GNC, LSA, TG], hollowness [Brd, HNTC], and aberration [MNTC]. People in this condition are led to pretensions [Brd] and imposture [TNTC], and do things which may be classed as madness [EBC, MNTC].

as[a] also the-(folly) of-those came-to-be-(plain).
LEXICON—a. ὡς (LN **64.12**): 'as' [HNTC, NTC; KJV, NASB], 'as with/in the case of (those men)' [NAB, NIV, NRSV], 'like' [NJB, REB], '(that is) just (what happened)' [TEV], 'just as (it was)' [Herm], 'exactly as' [ICC], 'even as' [Lns], not explicit [TNT].

DISCOURSE UNIT: 3:10–4:8 [Herm, NCBC, TG; NIV, TEV] The topic is a summary exhortation [Herm], last instructions [TEV], Paul's charge to Timothy [NIV].

DISCOURSE UNIT: 3:10–17 [EBC, GNC, Lns, LSA, NTC, TNTC; NAB]. The topic is further exhortation [TNTC], exhortation to believe what had been learned [LSA], an appeal to loyalty and endurance [GNC], Timothy's faithful stand with Paul in the past [Lns], the persecution of all Christians [EBC].

DISCOURSE UNIT: 3:10–14 [Brd]. The topic is commendation of Timothy's loyalty and encouragement to endure.

3:10 But[a] you have-followed[b] my teaching,[c] the conduct,[d] the purpose[e]
LEXICON—a. δέ (LN 89.87; 89.124): 'but' [Herm, ICC; KJV, NASB, REB, TEV], 'however' [HNTC, Lns, NTC; NIV], 'though' [NJB], 'not so (with you)' [TNT], 'now' [NRSV], not explicit [NAB].
  b. aorist act. indic. of παρακολουθέω (LN 36.32; 27.38) (BAGD 2. p. 619): 'to follow' [LN, Lns, NTC; NASB, NJB], 'to closely follow' [HNTC; NAB], 'to faithfully follow' [Herm], 'to follow with the mind' [BAGD], 'to know all about something' [NIV], 'to observe' [NRSV, REB], 'to fully know' [KJV], 'to conform to' [LN], 'to make one's own' [BAGD]. This verb is translated differently to collocate with the various nouns following it: 'to follow…to know all about…to know how' [TNT], 'to follow…to observe' [TEV], 'to heartily become a follower…to listen to…to imitate' [ICC]. The multiplicity of renderings derives not only from the word's being rich in connotations and implications [LSA, MNTC, NTC], but also from the fact that, in the context, Paul uses the word once to relate to nine words in the dative case plus two modifying clauses; a particular sense of the word is not applicable to all of the topics named, or even to their basic groupings: teachings, virtues, and events of life [ICC, NTC].
  c. διδασκαλία (LN 33.224; 33.236) (BAGD 2. p. 191): 'teaching' [BAGD, Herm, HNTC, ICC, LN, Lns, NTC; all versions except KJV], 'doctrine' [KJV]. It means his doctrine [TNTC], what he taught about the Christian faith [LSA, TG].
  d. ἀγωγή (LN **41.3**) (BAGD p. 15): 'conduct' [BAGD, Herm, LN, Lns, NTC; NAB, NASB, NRSV, TEV], 'way of life' [BAGD; NIV, NJB, TNT], 'manner of life' [HNTC, ICC; KJV, REB]. It refers to the external expression of his guiding principles [EGT, Herm].
  e. πρόθεσις (LN 30.63) (BAGD 2.a. p. 706): 'purpose' [BAGD, HNTC, LN, Lns, NTC; KJV, NASB, NIV, TNT], 'purpose in life' [TEV], 'resolution' [NAB, REB], 'resolve' [BAGD, Herm], 'way of thinking' [BAGD], 'aims' [ICC; NJB], 'aim in life' [NRSV].
QUESTION—What relationship is indicated by δέ 'but'?
This indicates a contrast with the false teachers and their heresy in the preceding verses [Alf, Brd, GNC, Herm, HNTC, ICC, Lns, LSA, MNTC, My, NTC, TG, TNTC; KJV, NASB, REB, TEV, TNT]. The 'you' is emphatic, contrasting Timothy with the false teachers [LSA, TG, TNTC].
QUESTION—In what way did he follow closely?
  1. He followed in mind and understanding [ICC], having carefully noted, watched, observed, investigated, or studied [MNTC, TNTC], thus being acquainted with [NCBC], and staying informed [TG], so as to know all about [EBC, LSA] Paul's teachings, virtues, and incidents in his life [ICC].
  2. He followed Paul's virtues and life as a pattern, model, or example to imitate or copy [Alf, HNTC, ICC, NTC]. But they were more than a pattern; they were guidelines for his practical Christian conduct throughout life [My, NTC].

3. He followed as a disciple [EGT, El, GNC, Lns]. It means to have a close relationship to his master [GNC, HNTC, Lns], accompanying him as a companion [ICC, MNTC] so as to learn all that was taught [El]. It is not implied that he copied Paul in all these respects [EGT].

QUESTION—What is meant by πρόθεσις 'purpose'?

It refers to 'what he was trying to do' [LSA], to his own chief aim in life [EGT, NTC, TNTC], his main purpose or concern in life [TG], his firm resolution [GNC, TNTC], his supreme spiritual objective of life [El]. It is his guiding purpose and motive on which his mode of life and work was based [HNTC, My]. To be specific, that aim or purpose could be to have a single-minded commitment to Christ [GNC], or to engender faith in others [Lns].

the faith/faithfulness,[a] the patience,[b] the love,[c] the endurance,[d]

LEXICON—a. πίστις (LN 31.85; 31.88) (BAGD 2.d.γ. p. 663): 'faith' [BAGD, Herm, HNTC, ICC, LN, Lns, NTC; all versions except NAB, REB], 'fidelity' [NAB], 'faithfulness' [REB].

b. μακροθυμία (LN 25.167) (BAGD 1. p. 488): 'patience' [BAGD, Herm, HNTC, LN; all versions except KJV, TNT], 'longsuffering' [Lns, NTC; KJV], 'forbearance' [ICC; TNT], 'steadfastness' [LN], 'endurance' [BAGD]. It is patience in respect to trouble and afflictions of every kind [Brd]. It is patience with respect to people [NTC].

c. ἀγάπη (LN 25.43) (BAGD I.1.a. p. 5): 'love' [BAGD, Herm, HNTC, ICC, LN, Lns, NTC; all versions except KJV, REB], 'charity' [KJV], 'spirit of love' [REB].

d. ὑπομονή (LN 25.174) (BAGD 1. p. 846): 'endurance' [BAGD, LN; NAB, NIV, TEV], 'perseverance' [BAGD; NASB, NJB], 'steadfastness' [BAGD; NRSV], 'fortitude' [BAGD; REB], 'patience' [BAGD; KJV]. This noun is also translated as a verb: 'to bear (persecution)' [TNT]. It is endurance with respect to adverse circumstances [NTC, TNTC].

QUESTION—What is meant by πίστις 'faith, faithfulness'?
1. It refers to his belief and trust in God [El, GNC, HNTC, Lns, LSA, My, NCBC, NTC, TNTC; all versions except NAB, REB]: how I believe.
2. It refers to the content of his beliefs [El, TG]: what I believe.
3. It refers to the quality of faithfulness [EBC; NAB, REB]: how I am faithful to the Christian faith.

3:11 the persecutions,[a] the sufferings,[b] which happened[c] to-me in Antioch, in Iconium, in Lystra,

LEXICON—a. διωγμός (LN 39.45) (BAGD p. 201): 'persecution' [BAGD, Herm, HNTC, ICC, LN, Lns, NTC; all versions].

b. πάθημα (LN 24.78) (BAGD 1. p. 602): 'suffering' [BAGD, Herm, HNTC, ICC, LN, Lns, NTC; all versions except KJV], 'affliction' [KJV].

c. aorist mid. indic. of γίνομαι (LN 13.107): 'to happen to' [BAGD, LN, NTC; NASB, NIV, NRSV, TEV], 'to befall' [BAGD, HNTC, ICC], 'to occur to' [LN, Lns], 'to come to' [KJV, NJB], 'to encounter' [Herm], 'to go through' [REB], 'as I did (bear)' [TNT], not explicit [NAB].

QUESTION—How is this verse related to the preceding one?
1. It continues the list of things Timothy has followed [Alf, Herm, HNTC, ICC, Lns, NTC; KJV, NASB, NIV, NJB, NRSV, TEV, TNT]. After listing expressions of active obedience, Paul now lists expressions of passive obedience [NTC].
2. It gives the circumstances in which all the nouns in the list in 3:10 were exercised [MNTC; NAB]: you followed my...patience, love, and endurance through persecution and sufferings. Paul's character was tested by these [MNTC].
3. It gives the circumstances in which the last noun in 3:10 was exercised [Brd, GNC, LSA, My; REB, TNT]: you followed my...patience, love, and my endurance under persecution and suffering.

QUESTION—What does οἷα 'which' refer to?
1. It refers to the preceding word 'sufferings' [Alf, El, ICC, LSA, My; NRSV]: my persecutions, and the sufferings which happened to me.
2. It refers to both 'persecutions' and 'sufferings' [HNTC, Lns, MNTC, NTC; NAB, NIV, NJB, REB, TEV]: my persecutions, my sufferings—what kinds of things happened to me.

what persecutions I-endured,[a]

LEXICON—a. aorist act. indic. of ὑποφέρω (LN **25.175**) (BAGD p. 848): 'to endure' [BAGD, Herm, **LN**; all versions except NAB, TNT], 'to bear' [TNT], 'to have to bear' [NAB], 'to bear up against/under' [BAGD, ICC, LN, Lns], 'to put up with' [HNTC, LN], 'to undergo' [NTC].

QUESTION—How is this clause connected to its context?
1. It amplifies the preceding clause by dwelling on the especially dangerous suffering he endured [HNTC, ICC, Lns]. It specifies more closely what he suffered in those places [Lns].
2. It is an exclamation inserted in the account [TG; NASB, NRSV, TNT]: what persecutions I endured! He adds this upon thinking about the persecutions in the cities just mentioned [TG].
3. It is the object of an implied verb: you saw what persecution I endured [Alf], you know what persecutions I endured [NAB].
4. It is a concessive clause joined with the following clause [LSA]: although I suffered such persecutions, yet the Lord saved me out of them all.

and/yet[a] **out-of**[b] **all (of them) the Lord rescued**[c] **me.**

LEXICON—a. καί (LN 89.92; 91.12): 'and' [Herm, Lns; NAB, NASB, NJB, REB], 'yes' [ICC], 'but' [KJV, TEV], 'yet' [HNTC, NTC; NIV, NRSV, TNT].
  b. ἐκ with genitive object (LN 84.4): 'out of' [ICC, Lns; KJV, NASB], 'from' [BAGD, Herm, HNTC, NTC; all versions except KJV, NASB]. The Lord did not rescue him from experiencing the persecutions, but from the death that was likely to follow [GNC].
  c. aorist mid. indic. of ῥύομαι (LN 21.23) (BAGD p. 737): 'to rescue' [BAGD, Herm, HNTC, LN, Lns, NTC; NIV, NJB, NRSV, REB, TEV],

'to deliver' [BAGD, ICC, LN; KJV, NASB, TNT], 'to save' [NAB], 'to preserve' [BAGD].

QUESTION—What relationship is indicated by καί 'and, yet'?
1. It indicates sequence [Herm, ICC, Lns, NTC; NAB, NASB, NJB, REB]: and. As was to be expected, the Lord rescued him [Lns].
2. It indicates contrast [Brd, EGT, El, HNTC, NTC; NIV, TEV]: yet. It expresses Paul's gratitude as he looks back. He also means this to be an encouragement to Timothy, who can rely on similar help [HNTC]. Despite the great danger, the Lord delivered him [Brd].

QUESTION—To whom does 'Lord' refer?
It refers to Christ [Brd, TG].

3:12 And^a indeed^b all the (ones) wanting^c to-live^d godly^e in^f Christ Jesus will-be-persecuted.^{g}

LEXICON—a. δέ (LN 89.87; 89.124): 'and' [ICC; KJV, NASB], 'but' [Herm; NJB], 'moreover' [Lns], not explicit [HNTC, NTC; NAB, NIV, NRSV, REB, TEV, TNT].
- b. καί (LN 91.12; 89.93): 'indeed' [HNTC; NASB, NRSV, REB], 'in fact' [NTC; NIV], 'yea' [KJV], 'aye' [ICC], 'also' [Lns], not explicit [NAB, NJB, TEV, TNT].
- c. pres. act. participle of θέλω (LN 25.1; 30.58): 'to want to' [Herm, LN; NAB, NIV, NRSV, REB, TEV, TNT], 'to will' [LN; KJV], 'to be minded' [ICC], 'to intend' [Lns], 'to desire' [LN, NTC; NASB], 'to wish' [HNTC], 'to try to' [NJB].
- d. pres. act. inf. of ζάω (LN **41.2**) (BAGD 3.a. p. 336): 'to live' [BAGD, Lns, NTC; KJV, NASB, NJB], 'to live a life' [ICC, LN; NAB, NIV, NRSV, REB, TEV, TNT], 'to lead a life' [Herm, HNTC].
- e. εὐσεβῶς (LN 53.6) (BAGD p. 326): 'godly' [Lns; KJV, NASB], 'in a godly manner' [BAGD], 'devoutly' [NTC], 'in a devout manner' [LN], 'in devotion (to Christ)' [NJB], cf. parallel usage Titus 2:12. This adverb is also rendered as an adjective modifying 'life': 'godly' [HNTC; NAB, NIV, NRSV, REB, TEV, TNT], 'pious' [Herm], 'religious' [ICC].
- f. ἐν with dative object (LN 89.119): 'in' [Herm, HNTC, Lns, NTC; KJV, NAB, NASB, NIV, NRSV], 'in union with' [ICC, LN; TEV], 'to' [NJB], It is also translated as an adverbial phrase: 'as a follower of (Christ)' [REB], 'as (a Christian)' [TNT].
- g. fut. pass. indic. of διώκω (LN 39.45) (BAGD 2. p. 201): 'to be persecuted' [BAGD, HNTC, ICC, Lns, NTC; NAB, NASB, NIV, NJB, NRSV, TEV, TNT], 'to suffer persecution' [Herm; KJV]. It is also translated 'persecutions will come' [REB].

QUESTION—What relationship is indicated by δέ 'and, but'?
1. This adds a comment to the previous verse [Brd, El, GNC, HNTC, Lns, LSA, My, NTC; NASB, NIV, NRSV, REB]: and. It is a reminder that persecution is not confined to Paul alone [GNT, HNTC], and this general

statement is given to prepare Timothy for the persecution that will come to him [El, My].
2. It indicates a contrast [Alf, Herm; NJB]: but. Not only has Paul been persecuted, but all who want to live godly lives will be persecuted [Alf].

QUESTION—What is meant by the phrase ἐν Χριστοῦ Ἰησοῦ 'in Christ Jesus'?

It gives the circumstance of living a godly life and means to be in union with Christ [ICC, LN, TG; TEV], in fellowship with him [El, NTC], in a spiritual relationship with him [Brd, HNTC, MNTC]. It means that the pious life is Christian in its nature and that it is only possible in communion with Christ [My]. It also gives the reason they want to live a godly life [LSA].

3:13 But/And[a] evil[b] men and imposters[c] will-progress[d] to the worse,[e]

LEXICON—a. δέ (LN 89.87; 89.124): 'but' [HNTC; KJV, NASB, NRSV, TNT], 'but all the while' [NAB], 'while' [NIV, NJB], 'whereas' [REB], 'however' [Herm, Lns], 'moreover' [NTC], 'and' [ICC; TEV].

b. πονηρός (LN 88.110) (BAGD 1.b.α. p. 690): 'evil' [BAGD, LN, NTC; KJV, NAB, NASB, NIV, TEV, TNT], 'wicked' [BAGD, HNTC, LN, Lns; NRSV], 'bad' [BAGD, Herm], 'malicious' [ICC]. The phrase 'evil men' is translated 'evil-doers' [REB]. The phrase 'evil men and imposters' is translated 'wicked impostors' [NJB].

c. γόης (LN **88.232**): 'impostor' [HNTC, ICC, LN, Lns, NTC; NASB, NIV, NJB, NRSV, TEV, TNT], 'seducer' [KJV], 'charlatan' [NAB, REB], 'sorcerer' [Herm], 'swindler, cheat' [BAGD].

d. fut. act. indic. of προκόπτω (LN 59.64) (BAGD 2. p. 708): 'to progress' [BAGD, Herm, Lns; REB], 'to proceed' [NTC; NASB], 'to advance' [BAGD, HNTC, LN], 'to increase' [LN], 'to go' [NAB, NIV, NJB, NRSV, TEV, TNT], 'to get' [ICC], 'to wax' [KJV]. See this word at 3:9.

e. χείρων (LN **88.107**) (BAGD p. 881): 'worse' [BAGD, LN, Lns]. The phrase ἐπὶ τὸ χεῖρον 'to the worse' is translated 'from bad to worse' [Herm, HNTC, LN, NTC; all versions except KJV], 'worse and worse' [ICC; KJV].

QUESTION—What relationship is indicated by δέ 'but, and'?
1. It indicates a contrast with those who want to live godly lives (3:12) [Brd, EGT, El, GNC, Herm, HNTC, ICC, Lns, My, TNTC; KJV, NAB, NASB, NRSV, TEV, TNT]. People who want to be godly will be opposed, but evil men will be unrestrained as they become worse and worse [EGT]. This continues the description of the heretics which was interrupted at 3:10 [My]. At the same time, it contrasts Timothy with the false teachers [El].
2. It introduces a circumstance to the preceding verse [NIV, NJB, REB]: they will be persecuted while evil men and imposters become worse and worse.

3. It introduces a reason why persecution continues [Alf, MNTC, NTC]: they will be persecuted because evil men and imposters will become worse and worse.

QUESTION—How are 'evil men' related to the 'impostors'?
1. They are the same group [NTC, TG; NJB]: evil imposters will progress to the worse.
2. The evil men are a general classification of the whole group, while the imposters are a part of the group singled out for special mention [Alf, El, MNTC, My].
3. They are two classes of people [GNC, Lns, LSA]. The 'evil men' are those referred to in 3:2–5 and the imposters are those referred to 3:6–9 [GNC, Lns, LSA].

QUESTION—What is meant by ἐπὶ τὸ χεῖρον 'to the worse'?
This is an increase of degradation, not of influence [EGT, ICC]. Although 3:9 states that they will not progress farther before they are exposed, here it refers to progressing inwardly, degenerating more and more [Lns]. Their spiritual progress is downward [TG]. This refers to them morally and spiritually [NTC] and refers to their degree of wickedness [El]. They will go deeper in sin [GNC].

deceiving[a] and being-deceived.
LEXICON—a. pres. act. participle of πλανάω (LN **31.8**) (BAGD 2.c.δ. p. 665): 'to deceive' [BAGD, LN, Lns, NTC; all versions], 'to mislead' [BAGD]. The participle is also nominal zed: 'deceivers and deceived' [HNTC], 'deceived deceivers' [Herm].

QUESTION—How are the two participles related to the main verb: 'to get worse and worse'?
They indicate means and show how this growing wickedness comes about through the corrupting of their minds, which increasingly are unable to discern truth [MNTC, My, NTC]. The resultant state of their advancing in evil is to end up being deceived [El, Lns, My, NTC, TG].

QUESTION—Are the 'deceiving ones' the same people as the 'ones being deceived'?
1. They are the same people.
   1.1 They were first deceived and then they deceived others [Brd, EBC, EGT, El, Herm]. False teachers deceived those who now deceive others [Brd, EBC].
   1.2 They deceived others and then they themselves were deceived. Others deceived them [El, ICC, My] or became self-deceived [EGT, MNTC, NCBC, NTC]. They become deluded by their own pretense [MNTC].
2. They are two groups: the imposters deceiving, and the wicked men being deceived [Lns, LSA].

2 TIMOTHY 3:14

3:14 But[a] you continue[b] in what-things[c] you-learned[d] and were-assured-of,[e]

LEXICON—a. δέ (LN 89.124): 'but' [Herm, HNTC, ICC; KJV, NIV, NRSV, REB, TEV, TNT], 'for your part' [NAB], 'however' [Lns, NTC; NASB], not explicit [NJB].

b. pres. act. impera. of μένω (LN 68.11) (BAGD 1.a.β. p. 504): 'to continue' [BAGD, LN, NTC; KJV, NASB, NIV, NRSV, TEV], 'to remain' [BAGD, LN, Lns], 'to remain faithful to' [NAB], 'to keep to' [NJB], 'to keep on' [LN], 'to stand by' [Herm, HNTC; REB], 'to stand firm' [ICC], 'to be loyal to' [TNT]

c. ὅς (LN 92.27): 'what' [BAGD; NAB, NIV, NJB, NRSV], 'the things' [HNTC, Lns; NASB], 'the/these things which' [Herm, NTC; KJV], 'the truths' [REB, TNT], 'the truths that' [TEV], 'those truths that' [ICC].

d. aorist act. indic. of μανθάνω (LN 27.12) (BAGD 1. p. 490): 'to learn' [BAGD, Herm, HNTC, LN, Lns, NTC; KJV, NAB, NASB, NIV, NRSV, REB], 'to first learn' [ICC], 'to be taught' [LN; NJB, TEV, TNT], 'to be instructed' [LN].

e. aorist pass. indic. of πιστόω, πιστόομαι (LN **31.36**): 'to be assured of' [Lns; KJV, REB], 'to be convinced of' [BAGD, Herm, HNTC, NTC; NASB, NIV], 'to firmly come to believe' [LN], 'to firmly believe' [NRSV, TEV], 'to believe' [NAB], 'to know to be true' [NJB], 'to fully accept' [TNT].

QUESTION—What is meant by 'continuing in these things'?

Timothy was to remain loyal to the truth [ICC], to stay by the apostolic gospel [GNC]. He must not move away from Paul's message to accept the false teaching [MNTC]. He must continue believing what he had been taught [LSA].

knowing[a] from[b] whom you-learned,[c]

LEXICON—a. perf. act. participle of οἶδα (LN 28.1; 29.6) (BAGD 1.f. p. 556): 'to know' [BAGD, ICC, LN, Lns, NTC; KJV, NAB, NASB, NIV, NRSV, TEV, TNT], 'to realize' [HNTC], 'to remember' [LN; NJB, REB], 'to consider' [Herm].

b. παρά with genitive object (LN 90.14): 'from' [Herm, HNTC, Lns, NTC; NASB, NIV, NRSV, REB], 'of' [KJV], not explicit [ICC; NAB, NJB, TEV, TNT].

c. aorist act. indic. of μανθάνω (LN 27.12) (BAGD 1. p. 490): 'to learn' [Herm, HNTC, Lns, NTC; KJV, NASB, NIV, NRSV, REB]. This word is also rendered as '(who) your teachers were' [ICC; NAB, NJB, TEV, TNT].

QUESTION—What relationship is indicated by the use of the participial form εἰδώς 'knowing'?

It indicates a reason for continuing in what he had learned [HNTC, Lns, LSA, MNTC, My, NTC, TG, TNTC; NAB, NIV, TNT]: continue in what you learned because you know who taught you this. He can trust them

[GNC] because he knew their trustworthy characters [LSA, MNTC, NTC], their integrity [TNTC], their reliability [HNTC].

QUESTION—To whom does τίνων 'whom' (plural) refer?

It refers to Paul [Brd, EGT, GNC, Herm, HNTC, ICC, LSA, MNTC, My, NCBC, NTC, TG, TNTC], to his mother Lois and grandmother Eunice [Alf, Brd, EBC, EGT, GNC, Herm, HNTC, ICC, LSA, MNTC, NTC, TG, TNTC], to other teachers [Herm, NCBC, NTC, TNTC], to other witnesses (2:2) [HNTC, ICC, LSA, TG], to the prophets [EGT], to other devoted Christians [MNTC].

3:15 and that from[a] childhood[b] you knew[c] the sacred[d] writings,[e]

LEXICON—a. ἀπό with genitive object (LN 67.131): 'from' [HNTC, ICC, Lns, NTC; all versions except NJB, TEV], 'ever since' [Herm; NJB, TEV].
- b. βρέφος (LN **67.152**) (BAGD 2. p. 147): 'childhood' [BAGD, LN; NASB, NRSV], 'early childhood' [REB], 'a child' [Herm, HNTC; KJV], 'a babe' [Lns], 'infancy' [NTC; NAB, NIV], 'one's earliest days' [TNT], 'one's cradle' [ICC]. The phrase 'from childhood' is translated 'since you were a child' [NJB, TEV].
- c. perf. indic. act. of οἶδα (LN 28.1; 32.4): 'to know' [Herm, LN, Lns, NTC; all versions except REB, TNT], 'to be familiar with' [HNTC; REB, TNT], 'to be taught' [ICC].
- d. ἱερός (LN **53.9**) (BAGD 1. p. 372): 'holy' [BAGD, Herm, LN; KJV, NIV, NJB, TEV, TNT], 'sacred' [HNTC, Lns, NTC; NAB, NASB, NRSV, REB], 'religious' [ICC].
- e. γράμμα (LN 33.50) (BAGD 2.c. p. 165): 'writings' [BAGD, Herm, HNTC, NTC; NASB, NRSV, REB], 'scriptures' [KJV, NAB, NIV, NJB, TEV, TNT], 'teaching from scriptures' [ICC], 'letters' [Lns].

QUESTION—What relationship is indicated by καί 'and'?
1. It indicates coordination with the object of εἰδώς 'knowing' in the preceding clause [Alf, Brd, EGT, El, Herm, ICC, My]: continue in these things, because you know from whom you learned them and you know that you learned the sacred writings from childhood.
2. It indicates coordination with the preceding clause, both giving reasons for the main clause [GNC, HNTC, MNTC, NTC]: continue in these things, because you know from whom you learned them, and because you have known the sacred writings from childhood.
3. It explains the preceding clause [Lns]: you know from whom you learned these things, namely, that from childhood you have known the sacred writings. His authority for being certain was not that he loved the people who taught him, but that they taught him the sacred writings [Lns].

QUESTION—About what age does the term 'from childhood' indicate?
1. It indicates a very early age [Alf, Brd, EBC, El, MNTC, NTC], from infancy [EBC, El, Lns, NTC]. This is a hyperbolic expression indicating that his Scripture knowledge was coterminous with all of his conscious existence [EGT]. He refers to Timothy's life from the days he was an

infant to the present moment and means that Timothy had known the Scriptures the entire period, learning more and more as time went on [TNTC].
2. It refers to the time of training as a 'child' [GNC, Herm, ICC, LSA, My, NCBC, TG], and specifically from the age of five years [GNC, HNTC, ICC, TG].

the (ones) being-able[a] to-make you wise[b] to[c] salvation[d] through[e] faith[f] the (one) in Christ Jesus.

LEXICON—a. pres. pass. participle of δύναμαι (LN 74.5): 'to be able' [LN, Lns, NTC; KJV, NASB, NIV, NRSV, TEV], 'to have power to' [REB], 'to have it in them' [ICC]. The phrase 'being able to make wise' is translated 'the source of wisdom' [NAB], 'from these you can learn wisdom' [NJB], 'these can give you wisdom' [TNT].
b. aorist act. infin. of σοφίζω (LN **32.36**) (BAGD 1.a. p. 760): 'to make wise' [BAGD, LN, Lns, NTC; KJV, NIV, REB], 'to give wisdom' [HNTC; NASB, TEV, TNT], 'to give true wisdom' [ICC], 'to learn the wisdom' [NJB], 'to have wisdom' [Herm, LN], 'to instruct' [BAGD; NRSV], 'to teach' [BAGD].
c. εἰς with accusative object (LN 89.48): 'unto' [LN (32.36); KJV], 'for' [Herm, Lns, NTC; NIV, NRSV], 'to lead to' [HNTC, ICC, LN (32.36); NAB, NASB, NJB, REB, TEV, TNT].
d. σωτηρία (LN 21.25; 21.26) (BAGD 2. p. 801): 'salvation' [BAGD, Herm, HNTC, ICC, LN, Lns, NTC; all versions].
e. διά with genitive object (LN 89.76): 'through' [Herm, HNTC, Lns, NTC; all versions except TNT]. This preposition with its object 'faith' is also translated by a conditional clause: 'if you believe' [TNT], 'if you have true faith' [ICC].
f. πίστις (LN 31.102) (BAGD 2.b.α. p. 663): 'faith' [BAGD, Herm, HNTC, ICC, LN, Lns, NTC; all versions except TNT]. This noun is also rendered as a verb 'to believe' [TNT].

QUESTION—What relationship is indicated by εἰς 'to'?
It indicates the expected result of knowing Scripture [LSA]. It expresses the kind of wisdom the Scriptures supply [Brd].

QUESTION—What relationship is indicated by διά 'through'?
It indicates the means by which people are saved [Alf, Brd, HNTC, LSA].

3:16 All/Every[a] scripture[b] God-breathed[c] and/also useful[d]

LEXICON—a. πᾶς, πᾶσα (LN 59.23): 'all' [ICC, LN, Lns, NTC; all versions except TNT], 'every' [BAGD, Herm, HNTC; TNT].
b. γραφή (LN 33.53) (BAGD 2.a. p. 166): 'Scripture' [Herm, HNTC, ICC, LN, Lns, NTC; all versions], 'the individual Scripture passage' [BAGD].
c. θεόπνευστος (LN **33.261**) (BAGD p. 356): 'God-breathed' [NTC; NIV], 'inspired of God' [Lns; NAB], 'inspired by God' [BAGD, Herm, HNTC, ICC, LN; NASB, NJB, NRSV, TEV], 'divinely inspired' [LN], 'inspired' [REB, TNT], 'given by inspiration of God' [KJV].

d. ὠφέλιμος (LN 65.40) (BAGD p. 900): 'profitable' [HNTC, Lns; KJV, NASB], 'useful' [BAGD, ICC, NTC; NAB, NIV, NJB, NRSV, TEV, TNT], 'salutary' [Herm], 'beneficial' [BAGD, LN], 'advantageous' [BAGD]. It is also translated as a verb phrase: 'has its use' [REB].

QUESTION—What is the relation of the adjective θεόπνευστος 'God-breathed' to the noun γραφή 'Scripture'?

1. It is predicative. The verb 'is' is implied and the word καί means 'and'. The word πᾶσα may mean 'all' or 'every'.
  1.1 All Scripture is God-breathed and useful [EBC, GNC, ICC, NTC, TNTC; KJV, NAB, NASB, NIV, NJB, NRSV, TEV]. This is a reminder that the usefulness lies in its inspired character [TNTC]. Since it is inspired, it is therefore useful [ICC, NTC].
  1.2 Every Scripture is God-breathed and useful [HNTC, NCBC]. Having spoken generally of the sacred writings, Paul now emphasizes their usefulness in all the individual passages that make up the whole [HNTC]. Every passage, and not only some as the heretics argued, is inspired and therefore may be used for teaching [NCBC].
2. It is attributive. The verb 'is' is implied and the word καί means 'also'. The word πᾶσα may mean 'all' or 'every'.
  2.1 Every God-breathed Scripture is also useful [Alf, Brd, EGT, El, Herm, MNTC; TNT]. It is 'also' useful, besides its quality of inspiration [Alf]. This is a repetition and expansion of the preceding clause in 3:15 [EGT].
  2.2 All God-breathed Scripture is also useful [Lns, My; REB]. This confirms the preceding clause by stating that it is useful [My]. The meaning is the same as saying every Scripture is inspired by God and therefore useful [Lns].

for[a] teaching,[b] for reproof,[c] for correction,[d] for instruction[e] in righteousness,[f]

LEXICON—a. πρός with accusative object (LN 89.60): 'for' [Herm, HNTC, ICC, Lns, NTC; all versions].
  b. διδασκαλία (LN 33.224) (BAGD 1. p. 191): 'teaching' [BAGD, Herm, ICC, LN, Lns, NTC; NAB, NASB, NIV, NRSV, REB, TEV, TNT], 'instruction' [BAGD, HNTC], 'doctrine' [KJV], not explicit [NJB].
  c. ἐλεγμός (LN **33.417**) (BAGD p. 249): 'reproof' [BAGD, Herm, HNTC, NTC; KJV, NAB, NASB, NRSV, TNT], 'refutation' [Lns]. This word is also translated as a participle: 'rebuking' [LN; NIV, TEV], 'refuting' [ICC; REB], 'refuting error' [NJB].
  d. ἐπανόρθωσις (LN **72.16**) (BAGD p. 283): 'correction' [HNTC, ICC, NTC; KJV, NAB, NASB, NRSV], 'improvement' [BAGD, Herm], 'restoration' [Lns], 'reformation of manners' [REB]. This word is also translated as a participle: 'correcting' [LN; NIV, TEV, TNT], 'guiding people's lives' [NJB].
  e. παιδεία (LN **33.226**) (BAGD 1. p. 603): 'instruction' [LN; KJV], 'training' [BAGD, HNTC, NTC; NAB, NASB, NIV, NRSV, TNT],

'education' [Herm, Lns], 'discipline' [REB], 'discipline of character' [ICC]. This word is also translated as a participle: 'teaching' [NJB], 'giving instruction' [TEV].
  f. δικαιοσύνη (LN 88.13) (BAGD 2.b. p. 196): 'righteousness' [BAGD, Herm, LN, Lns, NTC; KJV, NASB, NIV, NRSV], 'holiness' [NAB], 'the right way' [ICC], 'uprightness' [BAGD, HNTC], 'right living' [REB, TEV, TNT], 'to be upright' [NJB].

QUESTION—Does the phrase 'for teaching', etc., refer to making Timothy (or anyone) a better teacher, refuter, etc., by using the Scripture, or to the effect Scripture has on the reader?

1. It means that Scripture is useful when Timothy teaches, reproves, corrects, and instructs others [GNC, Herm, HNTC, ICC, MNTC, NCBC, NTC, TG]: all Scripture is useful in your teaching and reproving, correcting, and instructing others.
2. It means that Scripture has a useful effect on the reader [Alf, Brd, Lns, LSA, My]: all Scripture is useful in that it teaches, reproves, corrects, and instructs the one who reads it. The concern here is for Timothy's upbuilding and reliability as a Christian, not for his extended ability as a teacher [Alf].

QUESTION—What is meant by διδασκαλίαν 'teaching'?

It is the most general word of the four [EBC]. It means to teach the truth [GNC, ICC; REB, TEV], the gospel [GNC], and Christian doctrine [HNTC]. It is to teach all that is needed to make a person wise for salvation [Lns]. It is needed by the ignorant [El], and is used to advance the knowledge of all [My].

QUESTION—What is meant by ἐλεγμόν 'reproof'?

Reproof is needed by sinners [EBC], the evil, and prejudiced [El]. It means to convince people of sin [My]. It means to reprove people who are in the wrong [LSA]. It is to reprove error [GNC, TG; TEV], and sin [HNTC, ICC]. It is to refute error [NJB, REB], false teaching [ICC], religious lies [Lns], and errors in doctrine and conduct [NTC]. It is to expose the errors of false teachers [GNC].

QUESTION—What is meant by ἐπανόρθωσιν 'correction'?

It means to convince those who are misguided by their errors [ICC], and set them on the right path [ICC, NTC]. It means to correct mistakes [TG], errors [TNT], and faults [GNC, ICC, LN; TEV], both behavioral and ethical [GNC, ICC]. It is the positive side of reproof [NTC].

QUESTION—What is meant by παιδείαν τὴν ἐν δικαιοσύνῃ 'instruction in righteousness'?

This is needed by all Christians to bring them to a fuller measure of perfection [El]. It is the positive side to the correction of faults [GNC, TNTC]. It means to train Christians to do right [LSA], to instruct them in how to live according to God's will [TG], and to develop their Christian lives [My].

2 TIMOTHY 3:17

3:17 so-that^a the man of-God may-be qualified/competent,^b

LEXICON—a. ἵνα (LN 89.59): 'so that/that' [Herm, HNTC, Lns, NTC; all versions except NJB, TNT], 'in order that' [LN]. It is also translated as a clause starting a new sentence: 'This is how someone becomes' [NJB], 'If he obeys it, he will be' [TNT], 'It was given to make' [ICC].

b. ἄρτιος (LN **75.4**) (BAGD p. 110): 'qualified' [LN], 'fully qualified' [TEV], 'competent' [TNT], 'fully competent' [NAB], 'equipped' [NTC], 'fully equipped' [NJB], 'fit' [Herm, Lns], 'fit for his task' [ICC], 'capable' [BAGD; REB], 'adequate' [NASB], 'complete' [BAGD, HNTC], 'perfect' [KJV], 'proficient' [BAGD; NRSV]. It means to be able to meet all demands [BAGD]. It is also joined with the verb 'equipped' in the following clause: 'thoroughly equipped' [NIV].

QUESTION—What relationship is indicated by ἵνα 'so that'?

It indicates the purpose for which Scripture is useful [EBC, GNC, My, NTC, TNTC], or the contemplated result for one who receives its benefits [Alf, HNTC, Lns, TNTC].

QUESTION—What is meant by the genitive construction ὁ τοῦ θεοῦ 'the man of God'?

It is translated 'the man of God' [Herm, HNTC, Lns, NTC; KJV, NAB, NASB, NIV, REB, TNT], 'someone who is dedicated to God' [NJB], 'everyone who belongs to God' [NRSV], 'every one of God's men' [ICC], 'the person who serves God' [TEV].

1. This phrase refers to Christians in general [Brd, El, ICC, Lns, My, NTC]. It is any devout person [Brd]. It means a person who belongs to God [Lns, NTC].
2. This phrase refers to a minister of the gospel [EGT, GNC, Herm, HNTC, MNTC, NCBC, TG, TNTC]. The phrase is an Old Testament one that was applied to a prophet as a man who spoke in the name of God [MNTC, TNTC]. He is God's servant [TG].

QUESTION—What is meant by ἄρτιος 'qualified'?

It means to be made able to meet all demands [EBC], to be completely equipped for one's work as a man of God [EGT], ready at every point [Alf]. Such a person will be capable of doing his work well [TG], in a state of readiness to serve [LSA].

for^a every^b work^c good having-been-equipped.^d

LEXICON—a. πρός with accusative object (LN 89.44; 89.60) (BAGD III.3.c. p. 710): 'for' [Herm, HNTC, ICC, Lns, NTC; all versions except KJV, TEV], 'unto' [KJV]. It is also translated by an infinitive: 'to do' [TEV].

b. πᾶς, πᾶσα, πᾶν (LN 58.28; 59.23; 59.24): 'every' [NAB, NASB, NIV, NRSV, REB, TNT], 'every kind of' [LN; TEV], 'all' [LN; KJV], 'any' [LN; NJB].

c. ἔργον (LN 42.11, 42.42): 'work' [Herm, HNTC, ICC, Lns, NTC; all versions except TEV], 'deed' [LN (75.5); TEV].

d. perf. pass. participle of ἐξαρτίζω (LN **75.5**) (BAGD 2. p. 273): 'to be equipped' [BAGD; NAB, NASB, NIV, NRSV, REB, TEV], 'to be completely equipped' [HNTC], 'to be thoroughly equipped' [NTC], 'to be fully equipped' [TNT], 'to be completely qualified' [LN], 'to be fully fit' [Lns], 'to fit (him) completely' [ICC], 'to be ready' [NJB], 'to be prepared' [Herm], 'to be furnished' [BAGD; KJV].

QUESTION—What is the relation between the adjective ἄρτιος 'qualified, competent' and the perfect passive participle ἐξηρτισμένος 'having been equipped'?

1. It is a coordinate relationship, describing two reasons for the usefulness of Scripture [Alf, GNC, Herm, HNTC, TG; NAB, NJB, REB, TEV, TNT]. He is qualified so as to meet all demands and is equipped to do every good work [GNC], perfectly fitted to his work and completely equipped to take on all responsibilities [HNTC], fully trained and completely capable of doing every kind of good work [TG].
2. The second term is a cognate form of the adjective and is used to emphasize the idea [Lns, NTC, TNTC]: so that he may be equipped, yes once for all thoroughly equipped [NTC], that he may be fitted up as having been fully fitted for every good work [Lns].
3. It is an explanatory relation, defining more precisely the first term [El, MNTC, My].
4. The second term gives the grounds for the first term [ICC, LSA]: the Scriptures are profitable to a man, making him suitable for specific tasks, because it can make (or has already made) him completely fit for every kind of good work.
5. The two words are to be combined as one expression with an intensified meaning: 'complete/capable/proficient' joined with 'having been furnished/prepared' is rendered 'thoroughly equipped' [EBC; NIV].

DISCOURSE UNIT: 4:1–18 [TNTC]. The topic is Paul's farewell message.

DISCOURSE UNIT: 4:1–8 [Brd, EGT, HNTC, ICC, Lns, LSA, My, NTC; NASB]. The topic is Paul's final appeal and solemn charge to preach the Word [EGT, HNTC, ICC, Lns, LSA, My, NTC; NASB], a charge to be diligent in his duties [Brd].

DISCOURSE UNIT: 4:1–5 [Brd, EBC, GNC, MNTC, TNTC; NAB, NJB]. The topic is the final solemn apostolic charge [GNC, TNTC; NAB, NJB], a charge to preach the Word [EBC], diligence to duty of his office [Brd], a plea for steadfastness [MNTC].

4:1 I-charge[a] before[b] God and Christ Jesus, the (one) being-about[c] to-judge[d] living-(ones)[e] and dead-(ones),[f]

TEXT—Instead of Χριστοῦ Ἰησοῦ 'Christ Jesus', some manuscripts have τοῦ κυρίου Ἰησοῦ Χριστοῦ 'the Lord Jesus Christ'. GNT does not mention this other reading. 'The Lord Jesus Christ' is accepted only by KJV.

2 TIMOTHY 4:1

LEXICON—a. pres. mid. indic. of διαμαρτύρομαι (LN 33.319) (BAGD 1. p. 186): 'to charge' [BAGD, ICC, NTC; KJV, NAB, NJB], 'to solemnly charge' [NASB, REB, TNT], 'to give a charge' [NIV], 'to solemnly urge' [NRSV, TEV], 'to adjure' [Herm, HNTC], 'to earnestly testify' [Lns], 'to insist' [LN].
  b. ἐνώπιον with genitive object (LN 83.33) (BAGD 2.b. p. 270): 'before' [Herm, LN; KJV, NJB, REB], 'in the presence of' [BAGD; NAB, NASB, NIV, NRSV, TEV, TNT], 'in the sight of' [BAGD, HNTC, Lns, NTC], 'as in the sight of' [BAGD, ICC].
  c. pres. act. participle of μέλλω (LN 67.62): 'to be about to' [LN, Lns], 'to be coming/shall come (to judge)' [ICC; NAB], 'to be going (to judge)' [BAGD, HNTC], 'is (to judge)' [NASB, NRSV, REB, TNT], 'is (to be judge)' [NJB]. This word is also conflated with the following infinitive 'to judge' and rendered 'will judge' [Herm, NTC; KJV, NIV, TEV]. The word μέλλω with the present infinitive is at times referred to as a periphrasis for the future tense [BAGD].
  d. pres. act. infin. of κρίνω (LN 56.20) (BAGD 4.b.α. p. 452): 'to judge' [BAGD, Herm, HNTC, ICC, LN, Lns, NTC; all versions except NJB], 'to be a judge' [NJB].
  e. pres. act. participle of ζάω (LN 23.88) (BAGD 1.a.α. p. 336): 'to live' [BAGD, HNTC, ICC, LN, Lns]. It is often translated as a substantive: 'the living' [BAGD, Herm, NTC; all versions except KJV], 'the quick' [KJV].
  f. νεκρός (LN 23.121) (BAGD 2.a. p. 535): 'dead' [BAGD, HNTC, ICC, LN, Lns]. This adjective is translated as a substantive: 'the dead' [BAGD, Herm, NTC; all versions].

QUESTION—What is the significance of giving this charge in the sight of God and of Christ Jesus?
  Paul calls on God and Christ to be witnesses to what he is going to charge Timothy with [HNTC]. Timothy lives in the presence of God and Christ and is accountable to them [GNC, NTC]. Christ is called to witness as the coming judge who will know whether Timothy fulfils the charge and who will call Timothy to account if he fails to heed it [HNTC, MNTC].

QUESTION—To whom does 'the living' and 'the dead' refer?
  These designations comprise all those who will be alive at the time of his coming and all those who have died before that coming [El, GNC, Lns, NTC].

and his appearance[a] and his kingdom:[b]

TEXT—Instead of καί 'and' at the beginning of the phrase, some manuscripts have κατά 'at'. GNT selects the reading καί 'and' with a C rating, indicating a considerable degree of doubt. The reading κατά 'at' is selected only by KJV, making this last phrase the time of judgment: 'who shall judge the quick and the dead at his appearing and his kingdom'. All others select καί 'and' so that there are four items in the charge. The first two are introduced by ἐνώπιον 'before' and the last two are in the accusative case, which is used in adjurations [Brd, EBC, El, Lns, NTC] and is translated 'by' [HNTC, NTC; NAB, NASB, REB], 'in view of' [NIV, NRSV], 'in the name of' [NJB], 'because' [TEV], 'remembering' [TNT], '(and) at' [Herm].

LEXICON—a. ἐπιφάνεια (LN 24.21) (BAGD 1. p. 304): 'appearing' [BAGD, ICC, LN, NTC; all versions except REB, TEV, TNT], 'appearance' [Herm], 'coming appearance' [REB], 'manifestation' [HNTC], 'epiphany' [Lns]. This word is also translated as a finite verb: '(he) is coming' [TEV], 'will come again' [TNT].

b. βασιλεία (LN 37.64) (BAGD 3.g. p. 135): 'kingdom' [BAGD, Herm, HNTC, ICC, Lns, NTC; KJV, NASB, NIV, NJB, NRSV], 'kingly power' [NAB], 'reign' [LN; REB], 'rule' [LN]. This word is also translated as a verb: 'to rule as king' [TEV], 'to come to rule' [TNT].

QUESTION—What is the significance of making the charge with the mention of his coming and his kingdom?

Not only is the presence of God and Christ invoked with the preposition ἐνώπιον with the genitive 'in the sight of, before' (as in the formula in 1 Tim. 5:21 and 2 Tim. 2:14 [Alf, Herm, MNTC]), but these two other factors are given as additional grounds for the solemn charge [GNC, LSA, TG, TNTC]. Timothy should heed this final charge, since he, the false teachers, and all the people will have to give a final account at Christ's coming [GNC]. To urge someone by an event is to cite the happening as a reason why the command is given and why it must be obeyed [TG]. The coming of Christ and the subsequent perfect kingdom are two articles of the Christian hope which should strengthen Timothy's resolution [HNTC]. If Timothy obeys, he will share in the coming and in the reign [NTC]. It will be great glory for Timothy to be acknowledged by Christ and then to reign with him [Lns]. The hope of such future glories should inspire him to present fortitude [TNTC]. Timothy is warned to do his duty on pain of losing this great goal of the Christian life [MNTC].

4:2 preach[a] the word,[b] be-persistent/ready[c] (whether) convenient[d] (whether) inconvenient,[e]

LEXICON—a. aorist act. impera. of κηρύσσω (LN 33.207; 33.256) (BAGD 2.b.β. p. 431): to 'preach' [BAGD, Herm, LN; KJV, NAB, NASB, NIV, TEV], 'to proclaim' [HNTC, LN; NJB, NRSV, REB, TNT], 'to herald' [Lns, NTC].

b. λόγος (LN 33.260) (BAGD 1.b.β. p. 478): 'word' [BAGD, Herm, Lns, NTC; KJV, NAB, NASB, NIV], 'message' [HNTC; NJB, NRSV, REB, TEV, TNT], 'message of the Gospel' [ICC].

c. aorist act. impera. of ἐφίστημι, ἐφίσταμαι (LN 68.14) (BAGD 1.a. p. 330): 'to be persistent' [NRSV], 'to do with persistence' [LN], 'to press on' [TNT], 'to press home' [REB], 'to stay with one's task' [NAB], 'to stand up to one's task boldly' [ICC], 'to keep at (it)' [HNTC], 'to insist on' [NJB, TEV], 'to be instant' [KJV], 'to be ready' [BAGD; NASB], 'to

2 TIMOTHY 4:2

be prepared' [NIV], 'to stand by' [Herm], 'to stand at hand' [Lns], 'to be on hand' [BAGD, NTC].

d. εὐκαίρως (LN 67.6) (BAGD p. 321): 'convenient' [BAGD; NAB], 'favorable' [TNT], 'welcome' [NJB], 'in season' [BAGD, HNTC, ICC, NTC; KJV, NASB, NIV, REB], 'in good season' [Lns]. This word is also translated by a clause: '(whether) the time is favorable/right' [NRSV, TEV], '(whether) you are expected' [Herm], 'when it is convenient' [BAGD].

e. ἀκαίρως (LN **67.8**) (BAGD p. 29): 'inconvenient' [BAGD; NAB], 'unwelcome' [NJB], 'unfavorable' [NRSV, TNT], 'out of season' [BAGD, HNTC, ICC, NTC; KJV, NASB, NIV, REB], 'in no season' [Lns].

QUESTION—What is meant by ἐπίστηθι 'be persistent, be ready'?

1. It means to be persistent [Alf, Brd, GNC, HNTC, ICC, LN, MNTC, TG; KJV, NAB, NJB, NRSV, REB, TEV, TNT]. This relates to his preaching [Alf, MNTC] and to all of his pastoral duties [Alf, HNTC]. He is to be diligent [Alf, Brd] and keep at it [GNC].
2. It means to be ready [EBC, EGT, El, Herm, Lns, LSA, NCBC, NTC, TNTC; NASB, NIV]. This relates to always being ready to preach [EGT, El, Lns, LSA, NTC]. He is to be ready to act [EGT], on duty constantly, ready for any emergency [EBC]. He is to use every occasion as an opportunity to preach [LSA].

QUESTION—What is the unexpressed personal referent of the adverbs εὐκαίρως 'convenient' and ἀκαίρως 'inconvenient'?

1. It refers objectively to whether it is the right, convenient, opportune, favorable or desirable time for the hearers or not [BAGD, El, GNC, Herm, LSA, MNTC, My, NCBC, TG].
2. It refers to both the hearers and to Timothy [ICC]: whether you feel like it or not, and whether they want to hear you or not.
3. Its reference is not personal but to the opportunity to proclaim the message [EGT, TG], or serve in any and all of his different tasks [TNTC].

reprove,[a] admonish,[b] exhort,[c] with[d] all[e] patience[f] and teaching.[g]

LEXICON—a. aorist act. impera. of ἐλέγχω (LN 33.417) (BAGD 3. p. 249): 'to reprove' [BAGD, Herm, NTC; KJV, NASB, TNT], 'to rebuke' [LN], 'to correct' [BAGD; NAB, NIV], 'to refute' [HNTC], 'to refute falsehood/false teaching' [ICC; NJB], 'to use argument' [REB], 'to convince' [NRSV, TEV], 'to convict' [Lns]. He is to refute false teaching and to rebuke wrong-doers [ICC]. He is to reprove people who are in error [El, GNC], to correct them for their lack of holiness and truth [El]. He will tell them that they are doing wrong [LSA]. He refutes error with reasoned arguments [HNTC].

b. aorist act. impera. of ἐπιτιμάω (LN 33.419) (BAGD 1. p. 303): 'to rebuke' [BAGD, HNTC, LN, NTC; KJV, NASB, NIV, NRSV], 'to rebuke wrong-doers' [ICC], 'to reprove' [BAGD; NAB], 'to censure'

[BAGD], 'to reproach' [TEV], 'to chide' [Lns], 'to correct error' [NJB], 'to correct' [TNT], 'to threaten' [Herm], 'to use reproof' [REB], 'to pass censure on' [ICC]. He is to reproach or warn those who do not heed the rebuke [GNC, ICC] and tell them to stop doing wrong [LSA].

c. aorist act. impera. of παρακαλέω (LN 25.150) (BAGD 2. p. 617): 'to exhort' [BAGD, HNTC; KJV, NASB], 'to admonish' [Herm, Lns, NTC], 'to encourage' [BAGD, LN; NIV, NRSV, TEV, TNT], 'to encourage those who do (obey)' [ICC], 'to appeal to' [BAGD; NAB], 'to use appeal' [REB], 'to give encouragement' [NJB]. He is to encourage those who obey [ICC] and tell them what they ought to do [LSA]. Exhortation is for all [ICC].

d. ἐν with dative object (LN 89.84): 'with' [Herm, NTC; all versions except NAB], 'in' [Lns]. This preposition is also translated as a participle: 'using' [HNTC, ICC], or is conflated with the noun objects including the modifier 'all' and translated 'constantly teaching and never losing patience' [NAB], 'never failing in patience' [ICC].

e. πᾶς (LN 59.23): 'all' [Herm, NTC; KJV, REB, TEV, TNT], 'all' as a noun [NJB], 'utmost' [NRSV], 'great' [NASB], 'great and careful' [NIV], 'every' [ICC], 'every sort of' [HNTC]. This adjective is also translated as an adverb: 'constantly (teaching) and never (losing patience)' [NAB], 'never stop teaching' [TNT], 'never failing (in patience)' [ICC].

f. μακροθυμία (LN 25.167) (BAGD 2.a. p. 488): 'patience' [BAGD, Herm, ICC, LN; all versions except KJV], 'longsuffering' [Lns, NTC; KJV], 'forbearance' [BAGD, HNTC].

g. διδαχή (LN 33.224; 33.236) (BAGD 1. p. 192): 'teaching' [BAGD, HNTC, ICC, LN, NTC; NRSV, REB], 'instruction' [BAGD, Herm; NASB, NIV], 'doctrine' [Lns; KJV]. This noun is also translated as a verb: 'to teach' [NAB, TEV, TNT], 'to instruct' [NJB]. Most commentators take this to be the act of teaching [Alf, Brd, EBC, EGT, El, ICC, LSA, MNTC, My, NCBC, NTC, TG], but one takes it to be the doctrinal content of the word which is conveyed by teaching [Lns].

QUESTION—What does the phrase 'with all patience and teaching' modify?
1. It qualifies the three preceding imperatives [Alf, Brd, EBC, EGT, GNC, HNTC, LSA, NTC] and indicates manner [LSA].
2. It qualifies the immediately preceding imperative 'exhort!' [My].
3. It qualifies all five imperatives [Lns, TNTC], as to how they are to be effected, viz., subjectively (manner) 'with patience', and objectively (means) 'by continual teaching' [Lns, TNTC]. Some combine these two aspects of operation, so that 'patience' modifies 'teaching' with terms like 'always be patient as you teach', 'as you teach with all patience', 'all the patience good teaching needs', 'with patience and care to instruct', 'with utmost patience in teaching' [TG; NJB, NRSV, REB, TEV].

QUESTION—What does πᾶς 'all' modify?
1. It modifies both 'patience' and 'teaching' [EGT, El, ICC, MNTC, TNTC].

2. It modifies an implied verb: 'but do all with patience and care to instruct' [NJB].

4:3 For[a] there-will-be (a) time[b] when (they will) not accept[c] being-sound[d] teaching,[e]

LEXICON—a. γάρ (LN 89.23; 91.1): 'for' [Herm, HNTC, ICC, Lns, NTC; all versions except NJB, TEV], not explicit [NJB, TEV].
  b. καιρός (LN 67.1) (BAGD 1. p. 394): 'time' [BAGD, Herm, HNTC, ICC, LN; all versions], 'season' [Lns, NTC].
  c. pres. act. participle of ὑγιαίνω (LN 72.15) (BAGD 2. p. 832): 'sound' [Herm, ICC, LN, NTC; all versions], 'wholesome' [HNTC], 'healthy' [Lns], 'correct' [BAGD, LN]. It is reasonable and appeals to sound intelligence [BAGD]. See this word at 1:13.
  d. διδασκαλία (LN 33.224, 33.236) (BAGD 2. p. 191): 'teaching' [BAGD, Herm, HNTC, ICC, LN, Lns; NJB, REB], 'doctrine' [NTC; KJV, NAB, NASB, NIV, NRSV, TEV, TNT].
  e. fut. mid indic. of ἀνέχομαι (LN **31.54**) (BAGD 2. p. 66): 'to accept' [LN; NJB], 'to put up with' [BAGD, HNTC; NIV, NRSV], 'to endure' [BAGD, Herm, NTC; KJV, NASB], 'to stand' [Lns; REB], 'to listen to' [TEV, TNT], 'to listen to or to hear willingly' [BAGD], 'to tolerate' [ICC; NAB].

QUESTION—What relationship is indicated by γάρ 'for'?
It indicates the grounds for the preceding commands [Alf, EBC, El, GNC, HNTC, LSA, My, NTC, TNTC]. He must do these things at once because people will not always listen to the truth [Alf]. This justifies the need for diligence [EBC, El, NTC] and urgency [HNTC, TNTC].

QUESTION—Who is the subject of the verb?
The subject is professing Christians in the future [Alf].

but[a] according-to[b] their own desires[c] they-will-heap-up[d] teachers[e] itching[f] the ear,

LEXICON—a. ἀλλά (LN 89.125): 'but' [Herm, HNTC, Lns, NTC; all versions except NIV, TNT], 'instead' [NIV], 'nay' [ICC], not explicit [TNT].
  b. κατά with accusative object (LN 89.8): 'according to' [NJB], 'after' [Herm; KJV], 'following' [NAB], 'just as' [TNT], 'in accordance to' [NASB], 'in accordance with' [BAGD, Lns]. This preposition is also translated 'to suit' [HNTC, NTC; NIV, NRSV], '(each) will follow' [REB, TEV].
  c. ἐπιθυμία (LN 25.20) (BAGD 3. p. 293): 'desire' [BAGD, HNTC, LN; NAB, NASB, NIV, NRSV, TEV], 'lust' [LN, Lns; KJV], 'taste' [NJB], 'whim' [REB], 'caprice' [ICC], 'fancy' [Herm, NTC]. The phrase 'according to their own desires' is translated 'just as they like' [TNT]. See this word at 3:6.
  d. fut. act. indic. of ἐπισωρεύω (LN **59.65**) (BAGD p. 302): 'to heap up' [Lns], 'to heap' [KJV], 'to accumulate' [BAGD, NTC; NASB, NRSV], 'to greatly increase the number of' [LN], 'to surround (themselves) with'

[NAB], 'to gather around (them) a great number of' [NIV], 'to gather a crowd of' [REB], 'to gather together' [Herm], 'to amass' [HNTC], 'to pile' [ICC], 'to collect (themselves) a whole series of' [NJB], 'to collect (for themselves) more and more' [TEV, TNT].
  e. διδάσκαλος (LN 33.243): 'teachers' [Herm, HNTC, ICC, Lns, NTC; all versions].
  f. pres. mid. participle of κνήθω, κνήθομαι (LN **25.11**) (BAGD p. 437): 'to feel an itching' [BAGD]. The phrase 'itching ear' is translated 'having itching ears' [NTC; KJV], 'with their itching ears' [HNTC], 'wanting to have their ears tickled' [NASB], 'having an itch to get their hearing tickled' [Lns], 'with ears always itching for some novelty' [ICC], 'their ears will be itching for anything new' [NJB], 'because their ears are itching (for their wisdom)' [Herm], '(teachers) who tickle their ears' [NAB], '(teachers) to tickle his fancy' [REB], 'to say what their itching ears want to hear' [NIV], 'who will tell them what they are itching to hear' [TEV], 'to desire to hear what they want to hear' [LN], 'they will want to hear only what they fancy' [TNT], 'to suit their own desires' [NRSV].

QUESTION—What does 'according to their own desires' modify?
  1. It relates to, and tells why, they will gather many teachers to themselves who will tell them just what they want to hear. It is because of their lust to do evil [Brd, EBC, LSA]: because of their own desires to do evil they surround themselves with many ear-tickling teachers.
  2. It tells what kind of teachers they gather to themselves [HNTC, MNTC, NCBC, NTC]: teachers that fit, are according to and suit their own (the hearers') fancies or likings; compatible teachers who will condone their conduct.
  3. It relates to the preceding clause as a contrast to 'not listening to healthy teaching' so is joined by ἀλλά 'but, but rather, instead', with clauses like 'rather they will go after their own desires', 'instead of being obedient to the truth and God's providence they will do according to their own selfish and willful desires', 'not tolerating sound teaching but led by their own capricious whims' [Alf, GNC, ICC, My].

QUESTION—What is meant by having 'itching ears'?
  The listeners (not the false teachers) want to hear something new [Brd, El, ICC, MNTC, My, NCBC, TG], things that excite their fancies [HNTC]. They want to hear what pleases them [LSA, NCBC, NTC] and what they agree with [TG].

4:4 and from[a] the truth[b] they-will-turn-away[c] the ear,
LEXICON—a. ἀπό with genitive object (LN 89.122): 'from' [Herm, HNTC, Lns, NTC; KJV, NASB, NIV]. With a semantically negative verb form it is translated 'to': 'stop listening to' [NASB], 'refuse to listen to' [ICC], 'turn away from listening to' [NRSV, TEV], 'shut/stop their ears to' [NJB, REB, TNT].

b. ἀλήθεια (LN 72.2) (BAGD 2.b. p. 36): 'truth' [BAGD, Herm, HNTC, ICC, LN, Lns, NTC; all versions].
c. fut. act. indic. of ἀποστρέφω (LN **68.44**) (BAGD 1.a.α. p. 100): 'to turn away' [BAGD, Herm, HNTC, NTC; KJV, NASB, NIV], The phrase 'to turn away the ear' is translated 'to shut one's ears' [NJB, TNT], 'to stop one's ears' [REB], 'to stop listening' [LN; NAB], 'to refuse to listen' [ICC], 'to turn away from listening' [NRSV, TEV], 'to turn one's hearing away' [Lns]. It means that they will not listen to the truth [LSA].

QUESTION—What relationship is indicated by καί 'and'?
This indicates an explanation of the previous clause and means 'that is' [LSA].

and to[a] myths[b] they-will-turn-aside.[c]
LEXICON—a. ἐπί with accusative object (LN 84.17): 'to' [Herm, HNTC, ICC, NTC; all versions except KJV], 'unto' [KJV], 'upon' [Lns].
b. μῦθος (LN 33.13) (BAGD p. 529): 'myth' [BAGD, LN, Lns, NTC; NASB, NIV, NJB, NRSV], 'fable' [Herm, HNTC, LN; KJV, NAB, REB, TNT], 'legend' [LN; TEV], 'empty legend' [ICC].
c. fut. pass. indic. of ἐκτρέπω, ἐκτρέπομαι (LN **31.65**) (BAGD p. 246): 'to stray after' [LN], 'to wander off/away (to)' [NAB, NRSV], 'to turn away (to)' [BAGD, Herm, HNTC; NJB, REB], 'to turn aside (to)' [NTC; NASB, NIV, TNT], 'to turn aside to listen (to)' [ICC], 'to be turned (unto)' [KJV], 'to give their attention (to)' [TEV], 'to wrench it out (upon)' [Lns]. The passive voice has the sense of the middle voice [BAGD, El, ICC].

QUESTION—What are τοὺς μύθους 'the myths'?
The article implies that these myths are the ones Paul has already warned Timothy about in 1 Tim. 1:4 and 4:7 [Alf, Brd, NTC]. The errors in the future will be an intensification of present falsehoods [El, HNTC]. The term 'myths' does not describe the origins of the new teachings, but characterizes them as being empty and foolish [MNTC]. To turn aside to them is to take them seriously and believe them [TG].

4:5 But you be-self-controlled[a] in all,[b] endure suffering,[c] do[d] (the) work[e] of-(an) evangelist,[f] fulfill[g] your ministry.[h]
LEXICON—a. pres. act. impera. of νήφω (LN **88.86**) (BAGD p. 538): 'to be self-controlled' [BAGD, LN], 'to keep control of oneself' [LN; TEV], 'to be self-possessed' [BAGD], 'to keep steady' [NJB], 'to be steady and self possessed' [NAB], 'to keep calm, to keep self-restrained' [ICC], 'to keep one's head' [HNTC; NIV, REB, TNT], 'to be sober' [Herm, Lns, NTC; NASB, NRSV], 'to watch' [KJV].
b. πᾶσιν (LN 59.23) (BAGD 2.a.δ. p. 633): 'all'. The phrase ἐν πᾶσιν 'in all' is translated 'in all things/matters' [Herm, ICC, NTC; KJV, NASB], 'in all situations/circumstances' [HNTC; NIV, TEV], 'in all respects' [BAGD], 'in every way' [BAGD], 'in every respect' [Lns], 'all the time'

[NJB], not explicit [NAB]. It is also translated as an adverb: 'always' [NRSV], or as a verb phrase: 'whatever happens' [REB, TNT].
c. aorist act. impera. of κακοπαθέω (LN **24.89**) (BAGD 2. p. 397): 'to endure suffering' [LN; NRSV, TEV], 'to endure hardship' [HNTC; NASB, NIV], 'to endure affliction' [KJV], 'to endure in sufferings' [Herm], 'to put up with suffering' [NJB], 'to put up with hardship' [NAB, REB], 'to be ready to suffer' [TNT], 'to be ready to face suffering' [ICC], 'to suffer hardship' [NTC], 'to suffer what is bad' [Lns].
d. aorist act. impera. of ποιέω (LN 90.45) (BAGD I.1.b.α. p. 681): 'to do' [BAGD, Herm, LN, Lns, NTC; all versions except NAB, REB], 'to perform' [NAB], 'to carry out' [HNTC]. The phrase 'to do work' is translated 'to work' [REB], 'your work is' [ICC].
e. ἔργον (LN 42.42) (BAGD 2. p. 308): 'work' [BAGD, Herm, ICC, LN, Lns, NTC,; all versions except REB], 'job' [HNTC], 'task' [BAGD, LN]. This noun is also translated as an imperative verb: 'work (to spread the gospel)' [REB].
f. εὐαγγελιστής (LN 53.76) (BAGD p. 318): 'evangelist' [BAGD, Herm, HNTC, LN, Lns, NTC; KJV, NAB, NASB, NIV, NRSV, TNT], 'preacher of the gospel/Good News' [BAGD; TEV]. This noun is also translated as a verb phrase: 'to preach the gospel' [NJB], 'to spread the gospel' [REB], 'to preach good tidings' [ICC].
g. aorist act. impera. of πληροφορέω (LN **68.32**) (BAGD 1.a. p. 670): 'to fulfill' [BAGD, Herm, Lns; NAB, NASB, NJB], 'to fulfill completely' [LN], 'to carry out fully/to the full' [NRSV, TNT], 'to make full proof' [KJV], 'to discharge to the full' [HNTC, NTC], 'to discharge all (the duties)' [NIV, REB], 'to perform it to the full' [ICC], 'to perform your whole (duty)' [TEV].
h. διακονία (LN 35.21) (BAGD 3. p. 184): 'ministry' [HNTC, LN, Lns, NTC; KJV, NAB, NASB, NRSV], 'duties of your ministry/calling' [NIV, REB], 'duty as a servant of God' [TEV], 'duty' [TNT], 'task' [LN], 'task of ministry' [ICC], 'service' [BAGD, Herm; NJB].

QUESTION—What relationship is indicated by δέ 'but'?

It indicates contrast between the actions of those described in 3:4 and those commanded of Timothy [Alf, Brd, El, GNC, Herm, HNTC, ICC, Lns, MNTC, NTC; all versions]: but as for you.

QUESTION—What relation is there between his 'work of an evangelist' and his 'ministry'?

Although several commentators regard 'evangelist' as used of Timothy in a wide general sense of preaching, teaching, and expounding the gospel [Alf, Brd, Lns, NTC], it is a specific work and not an office [Brd, HNTC, NCBC] and it was his first calling [EGT, El, My]. His διακονία 'ministry' embraces a wide range of duties [MNTC, My, TG, TNTC] as the servant of God [LSA, TG] and of people [ICC, Lns, LSA].

DISCOURSE UNIT: 4:6–8 [Brd, EBC, GNC, MNTC, TNTC; NAB, NJB]. The topic is the reward for fidelity [NAB], the closing time of Paul's apostolic course [Brd; NJB], Paul's final testimony [EBC, GNC], a triumphant confession [NTC], the farewell [MNTC].

4:6 For[a] I already[b] am-being-poured-out,[c]
LEXICON—a. γάρ (LN 89.23; 91.1): 'for' [ICC, Lns, NTC; KJV, NAB, NASB, NIV], not explicit [Herm, HNTC; NJB, NRSV, REB, TEV, TNT].
   b. ἤδη (LN 67.20): 'already' [Herm, HNTC, LN, Lns, NTC; all versions except KJV, TEV], 'now ready' [KJV], 'the hour has come' [TEV], 'on the point of' [ICC].
   c. pres. pass. indic. of σπένδω (LN **53.27**) (BAGD p. 761): 'to be poured out', 'to be poured out as an offering' [LN], 'to be poured out as a drink offering' [Lns, NTC; NASB], 'to be poured out like a drink offering' [NIV], 'to be poured out like a libation' [NAB], 'to be poured out as a libation' [NRSV], 'to be poured away as a libation' [NJB], 'to be poured out as a libation to God' [ICC], 'to be poured out on the altar' [HNTC; REB], 'to be offered' [BAGD; KJV], 'to be sacrificed' [Herm; TEV], 'to begin the sacrificial ritual' [TNT].
QUESTION—What relationship is indicated by γάρ 'for'?
   It indicates the grounds for the preceding exhortation [GNC, HNTC, Lns, LSA, My, NTC]: you must be self-controlled and fulfill your ministry because I am about to die. All that is commanded of Timothy is done in view of what is happening to Paul [Lns]. Paul can do no more, so Timothy must carry on [HNTC, My, NTC].
QUESTION—At what time is the act of 'being poured out as libation' considered to occur?
   1. It is considered as already having begun [Alf, Brd, EBC, El, GNC, HNTC, Lns, MNTC, My, TNTC]: the end of my life has already begun, like the pouring out of a libation to God at the time of sacrifice.
   2. It is considered as imminent, being at the point of occurring [ICC, LSA, NCBC, TG]: the time has come so that my lifeblood is about to be poured out like a libation to God.
QUESTION—What is the picture and significance of σπένδομαι 'I am being poured out'?
   The picture is of a drink offering being poured on the lamb of sacrifice just before it was burned on the altar (Numbers 28:24) [EBC]. This pictures the process that leads to the shedding of his blood, his death as a martyr [Alf, EBC, GNC, HNTC, ICC, Lns, My, NCBC, TNTC], in which he considers himself as an offering to God [EGT, HNTC, LSA, MNTC, NTC, TG], the final concluding act of sacrifice being his imminent execution [Lns, NTC]. Paul's present sufferings constitute the commencement of the libation [El]. Paul's whole life has been a sacrifice offered to the Lord, and now the libation of his life's blood is ready to be poured on it [ICC, Lns, My, NTC]. He offers his life to God, as a wine offering is poured out on the altar [TG].

and the time^a of-my departure^b of me has-come.^c

LEXICON—a. καιρός (LN 67.1) (BAGD 3. p. 395): 'time' [BAGD, Herm, LN; all versions except REB], 'hour' [HNTC; REB], 'season' [NTC], 'moment' [ICC], 'period' [Lns].
   b. ἀνάλυσις (LN **23.101**) (BAGD p. 57): 'departure' [BAGD, Herm, HNTC, LN, Lns, NTC; KJV, NASB, NIV, NRSV, REB, TNT], 'death' [BAGD, **LN**], 'dissolution' [NAB]. This word is also translated as a verb 'to depart' [NJB], 'to leave (this life)' [TEV], 'to strike one's tent and be gone' [ICC].
   c. perf. act. indic. of ἐφίστημι, ἐφίσταμαι (LN **67.63**) (BAGD 2.b. p. 331): 'to be near' [NAB], 'to be very near' [LN], 'to be at hand' [HNTC; KJV, TNT], 'to be close at hand' [ICC], 'to be imminent' [BAGD, LN], 'to arrive' [NTC], 'to come' [Herm; NASB, NIV, NJB, NRSV], 'to be present' [Lns], 'to be here' [TEV], 'to be upon (me)' [REB].

QUESTION—Is the expression 'my departure' figurative or literal?
1. It is figurative, picturing the loosing of a ship from its moorings or of breaking camp [EBC, GNC, HNTC, ICC, LSA, NCBC, NTC, TNTC]. It is used here of leaving this life/physical body at death [EBC, GNC], getting free of all restricting ties [TNTC], and was a common metaphorical euphemism for death/dying [GNC, HNTC]. Paul must strike his tent and be gone [ICC].
2. The word is non-figurative [EGT, El, Lns, MNTC, My, TG], a perfectly general [El] and literal [Lns] usage of a word which by that time had lost any metaphorical significance [MNTC], meaning nothing more than leaving, setting out, departing for a long trip [MNTC, My]; a dead figure [LSA] and common euphemism for dying [EGT, LSA]: The time has now come for my leaving this life.

QUESTION—What time is implied in this context by ἐφέστηκεν 'has come'?
1. It indicates that the departure time has already arrived, [Brd, EGT, GNC, LSA, MNTC, NTC], paralleling his already being poured out [Brd], so the time is the present [GNC, Lns]: my departing time is now here.
2. It indicates that the departure time is near/at hand [Alf, El, HNTC, My, TG, TNTC], i.e. standing by (waiting to happen), all but here [El]: my time of departure is imminent.

4:7 The good^a fight/contest^b I-have fought/contended-in,^c the course^d I-have-finished,^e

LEXICON—a. καλός (LN 88.4) (BAGD 2.c.β. p. 400): 'good' [BAGD, Herm, LN; all versions except REB, TEV, TNT], 'great' [REB, TNT], 'grand' [NTC], 'noble' [HNTC, Lns], 'right' [ICC]. This adjective is also translated 'to do one's best' [TEV].
   b. ἀγών (LN 39.29; 50.4) (BAGD 2. p. 15): 'fight' [BAGD, Herm, ICC, LN, NTC; all versions except REB, TEV, TNT], 'struggle' [BAGD, LN], 'contest' [BAGD, Lns], 'race' [LN; REB, TEV, TNT], 'match' [HNTC].

c. perf. mid. indic. of ἀγωνίζομαι (LN 39.29; 50.1) (BAGD 2.b. p. 15): 'to fight' [Herm, HNTC, ICC, LN, NTC; KJV, NAB, NASB, NIV, NRSV], 'to struggle' [BAGD], 'to contend' [Lns], 'to compete' [LN], 'to run' [REB, TNT], 'to do (one's best) in the race' [TEV].
d. δρόμος (LN **50.5**) (BAGD 1. p. 206): 'course' [BAGD, Herm, ICC, LN; KJV, NASB, REB, TNT], 'race' [BAGD, HNTC, **LN**, Lns, NTC; NAB, NIV, NJB, NRSV], '(the) full distance' [TEV].
e. perf. act. indic. of τελέω (LN 68.22) (BAGD 1. p. 810): 'to finish' [BAGD, LN, Lns, NTC; all versions except NJB, TEV], 'to complete' [BAGD, Herm, HNTC, LN], 'to come to the end of' [ICC], 'to bring to an end' [BAGD], 'to run to the finish' [NJB], 'to run the full distance' [TEV].

QUESTION—What does the adjective καλόν 'good' modify?
1. It modifies the noun 'fight/contest' [Brd, El, GNC, HNTC, ICC, Lns, LSA, MNTC, TNTC; all versions except TEV]. It indicates that it is a noble, grand, or great contest in which he has contended [GNC, HNTC, MNTC, NTC].
2. It describes the quality of fighting/contending Paul exhibited in the contest of life and is translated adverbially: 'completed it well' [EBC], 'fought through it faithfully' [My], 'I have done my best' [TEV].

QUESTION—What is the significance and meaning of these two metaphors?
1. There are two different metaphors, one of fighting and one of racing [Herm, HNTC, ICC, MNTC, My, NTC; KJV, NAB, NASB, NIV, NRSV]. 'Fight' refers to a wrestling match [HNTC, MNTC]. The course is his ministry [My, NTC] or his life [MNTC].
2. There is one metaphor, that of racing [Alf, Brd, EBC, EGT, El, GNC, Lns, LSA, NCBC; REB, TEV, TNT]. The first clause refers to any contest and is specified as a race in the second clause [Alf, Brd, EGT, LSA, NCBC]. The course is the race of life [EBC, EGT, El], or the race of his ministry [GNC, LSA].

the faith[a] I-have-kept.[b]
LEXICON—a. πίστις (LN 31.102) (BAGD 3. p. 664): 'faith' [Lns, NTC; all versions], '(my) trust' [HNTC]. This noun is also translated as an adjective: 'faithful' [Herm]; or verb phrase: 'to keep faith' [ICC].
b. perf. act. indic. of τηρέω (LN 36.19) (BAGD 3. p. 815): 'to keep' [BAGD, NTC; all versions], 'to not lose' [BAGD], 'to guard' [Lns], 'to remain' [Herm], 'to be loyal to' [HNTC].

QUESTION—To what does τὴν πίστιν 'the faith' refer ?
1. This is objective faith, the body of truth believed by Christians [Alf, BAGD, Brd, EGT, Lns, LSA, My, TNTC], 'the Christian creed' [Brd]. Some see a metaphor in the verb and refer to faith as the deposit or trust (cf. 2 Tim. 1:14) he had received [Brd, EGT, El, Lns, MNTC, NCBC, TNTC]. Another classifies this as a dead figure [LSA]. Paul has been

loyal to what Christians believe [LSA]. He has kept the faith against all inducements to deny it [My]. He has preserved the faith intact [NCBC].
2. This is personal faith in God [NTC]. Paul's faith in Christ has never swerved and keeps ruling his life.
3. This is part of the athletic metaphor [EBC]. Paul has kept the rules and is not disqualified from winning the race [EBC].
4. This is part of the fixed phrase 'to keep faith' which refers to his fidelity, i.e., loyalty all through his ministry [GNC, Herm, HNTC, ICC]. Paul has remained faithful [Herm] and has been true to his promise to the Lord [ICC]. He has been loyal to the divine mandate [HNTC].

4:8 For-the-rest[a] there-is-stored-up[b] for-me the crown[c] of-righteousness,[d]
LEXICON—a. λοιπός (LN 67.134) (BAGD 3.a.α. or 3.b p. 480): 'for the rest', 'now' [Herm, HNTC; NIV, TNT], 'and now' [REB, TEV], 'all (there is) now' [NJB], 'as for the rest' [Lns], 'from now on' [BAGD, LN; NAB, NRSV], 'henceforth' [LN; KJV], 'so henceforth' [ICC], 'in/for the future' [BAGD, NTC; NASB], 'furthermore' [LN], 'therefore' [BAGD].
b. pres. mid. indic of ἀπόκειμαι (LN 85.53; 13.73) (BAGD 2. p. 92): 'to be in store' [HNTC; NIV], 'to be stored up safely' [ICC], 'to be safely stored away' [NTC], 'to be laid up' [Lns; KJV, NASB], 'to be reserved', [BAGD, Herm; NRSV], 'to await/wait' [NAB, REB, TEV], 'to remain' [TNT], 'there is to come' [NJB].
c. στέφανος (LN **57.121**) (BAGD 2.a. p. 767): 'crown' [Herm, ICC; all versions except REB, TEV], 'garland' [HNTC; REB], 'wreath' [NTC], 'victory wreath' [Lns], 'prize of victory' [TEV], 'prize' [LN], 'reward' [BAGD]. This is the laurel wreath given to the winner of the race [EBC, GNC, HNTC].
d. δικαιοσύνη (LN 88.13) (BAGD 2.b. p. 196): 'righteousness' [BAGD, Herm, HNTC, LN, Lns, NTC; KJV, NASB, NIV, NRSV, REB, TNT], 'a righteous life' [ICC; TEV], 'uprightness' [BAGD; NJB]. It is also translated 'merited' [NAB], 'awarded for a righteous life' [TEV].
QUESTION—What is meant by λοιπόν 'for the rest'?
It is taken by many to mean 'from now on, henceforth' [Alf, Brd, El, NTC; KJV, NAB, NASB, NRSV]. Others think that there is no notion of duration and that it means 'for the rest, now' [EGT, Herm, HNTC, Lns, MNTC, My, TNTC; NIV, REB, TEV, TNT]. Paul is at the end of his life and now nothing remains other than to receive his reward [HNTC, My]. Paul has nothing more to do than to receive the crown [EGT]. This contrasts what remains to be realized with what has been accomplished [TNTC].
QUESTION—In what sense is the crown stored up?
The verb describes something that is set aside for future use [El]. God has kept it for him [TG]. The crown was reserved in anticipation of the completion of the race and the time of presenting it to the winner [Lns]. It has been promised to him and Christ has earned it for him [NTC].

2 TIMOTHY 4:8

QUESTION—How are the nouns related in the genitive construction ὁ τῆς δικαιοσύνης στέφανος 'the crown of righteousness'?

Paul has resumed the athletic metaphor, and the στέφανος 'crown' refers to the garland or winner's wreath [EBC, Lns, LSA, NTC, TG], awarded in recognition of achievement [LSA], at the end of the race, which in this case was the end of his victorious life [EBC]

1. It means the crown that is awarded for righteousness [Alf, Brd, EGT, El, GNC, HNTC, Lns, MNTC, NCBC, NTC, TNTC; TEV]: the crown that is awarded to those who are righteous. The crown is eternal life and is given as a fitting recompense for an upright life [HNTC, NTC]. The crown goes with and belongs to imputed righteousness and to acquired righteousness manifested in the life [Lns].
2. It means the crown that consists of righteousness [LN, My]: the crown, that is, righteousness. Righteousness is that perfect state granted at the judgment by the sentence that justifies him [My]. The prize is being declared righteous or being put right with God [LN (57.121)].

which the Lord will-give[a] to-me on that day, the righteous[b] judge,[c]

LEXICON—a. fut. act. indic. of ἀποδίδωμι (LN 38.16) (BAGD 1. p. 90): 'to give' [KJV, NJB, NRSV, TEV, TNT], 'to duly give' [Lns], 'to award' [BAGD, HNTC, ICC, NTC; NAB, NASB, NIV, REB], 'to reward' [LN], 'to bestow' [Herm].

b. δίκαιος (LN 88.12) (BAGD 2. p. 195): 'righteous' [BAGD, HNTC, LN, Lns, NTC; KJV, NASB, NIV, NRSV, REB, TEV], 'upright' [NJB], 'just' [Herm, LN; NAB], not explicit [ICC]. It is also translated as an adverb: '(who judges) rightly' [TNT].

c. κριτής (LN **56.28**) (BAGD 1.a.β. p. 453): 'judge' [BAGD, Herm, HNTC, LN, Lns, NTC; all versions except TNT]. This noun is also translated by a relative clause 'who judges' [TNT]. Not explicit [ICC].

QUESTION—Who is the Lord?

The Lord is Christ [Alf, Brd, HNTC, MNTC, NTC, TG].

QUESTION—What day is referred to?

It is the day Christ comes again [EGT, HNTC, My], the day of the last judgment [Brd, El, TG], the day of resurrection [Lns].

and not only[a] to-me but also to-all the (ones) having-loved[b] the appearing[c] of-him.

LEXICON—a. μόνος (LN 58.50): 'only' [Herm, HNTC, ICC; all versions except REB, TNT], 'alone' [Lns, NTC; REB, TNT].

b. perf. act. participle of ἀγαπάω (LN 25.104) (BAGD 2. p. 5): 'to love' [LN; KJV], 'to have loved' [HNTC, NTC; NASB], 'to have been loving' [Lns], 'to look for with eager longing' [NAB], 'to long for' [BAGD, Herm], 'to have longed for' [NIV, NJB, NRSV], 'to set their hearts on' [ICC; REB, TNT], 'to wait with love for' [TEV]. The perfect tense refers to their love having continued up to the moment of receiving the crown [Alf, EGT, TNTC]. This views their love from the viewpoint of the time of the judgment [ICC]. To love the Lord's appearing means to look forward to it with earnest joy [Alf]. They long for it to take place [HNTC, MNTC, NCBC, TNTC]. Love for Christ is a motive for this longing [MNTC]. They long for Christ's complete triumph [TNTC].

c. ἐπιφάνεια (LN **24.21**) (BAGD 1. p. 304): 'appearing' [BAGD, ICC, LN, NTC; KJV, NAB, NASB, NIV, NJB, NRSV], 'manifestation' [HNTC], 'appearance' [Herm], 'coming appearance' [REB], 'coming again' [TNT], 'coming in judgment' [BAGD], 'epiphany' [Lns]. It is also translated as a verb: 'to appear' [TEV]. See this word at 4:1.

DISCOURSE UNIT: 4:9–22 [EGT, Lns, My, NTC; NASB, REB]. The topic is personal concerns and details [EGT, My, NTC; NASB], final instructions [REB], addenda to the body of letter [Lns].

DISCOURSE UNIT: 4:9–18 [GNC, HNTC, ICC; NIV, NJB, TEV]. The topic is a personal request, remarks, and warning instructions [GNC, HNTC; NIV, TEV], an appeal to come and assurance of God's protection [ICC], final advice [NJB].

DISCOURSE UNIT: 4:9–15 [LSA, NCBC]. The topic is being diligent to come to Paul soon [LSA], instructions and information regarding Paul's co-workers [NCBC].

DISCOURSE UNIT: 4:9–13 [EBC, MNTC, TNTC; NAB]. The topic is Paul's loneliness [NAB], Paul's final plea [EBC], a personal request [TNTC], instructions relative to Timothy's visit [MNTC].

DISCOURSE UNIT: 4:9–12 [Brd, Herm]. The topic is an invitation for Timothy to come to his lonely situation [Brd], a description of Paul's situation [Herm].

4:9 **Do-your-best/Hasten**[a] **to come to me soon:**[b]
LEXICON—a. aorist act. impera. of σπουδάζω (LN 68.63; 68.79) (BAGD 1. p. 763): 'to do one's best' [HNTC, LN, NTC; NAB, NIV, NRSV, REB, TEV, TNT], 'to make every effort' [Herm, ICC; NASB, NJB], 'to be diligent' [Lns], 'to do one's diligence' [KJV], 'to endeavor' [LN], 'to hasten, to hurry' [BAGD, LN].

b. ταχέως (LN 67.56) (BAGD 1.a. p. 806): 'soon' [BAGD, LN; NAB, NASB, NRSV, REB, TEV, TNT], 'quickly' [BAGD, Herm, HNTC, Lns, NTC; NIV], 'at once' [BAGD], 'speedily' [ICC], 'shortly' [KJV], 'without delay' [BAGD]. It is also translated 'as soon as you can' [NJB].

QUESTION—What is meant by σπούδασον 'do your best, hasten'?
1. It means that Timothy is to do his best to come soon [Brd, El, GNC, Herm, HNTC, ICC, Lns, LSA, NTC; all versions]. Timothy has to conclude his work before setting out [Lns], and travel conditions are taken into account [GNC].
2. It means that he is to hasten and come soon [BAGD, EBC].

4:10 for[a] **Demas has-deserted**[b] **me, having-loved**[c] **the present**[d] **age,**[e] **and went**[f] **to Thessalonica, Crescens to Galatia, Titus to Dalmatia.**

TEXT Instead of Γαλατίαν 'Galatia', some manuscripts have Γαλλίαν 'Gaul'. GNT selects the reading 'Galatia' with a B rating, indicating some degree of doubt. The reading 'Gaul' is selected only by HNTC.

LEXICON—a. γάρ (LN 89.23): 'for' [Herm, HNTC, LN, Lns, NTC; all versions except NJB, REB, TEV], 'as it is' [NJB], not explicit [ICC; REB, TEV].
- b. aorist act. indic. of ἐγκαταλείπω (LN 35.54) (BAGD 2. p. 215): 'to desert' [BAGD, HNTC, ICC, LN, NTC; NASB, NIV, NJB, NRSV, REB, TEV], 'to forsake' [KJV], 'to leave' [Herm; NAB, TNT], 'to abandon' [Lns].
- c. aorist act. participle of ἀγαπάω (LN 25.104) (BAGD 2. p. 5): 'to love' [LN; KJV, NASB, NIV], 'to be in love with' [NRSV], 'to fall in love with' [TEV], 'to love too much' [TNT], 'to be enamored' [NAB], 'to have one's heart set on' [REB]. It is also translated as a noun: '(for) love (of this life)' [NJB].
- d. νῦν (LN 67.38) (BAGD 3.a. p. 546): 'present' [HNTC, ICC, Lns, NTC; KJV, NAB, NASB, NRSV, REB, TEV], 'this' [Herm; NIV, NJB, TNT].
- e. αἰών (LN 41.38; 67.143) (BAGD 2.a. p. 27): 'age' [BAGD, LN], 'world' [Herm, HNTC, ICC, NTC; all versions except NJB], 'life' [NJB], 'eon' [Lns].
- f. aorist pass. indic. of πορεύομαι (LN 15.18, 15.34): 'to go off' [HNTC, ICC; TEV, TNT], 'to go' [Herm, Lns, NTC; NAB, NASB, NIV, NJB, NRSV, REB], 'to go away' [LN], 'to depart' [KJV].

QUESTION—What relationship is indicated by γάρ 'for'?

It indicates the grounds for the preceding command [Alf, EBC, GNC, Lns, LSA, NTC]: come soon because all except Luke have gone away.

QUESTION—What relationship is indicated by the use of the participle ἀγαπήσας 'having loved'?

It indicates the reason Demas deserted Paul [Brd, GNC, Herm, HNTC, LSA]: he deserted me because he loved the present age.

QUESTION—What does it mean 'to love this world/age'?

This is a somewhat figurative expression [LSA], indicating in its broadest sense predominate interest in worldly matters or pursuits [MNTC, TG], or it simply means he went into business and so left for Thessalonica, his probable home [Lns, NCBC]. However, it was a concern for present benefits at the neglect of future reward [LSA]. This dominating interest in the affairs of this life [TG], i.e., love of the present world this side of the grave [NTC] comes out in sharp contrast to the love of the appearing of Christ and the future world of 4:8 [GNC, HNTC, NTC, TNTC], the same words ἀγαπάω 'to love' and αἰών 'world/age' being used in both verses. The personal benefits for which he may have been concerned were ease, comfort, and pleasures [El, HNTC, NTC], the visible earthly blessings [My], and may well have included the transitory treasures of material wealth [NTC, TG].

From the negative point of view, this expression shows his lack of inclination to be a partner to the peril, danger, rigors, hardship, and privation attending the apostle [Brd, EBC, El, HNTC, TNTC]. Demas became discouraged, and finally his courage failed [ICC, NCBC], and he therefore deserted Paul [TNTC].

QUESTION—Why did Crescens and Titus leave Paul?

They are not reproached for having left him [EGT, LSA]. It is assumed that Paul sent them to do missionary work [EBC, GNC, HNTC, NTC, TNTC] or some other errands [Lns].

4:11 Luke alone[a] is with me.

LEXICON—a. μόνος (LN 58.50) (BAGD 1.a.α. p. 527): 'alone' [BAGD, LN, Lns; TNT], 'only' [BAGD, Herm; KJV, NASB, NIV, NJB, NRSV, TEV]. This clause is translated 'I have no one with me but Luke' [NAB], 'apart from Luke I have no one with me' [REB], 'Luke is the only one with me' [HNTC, NTC], 'Luke is with me, but he is single-handed' [ICC].

Having-gotten[a] Mark, bring[b] (him) with yourself, for he-is useful[c] to-me for[d] ministry.[e]

LEXICON—a. aorist act. participle of ἀναλαμβάνω (LN 15.168) (BAGD 4. p. 57): 'to get' [Herm; NAB, NIV, NRSV, TEV], 'to take' [KJV], 'to take along' [BAGD, LN], 'to bring along' [LN], 'to get hold of' [HNTC; REB], 'to pick up' [Lns, NTC; NASB, TNT], 'to pick up on your journey' [ICC], not explicit [NJB].

b. pres. act. impera. of ἄγω (LN **15.165**) (BAGD 1.b. p. 14): 'to bring' [Herm, HNTC, ICC, LN, NTC; all versions], 'to bring along' [BAGD, Lns].

c. εὔχρηστος (LN 65.31) (BAGD p. 329): 'useful' [BAGD, ICC, Lns; NASB, NRSV, TNT], 'very useful' [NTC], 'helpful' [NIV], 'profitable' [KJV]. This phrase is translated 'I find him a useful helper/assistant' [NJB, HNTC], 'he can help me' [TEV], 'he can be of great service' [NAB], 'I can make good use of his services' [Herm], 'he is a great help' [REB].

d. εἰς with accusative object (LN 90.23) (BAGD 5. p. 230): 'for' [BAGD, ICC, Lns, NTC; KJV, NASB], 'in' [NIV, NJB, NRSV, TEV, TNT], 'with respect to' [BAGD], not explicit [Herm, HNTC; NAB, REB].

e. διακονία (LN 35.19; 35.21) (BAGD 1. p. 184): 'ministry' [LN, Lns, NTC; KJV, NIV, NRSV], 'service' [BAGD, Herm, ICC, LN; NAB, NASB], 'work' [NJB, TEV, TNT], 'assistant' [HNTC], not explicit [REB].

QUESTION—From where is Timothy to take Mark and bring him with himself?

Mark might have been working with Timothy, but was away touring the churches in Asia Minor at the time [Lns, NTC]. Mark was not in Ephesus [GNC] where Timothy was, but somewhere between there and Rome [EGT], so on the way [Brd, EGT, HNTC, MNTC, My, NCBC, TNTC], Timothy was to pick him up and bring him along.

QUESTION—To what does διακονία 'ministry' refer?
1. It refers to the work of Paul's apostolic office [Alf, My], his Christian work for the kingdom [NTC, TG], the service of preaching the gospel [EGT, NCBC], and to the outreach ministry for the Gospel in Rome [Lns].
2. It refers to attendance to Paul's personal needs [Brd, HNTC].
3. It is a neutral [El], intentionally vague [MNTC], general term [TNTC], which includes both personal service to Paul and the gospel ministry [El, GNC, LSA; and probably MNTC]; in fact he will be useful for any kind of service [MNTC, TNTC].

4:12 And/But[a] Tychicus I-sent[b] to Ephesus.
LEXICON—a. δέ (LN 89.87; 89.124): 'and' [KJV], 'now' [Lns, NTC], 'as for' [ICC], 'but' [NASB], not explicit [Herm, HNTC; all versions except KJV, NASB].
b. aorist act. indic. of ἀποστέλλω (LN 15.66): 'to send' [Herm, ICC; all versions], 'to send away' [BAGD], 'to dispatch' [HNTC], 'to commission' [Lns, NTC].

QUESTION—What relationship is indicated by δέ 'and, but'?
1. It indicates a continuation [HNTC, ICC, Lns, NTC; KJV]: and. Paul interrupted the account of how short-handed he was by a comment about bringing along Mark, and now he resumes with the departure of Tychicus [HNTC]. It is not a contrast since Paul had also sent away Crescens and Titus [Lns]. This is a parenthetical remark to explain that he is sending a substitute while Timothy and Mark are away visiting Paul [Lns]. Another view is that this is a second grounds for bringing Mark to Paul [LSA].
2. It indicates a contrast to those mentioned in 4:10 who had left on their own accord [Alf, EGT].
3. It indicates a contrast to an implied statement [El, GNC]: I need Mark; I had a useful man in Tychicus, but I sent him to Ephesus.

QUESTION—What are the implications of the aorist form ἀπέστειλα 'I sent' in this situation?
1. It indicates a past action of sending Tychicus to Ephesus, and is represented by the English past tense 'I sent' [NIV, TEV], or more commonly by the perfect tense 'I have sent' [Herm; KJV, NAB, NASB, NJB, NRSV, REB, TNT], and 'I have dispatched' [HNTC].
2. This is an epistolary aorist (cf. Col. 4:8) [Alf, Brd, EBC, GNC, Lns, NTC, TNTC] and hence may be rendered: 'I am sending' [EBC, GNC, ICC], or 'I am commissioning' [Lns, NTC]. Paul is sending this letter with Tychicus [Alf, EBC, TNTC] or is sending him to take Timothy's place [Alf, EBC, TNTC].

4:13 The cloak,ª which I-leftᵇ in Troas with Carpus, comingᶜ bring,ᵈ and the books,ᵉ especiallyᶠ the parchments.ᵍ

LEXICON—a. φαιλόνης (LN **6.172**) (BAGD p. 851): 'cloak' [BAGD, HNTC, ICC, LN, Lns, NTC; all versions except TEV], 'coat' [Herm; TEV]. This means any type of outer garment [LN]. Probably it was little more than a blanket with a hole in the middle for the head [MNTC, NTC, TG].

  b. aorist act. ind. of ἀπολείπω (LN **85.65**) (BAGD 1. p. 94): 'to leave' [Herm, HNTC, LN, NTC; all versions], 'to leave behind' [BAGD, ICC].

  c. pres. mid. participle of ἔρχομαι (LN 15.81): 'to come' [LN]. This is translated as a temporal dependent clause 'when you come' [Herm, HNTC, ICC, NTC; all versions], or as a prepositional phrase 'on coming' [Lns].

  d. pres. act. impera. of φέρω (LN 15.166) (BAGD 4.a.α. p. 855): 'to bring' [BAGD, Herm, HNTC, LN; all versions except KJV], 'to fetch' [BAGD], 'to bring with you' [ICC; KJV], 'to bring along' [NTC], 'to be bringing along' [Lns].

  e. βιβλίον (LN 6.64) (BAGD 1. p. 141): 'book' [BAGD, Herm, HNTC, LN, Lns, NTC; all versions except NIV, NJB], 'scroll' [BAGD, LN; NIV, NJB], 'papers' [ICC]. This is a document consisting of a scroll or of scrolls bound in book form [LN]. They were papyrus rolls [Alf, EBC, El, Lns, MNTC, TG, TNTC].

  f. μάλιστα (LN 78.7) (BAGD 1. p. 489): 'especially' [BAGD, Herm, HNTC, LN, Lns, NTC; all versions except NRSV, REB], 'above all' [BAGD, ICC; NRSV], 'particularly' [BAGD, LN; REB], 'most of all' [BAGD].

  g. μεμβράνα (LN **6.59, 6.66**) (BAGD p. 502): 'parchment' [BAGD, Herm, LN (6.59), NTC; KJV, NAB, NASB, NIV, NRSV, TNT], 'notebook' [REB], 'book made of parchment' [LN (6.66); TEV], '(the) parchment ones' [HNTC; NJB], '(the) rolls' [ICC]. These were scrolls written on animal skins [Brd, EBC, Lns, LSA, NTC, TG] and were more expensive that the papyrus rolls [Alf, Brd, EBC, EGT, Lns, LSA, My].

DISCOURSE UNIT: 4:14–18 [NAB, EBC]. The topic is comfort in trials [NAB], man's opposition and God's support [EBC].

DISCOURSE UNIT: 4:14–15 [LSA, TNTC]. The topic is a warning about Alexander [LSA], a specific warning [TNTC].

4:14 Alexander the coppersmithª didᵇ greatᶜ harmᵈ to-me;

LEXICON—a. χαλκεύς (LN **2.55**) (BAGD p. 874): 'coppersmith' [BAGD, Herm, HNTC, LN, Lns; all versions except NIV, TEV], 'metalworker' [BAGD, NTC; NIV, TEV], 'worker in bronze' [ICC]. This word came to be used in a general sense of any metal worker [TG], especially workers in iron [EBC].

2 TIMOTHY 4:14

b. aorist mid. indic. of ἐνδείκνυμι (LN **13.131**) (BAGD 2. p. 262): 'to do (to someone)' [BAGD, Herm, HNTC, ICC, LN, Lns, NTC; all versions], 'to show (ill-will) and to do (harm)' [ICC].

c. πολύς (LN 78.3): 'great' [LN; NRSV, TEV], 'a great deal of' [Herm; NAB, NIV, REB, TNT], 'much' [HNTC, ICC, Lns, NTC; KJV, NASB], 'a lot of' [NJB].

d. κακός (LN 20.18; 88.106; 65.26) (BAGD 3. p. 398): 'harm' [BAGD, Herm, ICC, LN; all versions except KJV], 'evil' [BAGD, LN; KJV], 'damage' [Lns, NTC], 'ill-will' [ICC], 'wrong' [BAGD].

QUESTION—Who was Alexander?

He was either the Alexander Paul excommunicated (1 Tim. 1:19–20), a Jew who tried to stop the rioting in Ephesus (Acts 19:33–34), or some other man named Alexander [GNC]. This was a very common name and many commentators do not think that he has been referred to elsewhere in Scripture [Brd, EBC, El, ICC, Lns, My, NCBC, NTC]. Some think that it could be the Alexander Paul wrote about in 1 Tim. 1:19–20 [Alf, EGT, GNC, HNTC, MNTC, TG].

the Lord will-repay[a] him according-to[b] his deeds,[c]

TEXT—Instead of the indicative form ἀποδώσει 'he will repay', some manuscripts have the optative form ἀποδῴη 'may he repay'. GNT does not mention this alternative. The optative is selected only by KJV.

LEXICON—a. fut. act. indic. of ἀποδίδωμι (LN 38.16) (BAGD 3. p. 90): 'to repay' [NTC; NAB, NASB, NIV, NJB], 'to recompense' [BAGD, LN], 'to reward' [BAGD, LN; KJV, TEV], 'to pay (him) back' [HNTC; NRSV], 'to deal with (him)' [REB, TNT], 'to give (him his) recompense' [Herm], 'to give (every man his due) reward' [ICC], 'to duly give (to him)' [Lns]. This is the same verb used in 4:8.

b. κατά with accusative object (LN 89.8) (BAGD II.5.a.β. p. 407): 'according to' [BAGD, Herm; KJV, NAB, NASB, TEV], 'in accordance with' [Lns, NTC], 'for (what he has done)' [NIV, NRSV, TNT], 'as (his actions/deeds/he) deserve(s)' [HNTC; NJB, REB]. The sense of this preposition is also translated by an adjective: 'due (reward)' [ICC]. This word introduces the norm according to which rewards or punishments are given [BAGD].

c. ἔργον (LN 42.11) (BAGD 1.c.β. p. 308): 'deed' [BAGD, Herm, NTC; NAB, NASB, NJB, NRSV], 'work' [Lns; KJV], 'action' [HNTC], 'act' [LN], 'what he has done' [NIV, TEV, TNT], not explicit [REB, ICC].

4:15 whom also you guard-against,[a] for greatly[b] he-opposed[c] our words.[d]

LEXICON—a. pres. mid. impera. of φυλάσσω (LN 37.120) (BAGD 2.a. p. 868): 'to guard against' [BAGD], 'to be on guard' [NAB, NASB], 'to be on one's guard' [Herm, HNTC, ICC, NTC; NIV, NJB, REB, TEV, TNT], 'to guard oneself' [Lns], 'to guard closely' [LN], 'to look out for' [BAGD], 'to beware' [KJV, NRSV], 'to avoid' [BAGD].

b. λίαν (LN 78.1) (BAGD 1. p. 473): 'greatly' [Lns; KJV], 'strongly' [NAB, NIV, NRSV], 'vigorously' [NTC; NASB], 'bitterly' [ICC; NJB, REB, TNT], 'violently' [HNTC; TEV], 'vehemently' [BAGD], 'very much' [Herm].
c. aorist act. indic. of ἀνθίστημι (LN 39.1) (BAGD 2. p. 67): 'to oppose' [BAGD, HNTC, ICC, LN, NTC; NASB, NIV, NRSV, REB, TEV, TNT], 'to withstand' [BAGD, Lns; KJV], 'to resist' [BAGD, Herm; NAB], 'to contest' [NJB].
d. λόγος (LN 33.98, 33.99) (BAGD 1.a.δ. p. 477): 'word' [BAGD, Herm, LN, NTC; KJV], 'statement' [Lns], 'preaching' [NAB], 'teaching' [NASB], 'message' [LN; NIV, NRSV, TEV, TNT], 'what I said' [HNTC], 'everything/all that we said' [ICC; NJB], 'everything we teach' [REB].

QUESTION—What is referred to by 'our words'?
1. It refers to the verbal presentation of the common faith [Alf], the words of the Christian gospel [El, TG], the message, preaching, teaching, and doctrine Paul and the church proclaimed [EGT, ICC, LSA, MNTC, NCBC], or in a very general sense 'the Truth' [My].
2. It refers just to the words of defense at Paul's trial [Lns, NTC].
3. It refers to both Paul's defense at the trial and the proclamation of the gospel by preaching [Brd, EBC]. Any explicit rendering of this partly depends on where this Alexander is thought to be, whether in Ephesus where Timothy was, or in Rome where Timothy was about to come. Commentaries differ and the text gives no conclusive evidence.

DISCOURSE UNIT: 4:16–18 [Herm, LSA, MNTC, NCBC]. The topic is personal matters regarding Paul and his trial [Herm, MNTC, NCBC], Paul's resources and safety [LSA].

4:16 At my first[a] defense[b] no-one by-me[c] was-at-my-side,[c] but all-deserted[d] me;

LEXICON—a. πρῶτος (LN 60.46) (BAGD 1.a. p. 725): 'first' [BAGD, Herm, HNTC, ICC, LN, Lns, NTC; all versions except NJB, TEV], 'first time' [NJB, TEV].
b. ἀπολογία (LN **33.435**) (BAGD 2.a. p. 96): 'defense' [BAGD, Herm, HNTC, Lns, NTC; NASB, NIV, NRSV], 'answer' [KJV], 'hearing (of my) case in court' [ICC; NAB, REB, TNT]. This noun is also translated as a verb: 'to defend oneself' [LN; TEV], 'to present one's defense' [NJB].
c. aorist mid. indic. of παραγίνομαι (LN **35.6**) (BAGD 3. p. 613): 'to be at one's side' [Lns, NTC], 'to stand by' [BAGD, Herm; TEV], 'to stand with' [KJV], 'to take one's part' [NAB], 'to support' [NASB, TNT], 'to appear to support' [ICC], 'to come to one's support' [NIV, NRSV], 'to come into court to support' [NJB, REB], 'to give someone support' [HNTC], 'to come to the aid of' [BAGD], 'to come to help' [LN].
d. aorist act. indic. of ἐγκαταλείπω: 'to desert'. See this word at 4:10

QUESTION—What was this first defense?
It was the preliminary hearing in court [Alf, EBC, ICC, Lns]. This was a preliminary investigation of the charges [EGT, GNC, HNTC, MNTC, TG, TNTC].

QUESTION—What did Paul expect by having people by his side?
They would be witnesses in his behalf [HNTC, ICC, NTC, TG], or friends who would show by their presence that they valued and respected him [Lns, MNTC].

(may-it) not be-held-against[a] them.
LEXICON—a. aorist pass. opt. of λογίζομαι (LN 29.4; 57.227) (BAGD 1.a. p. 476): 'to be held against' [NAB, NIV, TNT], 'to be counted against' [BAGD, Herm; NASB, NRSV, REB], 'to be laid to one's account' [HNTC], 'to be laid to one's charge' [ICC; KJV], 'to be held accountable' [NJB], 'to be reckoned to' [Lns]. The passive verb is also translated as active by supplying an actor for the optative mood: 'May God not count it against them' [TEV].

QUESTION—Why did Paul add this clause?
This is a prayer to God [KJV, REB]. Paul indicated that he forgave those who deserted him [GNC, HNTC] because they feared to stand by him [Brd, EBC, HNTC, Lns, MNTC].

4:17 But[a] the Lord stood-with[b] me and strengthened[c] me,
LEXICON—a. δέ (LN 89.124): 'but' [Herm, HNTC, ICC, Lns, NTC; all versions except KJV], 'notwithstanding' [KJV].
b. aorist act. indic. of παρίστημι or παρίσταμαι (LN 85.14; **85.13**) (BAGD 2.a.γ. p. 628): 'to stand with' [KJV, NASB], 'to stand by' [BAGD, Herm, HNTC; NJB, NRSV, REB, TNT], 'to stand by/at one's side' [ICC, Lns, NTC; NAB, NIV], 'to stay with' [TEV], 'to be with someone' [LN], 'to come to the aid of' [BAGD] 'to help' [BAGD].
c. aorist act. indic. of ἐνδυναμόω (LN 74.6) (BAGD 1. p. 263): 'to strengthen' [BAGD, LN; KJV, NASB], 'to empower' [LN], 'to give strength' [Herm, HNTC, NTC; NAB, NIV, NRSV, TEV, TNT], 'to give power' [NJB], 'to loan strength' [REB], 'to inspire with strength' [ICC], 'to put power in' [Lns].

QUESTION—What relationship is indicated by δέ 'but'?
This indicates contrast [Brd, EBC, El, GNC, Herm, HNTC, ICC, Lns, LSA, NTC; all versions]. It contrasts the Lord's faithfulness with man's unfaithfulness [Brd, El]. These people deserted him, but the Lord stood by him [EBC, GNC, ICC, LSA].

QUESTION—To whom does 'Lord' refer?
It refers to Jesus [Alf, GNC, TG].

2 TIMOTHY 4:17

so-that[a] **through**[b] **me the preaching**[c] **could-be-fully-accomplished,**[d] **and all the nations**[e] **could-hear,**[f]

LEXICON—a. ἵνα (LN 89.59): 'so that' [HNTC, Lns; NAB, NIV, NJB, NRSV, REB, TEV], 'in order that' [NTC; NASB], 'that' [Herm, ICC; KJV], not explicit [TNT].

b. διά with genitive object (LN 90.4): 'through' [Herm, HNTC, Lns, NTC; NAB, NASB, NIV, NJB, NRSV], 'by' [ICC; KJV]. This preposition with its object is also translated as a verb clause: 'I might be his instrument' [REB], 'I was able to' [TEV, TNT].

c. κήρυγμα (LN 33.258) (BAGD 2. p. 431): 'preaching' [BAGD, Herm; KJV], 'message' [NTC; NIV, NJB, NRSV, TEV, TNT], 'preaching task' [NAB], 'preaching of the gospel' [HNTC, ICC], 'proclamation' [NASB], 'proclamation of the gospel' [REB], 'herald proclamation' [Lns].

d. aorist pass. subj. of πληροφορέω (LN **33.199**): 'to be fully accomplished' [NASB], 'to be brought to completion' [HNTC], 'to be completed' [NAB], 'to be fully completed' [Lns], 'to be fully made' [ICC], 'to be fully proclaimed' [NIV, NJB, NRSV], 'to fully proclaim' [TNT], 'to be proclaimed far and wide' [Herm], 'to proclaim completely' [LN], 'to be fully heralded' [NTC], 'to be fully known' [KJV], 'to make full (proclamation of the gospel)' [REB], 'to proclaim the full (message)' [TEV].

e. ἔθνος (LN 11.37, 11.55): 'nation.' The plural form τὰ ἔθνη 'the nations' [Herm; NAB] is translated 'the Gentiles' [ICC, Lns, NTC; all versions except NAB, REB], 'the whole pagan world' [HNTC; REB], 'the heathen' [BAGD, LN].

f. aorist act. subj. of ἀκούω (LN 24.52): 'to hear' [Herm, HNTC, ICC, LN, Lns, NTC; all versions].

and I-was-delivered[a] **out-from**[b] **(a) lion's mouth.**[c]

LEXICON—a. aorist pass. indic. of ῥύομαι (LN 21.23) (BAGD p. 737): 'to be delivered' [BAGD, ICC, LN; KJV, NASB, NIV], 'to be saved' [BAGD; NAB, NJB], 'to be rescued' [BAGD, Herm, HNTC, LN, Lns, NTC; NRSV, REB, TEV, TNT].

b. ἐκ with genitive object (LN 84.4): 'out of' [Lns, NTC; KJV, NASB], 'from' [Herm, HNTC, ICC; all versions except KJV, NASB].

c. στόμα (LN 8.19) (BAGD 1.c. p. 770): 'mouth' [BAGD, Herm, HNTC, LN, Lns, NTC; KJV, NASB, NIV, NJB, NRSV, TNT], 'jaws' [BAGD, ICC; NAB, REB]. The metaphor 'mouth of a lion' is translated 'being sentenced to death' [TEV].

QUESTION—How is this clause related to its context?

It is the result of the Lord's helping and strengthening Paul [Alf, Herm; NAB, NJB, NRSV, REB, TNT]: and so I was delivered.

QUESTION—What is the significance of the expression 'saved from the lion's mouth'?

Since Paul was a Roman citizen and was exempt from the disgrace of being thrown to the lions, this is not to be taken literally [Alf, EGT, Lns]. The expression is metaphorical [Alf, EGT, El, GNC, Lns, LSA, My, NCBC, TG, TNTC], or proverbial [Brd, HNTC, ICC], or an idiom [NTC]. Though the "lion" has been thought to refer to Nero by many church fathers, to other Roman officials related to Paul's trial, to the Roman Empire, to Satan [Alf], or to death, the expression is usually viewed more generally.

1. In a physical sense it is said to refer to deliverance from any great or extreme danger [El, HNTC, ICC, LSA, MNTC, TNTC], deliverance from death by execution right after his first hearing [Brd, GNC, HNTC, LN, TG], to complete deliverance (even from prison) after his earlier trial so as to declare the gospel far and wide [NTC], or to gaining some respite and relief [Brd, NCBC].
2. In a physical and spiritual sense it is said to mean to escape unhurt in body and soul in his present situation as mentioned in 3:11 [My].
3. In a completely spiritual sense, it means to be delivered from failure [Alf, EGT], either not completing the proclamation [EGT], or giving up or denying the gospel from lack of strength and courage when all men had forsaken him [Alf].

4:18 **The Lord will-deliver^a me from^b every evil^c work^d**

LEXICON—a. fut. mid. indic. of ῥύομαι: 'to deliver' [BAGD; KJV, NASB], 'to deliver'. See this word at 4:17.
b. ἀπό with genitive object (LN 89.122): 'from' [Herm, HNTC, ICC, Lns, NTC; all versions].
c. πονηρός (LN 88.110) (BAGD 1.b.β. p. 691): 'evil' [BAGD, Herm, HNTC, LN, NTC; KJV, NASB, NIV, NJB, NRSV], 'wicked' [BAGD, LN, Lns], 'harmful' [ICC]. This word is also translated by an infinitive phrase: 'to do harm' [NAB, REB], or it is conflated with the noun ἔργον 'work' and translated 'evil' [TEV], 'harm' [TNT].
d. ἔργον (LN 42.11; 42.42): 'work' [Lns, NTC; KJV], 'deed' [BAGD, ICC, LN; NASB], 'act' [Herm], 'contrivance' [HNTC], 'attempts' [NAB, NJB, REB], 'attack' [NIV, NRSV], 'harm' [TNT]. This word is also conflated with the qualifying adjective 'wicked' and rendered by the substantive 'evil' [TEV].

QUESTION—How is this verse related to its context?

It is a conclusion drawn from the preceding verse; his experience of the Lord's strengthening him and delivering him gives him this confidence [LSA, NTC, TNTC].

QUESTION—What is meant by 'evil work'?

It means every wicked work that evil people [Lns, LSA, My] and Satan [LSA] will inflict on Paul. It refers to opposition of his adversaries [Brd], anything that would harm him [ICC, TG]. Or it means an undermining of his faith or courage by his enemies that would cause him to sin [HNTC], every danger of faint-heartedness [Alf], temptation to sin [Brd], and apostasy [Alf].

and will-save[a] **to his heavenly**[b] **kingdom;**[c]

LEXICON—a. fut. act. ind. of σῴζω (LN 21.27) (BAGD 2.a.α. p. 798): 'to save' [BAGD, LN, Lns, NTC; NRSV], 'to preserve' [BAGD; KJV], 'to bring safe/safely (to/into)' [HNTC; NAB, NASB, NIV, NJB, REB, TNT], 'to carry safe (into)' [ICC], 'to take safely (into)' [TEV], 'to give safe conduct (into)' [Herm].
  b. ἐπουράνιος (LN 1.12) (BAGD 1.a.γ. p. 306): 'heavenly' [BAGD, Herm, HNTC, LN, Lns, NTC; all versions], 'in the heavens' [ICC].
  c. βασιλεία (LN 1.82) (BAGD 3.f. p. 135): 'kingdom' [BAGD, Herm, HNTC, ICC, LN, Lns, NTC; all versions], 'royal reign' [BAGD].

QUESTION—In what way would the Lord save Paul to his heavenly kingdom?
This means to bring him into heaven even though he is martyred [Brd, HNTC, Lns, My, NTC]. It is the saving act of placing him into heaven and into the continuing safety that follows [Lns].

to-whom (be) the glory[a] **to the ages**[b] **of the ages. Amen.**

LEXICON—a. δόξα (LN 33.357; 87.4): 'glory' [Herm, HNTC; all versions except NASB, NRSV, TEV], 'the glory' [Lns, NTC; NASB, NRSV, TEV], 'all glory' [ICC], 'praise' [BAGD, LN], 'honor' [LN].
  b. αἰών (LN 67.95) (BAGD 1.b. p. 27): 'age'. The phrase εἰς τοὺς αἰῶνας τῶν αἰώνων 'to the ages of the ages' is translated 'for the eons of the eons' [Lns], 'age after age' [ICC], 'for ever and ever' [Herm, HNTC, NTC; all versions].

QUESTION—To whom does the pronoun ᾧ 'whom' refer?
  1. It refers to Christ [Alf, Brd, EBC, EGT, El, My, NCBC, NTC, TG, TNTC].
  2. It refers to God [HNTC, MNTC]. The other references to 'Lord' in this verse also refer to God [MNTC].

QUESTION—What aspect of glory does Paul wish to ascribe to the Lord here?
The preeminent component of 'glory' here seems to be praise [Brd, Lns, LSA, TG], the action that glorifies the Lord [LSA]. Some add honor or adoration to praise [Lns, TG]. One commentator sees it as an expression of reverence (following the mention of the Divine Name) [MNTC], and another relates it more generally to the radiating splendor of all the Lord's wonderful attributes [NTC].

DISCOURSE UNIT: 4:19–22 [Brd, EBC, EGT, GNC, HNTC, LSA, MNTC, TNTC; NAB, NIV, NJB, TEV]. The topic is final personal greetings and farewell wishes [EBC, EGT, GNC, HNTC, MNTC, TNTC; NAB, NIV, NJB, TEV], the epilogue [Brd], the closing of the letter [LSA].

DISCOURSE UNIT: 4:19–21 [Brd, ICC, NCBC]. The topic is special greetings [ICC, NCBC], salutations [Brd].

2 TIMOTHY 4:19

4:19 Greet[a] Prisca and Aquila and the household[b] of-Onesiphorus.

LEXICON—a. aorist mid. impera. of ἀσπάζομαι (LN 33.20) (BAGD 1.a. p. 116): 'to greet' [BAGD, Herm, NTC; NAB, NASB, NIV, NRSV, TNT], 'to salute' [Lns; KJV], 'to give one's regards' [HNTC]. This imperative is also rendered by an indicative clause: 'I send greetings to' [BAGD; TEV], or simply 'greetings to' [BAGD; NJB, REB].

b. οἶκος (LN 10.8) (BAGD 2. p. 560): 'household' [BAGD, HNTC; KJV, NASB, NIV, NRSV, REB], 'house' [Lns], 'family' [BAGD, Herm, NTC; NAB, NJB, TEV, TNT].

4:20 Erastus remained[a] in Corinth, but Trophimus I-left[b] in Miletus sick.[c]

LEXICON—a. aorist act. indic. of μένω (LN 85.55) (BAGD 1.a.α. p. 503): 'to remain' [BAGD, Herm, LN, Lns, NTC; NASB, NRSV, TNT], 'to abide' [KJV], 'to stay' [LN; NAB, NIV, TEV], 'to stay behind' [HNTC; NJB, REB].

b. aorist act. indic. of ἀπολείπω (LN 85.65) (BAGD 1. p. 94): 'to leave' [HNTC, LN, Lns, NTC; all versions except NAB], 'to leave behind' [BAGD, LN], 'to have to leave' [NAB], 'to have to leave behind' [Herm].

c. pres. act. participle of ἀσθενέω (LN 23.144) (BAGD 1.a. p. 115): 'to be sick' [BAGD, LN, Lns, NTC; KJV, NASB, NIV, TNT], 'to be ill' [HNTC, LN; NAB, NJB, NRSV, REB]. This participle is also translated by a clause: 'because he was sick' [Herm; TEV].

4:21 Do-your-best/Hasten[a] to come[b] before winter.[c]

LEXICON—a. aorist act. impera. of σπουδάζω: 'to do one's best', 'to hasten'. See this word at 4:9.

b. aorist inf. of ἔρχομαι (LN 15.7, 15.81): 'to come' [Herm, HNTC; KJV, NASB, NJB, NRSV, TEV, TNT], 'to come to me' [Lns], 'to get here' [NAB, NIV, REB].

c. χειμών (LN **67.165**) (BAGD 2. p. 879): 'winter' [BAGD, Herm, HNTC, LN, Lns, NTC; all versions].

QUESTION—Why was it important to come before winter?

The voyage would be impossible during the winter [Alf, GNC, TNTC], or very difficult and dangerous [Brd, EGT, El, HNTC, ICC, NTC, TG] because of storms [EGT, MNTC]. Without the coat Timothy was to bring, Paul would suffer in his cold, damp cell [EBC, GNC, ICC].

Greets[a] you Eubulus and Pudens and Linus and Claudia and all the brothers.

LEXICON—a. pres. mid. indic. of ἀσπάζομαι (LN 33.20) (BAGD 1.a. p. 116): 'to greet'. See this word at 4:19.

DISCOURSE UNIT: 4:22 [Brd, ICC, NCBC]. The topic is the benediction [Brd], the salutation to Timothy [ICC], final blessing [NCBC].

4:22 **The Lord (be) with[a] your(sg.) spirit.[b] Grace[c] (be) with[a] you-all.**

TEXT—After κύριος 'Lord', some manuscripts include Ἰησοῦς Χριστός 'Jesus Christ'. GNT does not mention the alternative reading. The reading 'the Lord Jesus Christ' is selected only by KJV.

TEXT—Some manuscripts terminate this final verse of the letter with ἀμήν 'Amen'. Only KJV includes this word.

LEXICON—a. μετά with genitive object (LN 90.60) (BAGD A.II.1.c.γ. p. 509): 'with' [BAGD, LN, Lns, NTC]. This preposition is also translated with the implied verb 'to be': 'be with' [Herm, HNTC; all versions]. This is a figurative use of 'with' which means aiding or helping someone [BAGD].

b. πνεῦμα (LN 26.9) (BAGD 3.b. p. 675): 'spirit' [BAGD, Herm, HNTC, LN, Lns, NTC; all versions]. It is a person's very self or ego [BAGD].

c. χάρις (LN 88.66) (BAGD 2.c. p. 877): 'grace' [BAGD, Herm, HNTC, LN, Lns, NTC; all versions].

QUESTION—To whom does the plural form ὑμῶν 'your' refer?

It refers to the members of the church where Timothy was [Alf, El, GNC, HNTC, Lns, MNTC]. They would hear this letter read to them [LSA, NCBC].

www.ingramcontent.com/pod-product-compliance
Lightning Source LLC
Chambersburg PA
CBHW051103230426
43667CB00013B/2417